Billie Holiday

P9-BAV-054

Billie Holiday

Essays on the Artistry and Legacy

Edited by
MICHAEL V. PEREZ *and*
JESSICA MCKEE

McFarland & Company, Inc., Publishers
Jefferson, North Carolina

LIBRARY OF CONGRESS CATALOGUING-IN-PUBLICATION DATA

Names: Perez, Michael V., 1963– editor. | McKee, Jessica, 1979– editor.
Title: Billie Holiday : essays on the artistry and legacy / edited by
    Michael V. Perez and Jessica McKee.
Description: Jefferson : McFarland & Company, Inc., Publishers, 2019. |
    Includes bibliographical references and index.
Identifiers: LCCN 2019037502 | ISBN 9781476674698 (paperback) |
    ISBN 9781476637082 (ebook) ∞
Subjects: LCSH: Holiday, Billie, 1915–1959. | Holiday, Billie, 1915–1959—
    Influence. | Holiday, Billie, 1915–1959—Criticism and interpretation. |
    Civil rights movements—United States—History—20th century |
    Civil rights movements—United States—History—21st century |
    African American women jazz singers—Biography. | Women jazz
    singers—Biography. | Jazz singers—United States—Biography.
Classification: LCC ML420.H58 B47 2019 | DDC 782.42165092—dc23
LC record available at https://lccn.loc.gov/2019037502

BRITISH LIBRARY CATALOGUING DATA ARE AVAILABLE

ISBN (print) 978-1-4766-7469-8
ISBN (ebook) 978-1-4766-3708-2

© 2019 Michael V. Perez and Jessica McKee. All rights reserved

*No part of this book may be reproduced or transmitted in any form
or by any means, electronic or mechanical, including photocopying
or recording, or by any information storage and retrieval system,
without permission in writing from the publisher.*

Front cover: portrait of Billie Holiday (Library of Congress)

Printed in the United States of America

McFarland & Company, Inc., Publishers
    Box 611, Jefferson, North Carolina 28640
    www.mcfarlandpub.com

For two great ladies,
Lynnette Porter and
Billie Holiday

Acknowledgments

We would like to thank Dr. Lynnette Porter for her invaluable mentorship and editorial savvy— this book would not have been made without her; Dr. Sally Blomstrom, whose gentle direction allowed this book to take shape and be realized with grace and purpose; our amazing colleagues in the Department of Humanities and Communication at Embry-Riddle Aeronautical University for their humor and brilliance in scholarship that continues to inspire; and the fierce and talented contributors that make this book so amazing.

Michael thanks his brother Tony, his mom, the poet Nola Perez, his sister-in-law Sally and his niece Elizabeth for their love and support during this book's genesis. Jessica thanks Molly for her continued support, Taylor for her unending faith in our abilities, and lastly, the constant artistry and empowering legacy of Billie Holiday, always the first reason for this book, always.

Table of Contents

Introduction

JESSICA MCKEE *and* MICHAEL V. PEREZ

Billie Holiday, both the person and her canon, has always resonated within American popular culture—which has, at times, reduced and conflated her image, voice, and legacy into a kind of cultural currency. Her name has become synonymous with the now-famous musical lament "Strange Fruit." This song not only criticized the violence against African Americans but also drew the ire of Harry Anslinger, the head of the Federal Bureau of Narcotics. For Anslinger, Holiday was "Public Enemy #1," the epitome of everything that was wrong with jazz music, which, he feared, could make "black people forget their place in the fabric of American society" (Weber). For Holiday, however, a single performance was a reclamation of herself: "I've got no understudy," Holiday said in an interview shortly before her death. "Every time I do a show I'm up against everything that has ever been written about me. I have to fight the whole scene to get people to listen to their own ears and believe in me again" (qtd. in Blackburn 11). Holiday's life and her life story, as told to longtime friend William Dufty in *Lady Sings the Blues*, is both a private and public performance—a performance that lends itself to multiple interpretations.

In Dufty's (re)telling, Holiday's feats are comparable to, and sometimes greater than, transformative moments in American history. Packed with "enough food to last Lindbergh across the Atlantic," a young Holiday "made it solo from Baltimore to New York" (20). Touring with Artie Shaw was akin to taming the wild west: "Don't tell me about those pioneer chicks hitting the trail in those slip-covered wagons with the hills full of redskins. I'm the girl who went West in 1937 with sixteen white cats, Artie Shaw and his Rolls-Royce—and the hills were full of white crackers" (79). Her film debut in Duke Ellington's *Symphony in Black* was "just a short subject. Something they filled in with when they couldn't get Mickey Mouse" (58). The loss of her cabaret card after a narcotics charge made her a refugee in her own country:

"Don't even think all the DP's [Displaced Persons] were in Europe. I've been one for years" (175). And finally, her escape from John Levy "had to be the kind of production that would make Liza crossing the ice look easy," a reference to *Uncle Tom's Cabin* in which Liza crosses the frozen Ohio River to freedom. In these instances, and others, Dufty asserts Holiday into American lore—from Mickey Mouse, to popular fiction, to Manifest Destiny, to Lindbergh's hop across the Atlantic.

Now, 60 years after her death, Holiday remains a prominent figure within American pop culture. Referencing her has become a fast, easily recognizable way to create a cultural citation that lends itself to a superficial exchange. Among many occurrences, her songs are included in the role playing, post-apocalyptic game *Fallout 3*; the graphic novel *Watchmen* devotes an entire panel to her; and her voice comments three times, with three different songs, in the series/season finale of the HBO series *The Leftovers*.

None of these representations can fully reflect the depths of the famous Lady Day and instead uses her image, at times, as mere background to a larger story. For example, in *Fallout 3*, an old-style radio sits next to a windowsill, outside of which graphically-imagined violence takes place, while Holiday starts her legendary plaintive love song "Crazy He Calls Me" in a voice not usually relegated to the background of anything, violence or otherwise. Billie's distinctive lilt, warm vibrato, and distinctive phrasing creates a cultural reference here that goes back some 80 years; it is the malleability of her image that we wish to examine, exult, and situate.

We argue that the fluidity of Holiday's image is an artistic triumph that deserves to be reexamined. Contributors to this collection deemphasize those biographical elements that seem to have hijacked components of Holiday's artistry—taking, perhaps, her flexibility as an artist hostage. The range of disciplines and interests covered by contributors—photography, poetry, film, activism—all intersect with Billie Holiday in important ways. Each contributor attempts to reclaim Holiday from the continuum of cultural commodification that reduces her image, sound, and legacy without honoring her natural place as a political artist.

We take as an integral premise that the analytical lens through which Holiday has most often been seen needs a new examination, one that is not simply predicated on tragedy, *sturm und drang*, and addiction narrative. We agree with the author John Szwed, who states in his 2016 biography *Billie Holiday: The Musician and the Myth* that there is a narrative pattern that assigns Holiday a rather rigid role, even as she "seemed consciously to choose songs that underlined what she had become: Our Lady of Sorrows" (3). Indeed, Szwed is right that "suffering and pain are neither necessary nor sufficient to produce a great artist" (3). This collection reclaims Holiday's image and legacy as derived from the rigid historicity of what Sady Doyle calls the "trainwreck persona":

> She's the girl who breaks the rules of the game and gets punished, which means she's actually the best indication of which game we're playing and what the rules are.... In her consistent violation of the accepted social codes—her ability to shock, to horrify, to upset, to draw down loud and powerful condemnations—she is a tremendously powerful force of cultural subversion [xxi].

In other words, the "trainwreck" reveals the social interplay of meeting expectations and defying them; in the case of Billie Holiday, this interplay can turn a song book into a spectator sport. Our purpose, then, is to examine the ways Holiday's performances (her own, impersonations of her, as well as the works she inspires) demonstrate the range of cultural subversion operating in Holiday's legacy. To provide a better overview of our objective, we have included 11 responses to the past, present, and future of Lady Day.

We begin with Michael V. Perez's "In Stereotragic Hi-Fidelity: Performing Billie Holiday," which challenges the "canon of performativity" that tends to only interpret Holiday, and her voice, as an artist in ruin. Perez characterizes Holiday's sound and compares it to performances from Audra MacDonald, David Sedaris, Joey Arias, José James, Zadie Smith and others. His purpose is to foster a more complete legacy of Holiday, to "understand mellifluously what it sounds like to be an African American artist who triumphs over adversity and appropriation ... all on her own terms." "We owe it to Holiday," Perez reasons, "to grow ourselves—as we hear her at all stages of her incomparable career, to hear it together."

Tammie Jenkins also asks readers to *hear more* in Holiday's voice. In "Billie Reverberates Her Blues: Advertising *Love for Sale* That Costs *More Than You Know*," Jenkins locates Holiday's use of "language games" within a blues tradition that has long imparted political significance to seemingly simple lyric. Using Holiday's biography as an analytical lens, Jenkins offers a close reading of two songs that she interprets as Holiday retelling her experiences with "abandonment, sexual assault, prostitution, and other abuses in ways that re-contextualized her past as discourses of the present."

In "Lady Sings the Blues? Tragedy, Autobiography and Reassessment," Anna Maria Barry agrees that Holiday's songs appear to reflect the troubles of her life, but "despite these truths," Barry prefers to dethrone the "Queen of Heartache," arguing that Holiday—as well as other singers like Nina Simone, Janis Joplin, and Amy Winehouse—are due a "radical reassessment" that recognizes the complexity of these artists as more than just heartbroken, tragic figures. Looking to Holiday and Dufty's *Lady Sings the Blues*, Barry interprets Holiday's autobiography as another kind of performance, one that presents a powerful voice that sheds light on "our most pressing contemporary concerns—from police brutality and the criminal justice system, to sexual abuse, drug policy and LGBTQIA+ rights." Barry asks readers to interrogate the "received truth about Holiday, with an acute awareness of how sexism and racism have shaped this."

Claudius Stemmler's "Merging Artists: The Legacy of Motown's *Lady Sings the Blues*" extends the discussion of the autobiography by focusing on the eponymously titled 1972 film that features Diana Ross as Holiday. Stemmler argues that Berry Gordy's production capitalized on Holiday's perceived authenticity to recast Motown and Diana Ross as culturally relevant to a changing political climate. More specifically, Stemmler argues, "they tried to harness the symbolic qualities of Billie Holiday in order to advance Ross' career." Stemmler locates this film within a larger "cultural continuity" that confirms "all participating artists … belong to larger authentic African American culture, despite the many changes each generation encompasses."

William Levine's "'Owning' Billie Holiday in Several Representative Jazz Poems" shifts the discussion from mass media responses to Holiday to the poetic representations of the artist. Levine interprets the latter as "an alternative economy, one that assigns a singular value to artistic accomplishments and musicians as a catalyst for personal insight and interpersonal identifications that are opposed to the values of mass culture." Looking at nine poetic tributes to Holiday, Levine reasons that these poems offer more to Holiday's "life and work" than more popular "forms of self-indulgent entertainment."

Fernando Gabriel Pagnoni Berns' essay, "Brigitte Loves Billie: Channeling Holiday in *Domino* (1988)," examines a type of self-indulgent entertainment that all too often relies on Holiday as savior, muse, and harlot, even sometimes conflating them with the artist herself. Pagnoni Berns reviews Holiday's "authenticity" as a proto-feminist persona in the 1988 Italian film *Domino*, in which the female protagonist (Domino) channels Holiday as a figure of empowerment. Pagnoni Berns situates the film within the femme fatale trope of the 1980s that served as a backlash against second-wave feminism. Pagnoni Berns argues that Domino relies on Holiday's "larger symbolic quality" as a means for "finding identity and agency in a world framed by ambiguity and empty visuality."

In "Seeing Is Believing? Reading Billie Holiday Through Photography," Matthew Duffus returns to Holiday's visuality to "complicate rather than clarify her image." As Duffus observes, Holiday is the most photographed jazz singer. The range of these images contributes to the "multiplicities of identities" that has come to define the Holiday mythos. Duffus employs Sontag's and Barthes' theories of photography to interpret four main images that he believes "support the Holiday legend—in keeping with so many … critics' references to photography and mythology—rather than coalescing into a definitive portrait of the singer." His purpose is to provide a deeper "understanding of how photography has contributed to the mythology of jazz and of Holiday."

As a complement to Duffus, Taylor Joy Mitchell, in "Shouting Back: Cohering Lady Day Through Kevin Young's Jazz Poem Anthology" reviews the Holiday poems Kevin Young published in his 2006 collection, *Jazz Poems*, and argues that, when analyzed collectively, the 13 poems that make up "Muting (for Billie Holiday)" act as a traditional jazz elegy—an instrumental tribute written for inspirational musicians. In their mourning for Holiday, the poets in Young's anthology fulfill the basic poetic goal of the elegy, with an added call-and-response strategy that invokes blues history. Young's organization forces readers to consider the way the poems speak to each other, and, in turn, provide a fuller image of Holiday. Each poet celebrates different aspects of Holiday's life and career and, as a unit, they recreate that very sacred space of performance as a fusion of language and musicality, illustrating the impermanence of jazz through a static form. Depending on the poem, Holiday's image mutates, creating a kaleidoscope of Holidays to fulfill the unique needs of the lamenting poet.

Moving from the page to the screen, Jesse Schlotterbeck's "Reevaluating *Lady Sings the Blues* and *What's Love Got to Do with It*: Ambivalent Representations of Black Female Artistry" eschews the question of authenticity and instead considers Diana Ross' performance of Holiday in *Lady Sings the Blues* and Angela Bassett's performance of Tina Turner in *What's Love Got to Do with It*. Schlotterbeck traces the "evolution of the musical biopic genre" and reconsiders the tendency to criticize the former while celebrating the latter. Both films reflect the ideology of the time, Schlotterbeck argues, "by striking an ideological balance between progressive and conservative aspects of representation."

In "Easy to Love: Representations of Billie Holiday in Contemporary American Poetry," Tara Betts reviews the broad range of poets that present Holiday as a central figure. Looking at the poems of Carole Weatherford, Angela Jackson, Rita Dove, Farah Jasmine Griffin and concluding with Kevin Young, Betts shows how these poets "allow Holiday to reveal her complexities as an artist and a human being." In these poetic forms, Betts reasons, Holiday "is not just a voice, a gardenia in her hair, or a persecuted drug addict," but rather an artist of great social and political import.

We conclude with Devona Mallory's "The Fruit Is on the Ground: The Impact of 'Strange Fruit' on Black Lives Matter." Mallory argues that the song, and the Black Lives Matter movement, demonstrate that the message of this ground-breaking song "remains as relevant today as the day it was first recorded." Mallory historicizes the history of lynching, of the movement, and of the song to demonstrate the myriad of ways that black bodies are subject to violence, racism, and systemic oppression.

Previous works on Holiday tend to offer biographic information or individualized meditations on their relationship to the singer and her songs; this collection examines the lasting impact of Holiday's legacy in order to not only complicate her image but also to sharpen it. Of the more than 40 full-length books published about Billie Holiday, all are single-authored. This collection, in contrast, is the first multi-authored text that attempts to create new critical parameters by not only considering the songs she performed but also the photographs, films, poetry, and impersonations she has inspired. In many ways, then, this collection is more about Holiday's lasting legacy than her life. As the celebrated actress Audra McDonald said in her 2014 acceptance speech for her performance as Holiday in *Lady Day at Emerson's Bar and Grill*, "most of all, Billie Holiday[,] you deserve so much more than you were given when you were on this planet. This is for you, Billie."

WORKS CITED

Cornish, Audie. "Audra McDonald Racks Up the Tonys, This Time as Billie Holiday." *All Things Considered,* NPR, 9 June 2014.

Doyle, Sady. *Trainwreck: The Women We Love to Hate, Mock, and Fear ... and Why.* Brooklyn: Melville House, 2016.

Dufty, William. *Lady Sings the Blues.* 1956. New York: Harlem Moon, 2006.

Weber, Brandon. "How Strange Fruit Killed Billie Holiday." *The Progressive,* 20 Feb. 2018. Accessed 4 May 2018.

In Stereotragic Hi-Fidelity

Performing Billie Holiday

Michael V. Perez

There's a relentless, legendary image that opens the second act of Samuel Beckett's celebrated, difficult play *Happy Days*. Winnie, Beckett's protagonist, who'd opened and performed the first act buried up to her waist in what could politely be called a mound in a scorched landfill, opens the second act (as the curtain rises) completely buried up to the top of her neck. Many have interpreted Winnie's incremental burying to speak for the (in)human condition and perseverance in the face of gradual, inevitable annihilation. This essay opens with Beckett's heroine forging on in the face of rising erasure to situate how performing Billie "Lady Day" Holiday has become in certain cases a problematic performative interpretation often delivered, either comically or in earnest, as a disembodiment of body from soul, a choice of vocalized isolation in the face of what can reductively be seen as speaking—and singing—through ruin.

In other words, the "trainwreck" persona—memorably examined by critic Sady Doyle, and so often referenced to chart Holiday's vocal career (and vocal) trajectory—reveals the social interplay of meeting expectations and defying them. In the case of Billie Holiday, this interplay can turn a songbook into a spectator sport. My purpose, then, is to examine the ways Holiday's performances (her own and impersonations of her as well as the works she inspires) demonstrate the range of cultural subversion operating in Holiday's legacy.

In referencing Lady Day to *Happy Days*, the idea of a vocalist as only a lit singing face is equally unbearable, in retrospect, though Michael Bennett used this lighting strategy to focus intensely on Jennifer Holliday as she sang her second act show-stopper "I Am Changing" from his renowned 1982 Broadway musical *Dreamgirls*. There, Jennifer Holliday's beatific face belted her modern-day torch song within the illumination of her spot-lit face to serve a clever purpose—she was actually changing, or being changed, into a new costume that was revealed at the song's key change and subsequent complete lighting of Holliday's body with her face. This example of costumed panache was a benign way to forefront the effect and perhaps, less so, the message, delivered via a Broadway power ballad about (both literally and figuratively) changing.

Regarding a different kind of change for Billie Holiday, as opposed to the much later example of Jennifer Holliday, it is relevant to mention that Lady Day's spotlight-encircled face is traditionally described as one memorable image in the performative legacy and gently relentless artistic vocal revolution known as "Strange Fruit." However, to take the political from the face (in, say, 1938, at Café Society) in any other song performed can disembody the voice itself from its inherently political message, in any given song. Herein the songbook is not Jerome Kern; the songbook is Billie Holiday, performing as an empowered African American artist and woman, visage, with both body *and* soul.

"Stereotragic"

Performing Holiday can be reductive, with Holiday as referenced mouthpiece—that disembodied face in that white circle of a spotlight. To mimic Holiday seems to come down to a repeated stretch of stitched-together vocal tics that sometimes ignore the woman behind the gardenia as vocally *stereotragic*, only capable of a limited vocal alchemy that demonstrates how to survive after a flame has been extinguished. Stereotragic interpretation is a coined phrase celebrated jazz artist Dee Dee Bridgewater might agree with, especially in the following observation: "I'm sure that her tragic life affected her singing but probably in an unconscious way, probably something she wasn't even aware of. You can hear the effects of her lifestyle in her late recordings. Her voice was very broken because of the ravages of the drugs that she had been taking and the hard life that she had been living, so that's kind of apparent" (qtd. in Primack).

It is this essay's aim to synthesize the voice, the face, the gardenia, and the body as one voice that is impossible to copy except as homage, or worse, in the case of some white male performers, unintentional minstrelsy. The problem with mimicking—not to mention performing—Holliday is the specter, or visual echo, of that Café Society disembodied head—Holiday must be given homage as body with soul, not one without the other. The voice without the apparent work of what generates it is what I intend to refute herein, as if an artist were just a mouth that contains the rote delivery of cumulative mannerisms. It's best to remember what can happen when only the body is assessed without the synthesis of it to the soul and artistic spirit of a performer, in this case regarding Holiday's much-discussed usage of drugs to forefront the body (in this case inferred perhaps by the phantom needle of heroin usage over the instrument forged from the marriage of body and soul, as if the abuse of Holiday's disembodied torso et al. "spoke" for her vocal legacy):

> When we think of Billie Holiday, most people think of her as a junkie rather than as a girl who grew up on the Baltimore waterfront to become one of the greatest jazz singers in the world. People using drugs? That happens every day. Becoming a great singer? Doesn't happen that much [qtd. in Himes, "What Makes Billie Holiday's Music So Powerful Today"].

This "read" comes from Justin Townes Earle, who wrote a terrific homage to Holiday entitled "White Gardenia." He gets to the core of the body/soul dichotomy in a figurative way—that Holiday is often defined by what she put into her body than the sound originating from her diaphragm and emerging from a face that became the gateway to how we understand her greatness. Body divorced from soul and its near–Aristotelean duplicity, unified, then split—this is the core of the problem of describing Holiday as only the sum of her parts, only a voice, only a junkie, only a body needled to fame, only a haphazard soul in either her recordings, performances, or "autobiography" (which may be the most potent example of Holiday being performed, where her voice is being used to write a history she may or may not have fully signed off on, despite the fact that it "sounds" like Holiday in many places. That is an analysis for another time, but a very good example, in its for-its-time shocking specificity, of "stereotragic" performance being bound to the written page).

Holiday as Song/Stress

What are the similarities and difference in constructing—or parroting—a Billie Holiday performance, and what elements comprise an imitation, be it tragic, comic, or both? What do these performances hold as commonalities, and in what way does a performance differ from its predecessors? Can these performances—or what I like to call *iterations*—form a timeline that represents both the legendary aspects as well as the less scrupulous choices contained in the Holiday songbook—and what components chosen by Holiday interpreters create Holiday in the most and least repetitious and/or reductive manner? Chasing a performative Holiday that combines the assumption of authenticity and myth—what I call *myth-ethnicity*—often forms the only visible marker when Holiday is interpreted. Indeed, many performances of Holiday often seem like fleshed-out versions of her autobiography *Lady Sings the Blues* and its notorious "truthiness."

Ultimately, I listen for what happens beyond the patterns involved in iterations of Billie: beyond the tics, elisions, stresses, "lazy" emphasis, and grit often put on as indication of a voice either in mint condition or decline (which is truthfully more prevalent as the latter). The term *songstresses* will be used to itself place stress on certain vocal similarities often delivered when Holiday is performed, creating a legacy of identifiable vocalisms that have been used to re-create Holiday *vocally*. The analysis of this essay aims to situate these unlikely song/stresses in a canon of performativity that is very much in need of reexamination, especially in terms of Lady Day's immense and under-examined vocal subtleties—as if creating Holiday referred only to a repertoire of vocalizations indicative of just a great artist in ruin.

What Lady Sounds Like, for Starters

Like no one else before or since her time on Earth—I would go as far as saying no one in the history of the recorded voice. But how do I know that?

An apt, brief description of Holiday's style comes from Farah Jasmine Griffin, who uses Holiday's voice to narrate her performing voice as a process: "Lady's singing style says, 'I'm going to take my time, be cool, laid back, and I will still get there on time without sweating'" (16–17). That way of bending notes and rhythm, sliding to a note, starting late after the beat without missing or distorting it. Griffin's description matches Lady Day's rhythmic innovations nicely, along with the way she would rehearse songs with Lester Young until she "felt" their tempo and construction and could improvise by ear, the song having gotten "into her ear" as a result of the thorough rehearsal process (qtd. in Griffin 18).

Sady Doyle nicely sums up how Holiday's style can still elude critics and can also include the obviously ubiquitous component of her "trainwreck" narrative—the idea being that the persona and the performer merge to more than just a sound:

> Critics are still figuring out exactly how she worked. Some of the things she did with tempo had no antecedent in Western music, outside a few experimental pieces by Chopin. [...] More than that, the archetype she created in the public consciousness, the tormented female singer who exorcised her demons onstage—[...] is found in every corner of music. She's responsible for everyone from Erykah Badu and Lauryn Hill to Tori Amos and Fiona Apple, from Amy and Lana to Joni and Janis.

How then can we hear Holiday without her narrative interfering and informing the sound, especially toward the end of her life, such as when

Johann Hari states, "[w]hen Billie sang 'Loverman, where can you be?' she wasn't crying for a man—she was crying for heroin" (Hari 23). John Szwed hears Chopin as well in a deft analysis of "Foolin' Myself" (from *Lady Day: The Complete Billie Holiday on Columbia, 1933–1944*) that also encapsulates what Lady Day's sound might be founded upon: her instinctively creative and intrinsic approach to rhythm mixed with phrasing:

> Preceded by first-rate musicians taking solos, Holiday has only one chorus left to sing when they finish. Her variations at first are minimal, though she announces her entry by immediately falling behind the beat. By the time she reaches the bridge, she is so extraordinarily behind the beat that the song seems about to fall apart. She had a sense of time that seems closer to what Mozart and Chopin called *tempo rubato*, the ability to stray far from a strict accompaniment while still managing to return to finish in time. Add to this her taste for stressing every syllable, giving her words a weight and a declamatory quality that captures the listener, even when the grain of her voice doesn't.

Any Holiday recording can be elucidated by the above analysis—such as an early (1936) song like the head-swinging pert version of "The Way You Look Tonight" from her Columbia Records period (especially each enunciation of "the way...," and the words "love—ly/never ever change"). The same signature tempo ownership and clarity of tone, changed as it may be at this point in her career, keeps the listener swinging to Holiday's subtle tempi embellishments running counter to the musicians in "Let's Call the Whole Thing Off" from 1957. Extra delight can be had as Holiday takes on the "ice cream" verse of the song ("You say vanilla...") to speak the refrain with a delightful "what the hell" tone ("Vanilluh, Vanillah, Chocolate! Strawberry! Let's call the whole thing off!"), coming back just in time for the bridge and having made the song hers with rhythmic suppleness and her signature pronunciation—elements that no amount of abuse or life can fully diminish.

The comparison here enables Holiday to make her own artistry span the best response for why a more rigid stereotragic analysis fails to encompass the subtleties and potency, not to mention the originality, of her voice at any stage of her career. It would be useful here to hear how Holiday explains her sound in quotes from the *Lady Sings the Blues* book where she sets the stage for the reader the way her early audiences heard her. Copying, yodeling, close order drill, horn playing instead of singing ... these are some of the negative references ("I don't think I'm singing...") that Holiday herself utilized in her autobiography-as-performance, as follows.

> I think I copied my style from Louis Armstrong. Because I used to like the big volume and the big sound that Bessie Smith got when she sang.... So I liked the feeling that Louis got and I wanted the big volume that Bessie Smith got [...] So anyway between the two of them I sorta got Billie Holiday.

I can't stand to sing the same song the same way two nights in succession. If you can, then it ain't music, it's close order drill, or exercise or yodeling or something, not music.

I don't think I'm singing. I feel like I'm playing a horn…. What comes out is what I feel [Holiday and Dufty].

Here is partially how Billie performs Billie, at least via William Dufty, if we follow the legend that Holiday *spoke* her book to Dufty as an interview and then allowed Dufty to "biographically" vocalize in her style. In this sense, Holiday used her own voice as a "guide vocal" for Dufty to follow. The actor Bill Murray may have expressed what I hear as another fundamental problem when approaching Holiday as homage: that she never sang the same way twice, as indicated from the excerpts taken from her autobiography. Indeed, this is the problem I hear with almost all current interpretations of Holiday, be they comic or earnest—there's an "in the moment" paint-by-numbers approach to the delivery that omits the spontaneity and immediacy Lady Day was known for—although a mimesis need not be aware of the soul driving the body and resort only to what an audience expects to hear in terms of signature tonality, mannerisms, scratches, elisions and upward slides between notes. I argue it should.

In fulfillment of my Lady Day performative comparison, Murray explains, "I don't believe that you can give the same performance every take. It's physically impossible, so why bother? If you don't do what is happening at that moment, then it's not real. Then you're holding something back." While I do not presume to state that Holiday performers are "holding back" in general, Murray understands what Holiday embodied—that the core to authenticity comes in the moment, perhaps as a result of (in Holiday's case) thorough rehearsal until a song is "in her ear," and then a delivery fully aware of its spatial reality and resonance—how it sounds in the moment. This integral aspect of a performative Holiday is not the main problem as I see it, however.

The Problem Is "Sui Generis"

The main problem inherent in attempting to perform Holiday may lie in the simple fact that her voice has often been described as *sui generis*—not like anyone else of her time or ours, not like anything before or (fully) since. Holiday herself considered, in her autobiography, her voice as founded upon a sonic blend of Louis Armstrong and Bessie Smith, though she is careful to point out that she always wanted Smith's big tone, which she didn't have. When Macy Gray became popular in America in the early 2000s with her neo-soul anthem "I Try," a friend of mine, who knew I hadn't yet heard the song, said that Gray sounded like a blend of Billie Holiday and Donald Duck—a description I wish I'd never heard. On that note, there have always been expectations connected to Holiday, especially when she is presented as the ultimate vocalist jazz will ever know, a claim that may have caused a degree of contempt prior to investigation in anyone uninitiated to Holiday's sound or legendary canon. I have had novice Holiday students at the university where I teach music courses state that they expected to hear a big voice as well—say, a Jennifer Hudson by way of Bessie Smith, perhaps, and not the percussive, expressive, contained coloratura phrasings heard in such Holiday recordings as "Travlin' Light," "Mandy Is Two," or "You Better Go Now" from Holiday's vocal heyday (pre–1955). No doubt unmet expectations lead to questions and transitions.

I Have Questions (Take It to the Bridge)

What do we recognize as the innate elements of a Billie Holiday performance, and what are our expectations from vocalists and performers who exhibit these elements? What do we hear when we hear Billie Holiday? What do we hear when Holiday is performed well, and not so well? What created Holiday's unique sound, and is it stable enough to elicit recognition and expectation? Why? And what is it about Holiday's vocal artistry that creates such a lasting impression of *sui generis* vocalization to this day?

I have more: What do we expect from artists who assume or impersonate Billie Holiday's singular, inimitable sound? Accurate vocal citation? Stretching the tempo to move in a supple delivery between the parentheses of a measure's groove? A seamless mesh of tics? A vocal assumption and translation of a "riff, a ba-deep, a ba-dop" (Holiday 69)? A "burned" scratch (Dove) that "whispered along a keyboard" (O'Hara)? Fidelity, "hi" or otherwise? The less-than-subtle familiarity of distorted mannerisms? The answer is *Yes, yes, and yes*—but discussed herein as a stereotragic stereo/type of isolated song/stresses that disembody body from soul as an (albeit unaware) reference point for many audiences. *New York Times* arts critic John Leland stated in 2017 that "Billie Holiday was a great American storyteller and a great American story. Her working materials were simple pop songs and standards—rarely blues—but her medium was her body itself: her voice, her back story. The past imprinted its lines on her skin; the future seemed to be running out." This is a lot of recurrent emphasis on corporeal "fair use" of a performer's body disengaged from its locus—the body becoming objectified and thus appropriated in more ways than one.

Whose body is this anyway? Performing Lady Day as all body and less soul (though, to clarify, Leland does not disembody Holiday so much as stress her self-contained physical instrument) conjures only a sequence of physical attributes assigned to her developing instrument over her lifetime. It also limits the performance to a specific vocal period, where Holiday did not differentiate whether or not her voice was in decline. In short, performing Holiday as all body and less soul distorts the impression and the impetus so well documented in *Lady Sings the Blues*: feeling. Can soul be only felt? Or is it something more ethereal that exists outside of corporeal limitations? Soul, for the sake of this argument, is the element founded in feeling that cannot be replicated as vocal tics in an uncadenced delivery. Cadence, rhythm, phrasing, improvisation, with feeling—this list starts to capture some of Holiday at effortless work, where soul dictates the felt notations of the body, rendering any homage performance as merely a phantasmagorical machine. We are more than the isolated delivery of our mannerisms and tics; a few of these go far as a sound bite, but what of the sound being carried by these sound bites that survive beyond equation and astute re-assembly?

The Divine Audra as Lady Day

Audra McDonald, the most awarded female actor in Tony award history, created an indelible impression in the 2016 HBO revival of *Lady Day at Emerson's Bar and Grill*. Her Lady Day is technically flawless, especially as an uncanny re-creation of the later stereotragic song/stress Holiday became. Every inflection, elongated forced vibrato, edged growl, and abrasion is present in this almost-one-woman show of Holiday in performance—so much so that the performance seems calibrated only to the worn range and vocal mannerisms apparent in the LP *Lady in Satin*. This of course is to be expected—the libretto of this musical play occurs toward the end of Holiday's career. McDonald's choices are perfectly logical, if not perfectly in the moment and perfectly resonant to how Billie herself may have performed Billie, given the limited vocal palette she had to work with. The delivery seems adjusted to the same set of vocal "calling cards" that clearly announce Holiday to a somewhat-discerning ear. McDonald is sublime, but perhaps as an uncanny avatar that stays with the boundaries of expectations we have come to recognize as the tragic "Lady in Satined Decline."

To be fair to the indisputably great artist that McDonald is and will continue to be, the performance in *Lady Day* is predicated on a foundation of ruin, as the concert being performed is ostensibly happening at one of Holiday's last gigs. A performance such as this surely makes sense if displaying the worn nature of Holiday's voice—thus, what choice would she, and McDonald, have in terms of vocal and dramatic range this late in a career most mimicked as a voice worn by life and by vice (squad) itself? McDonald brilliantly knows her range, her affects, her tics, her jumps and elisions, her gorgeously lazy way with tempo and phrasing—the problem is, these individually and effectively rendered parts do not seem to add up to a coherent whole, more so a vocalized "impression" at one volume primarily with each element given equal weight and application. For that, we have to thank—or not thank, perhaps—David Sedaris to understand the difference between Holiday homage and Holiday as a recognizable and limited impression.

The Guys (Sedaris, etc.)

It's also unfair to compare the incomparable McDonald with the brief snippets of Holiday imitation that Sedaris has famously delivered in the audiobook and NPR audiocast of his "Santa Land Diaries" as well as an isolated YouTube performance under a minute where Sedaris sings the Oscar Mayer Bologna jingle as Holiday might have performed it. Sedaris also goes for the joke factor yet delivers a strikingly similar brief rendition of Holiday singing "Away in a Manger" as a Macy's Santa Land elf, in defiance of a despotic Santa Claus who asked him to sing the carol for a group of Macy's patrons. It bears mentioning that Sedaris and McDonald have similarities in the vocal mannerisms they deploy: the scratch, the upward swoops between notes, the fluttered vibrato and punched enunciation in between slides, and ultimately the somewhat-mumbly timbre and fidelity to a stereotragic presence, meaning the vocalized Holiday after 1950. Sedaris' mimicry of Holiday—delivered as part of his reading of "Santa Land Diaries" on NPR's *This American Life*—may have delivered more than a snippet of distilled Holiday mannerisms played for comic effect; Sedaris' exposure in Holiday vocal "drag" actually may have started anyone with an ear for Holiday's unmatchable artistry to try and achieve it through purely mimetic efforts.

Thus, the sound exposed to a larger radio audience (or only, and it should be mentioned apocryphally, performed at Sedaris book signings with a tip jar that said "Billie Holiday Singing $10.00") became inadvertently, and without any contextual explanation, the Billie Holiday Sound. Almost as fulfillment of this effect, YouTuber J.L. Spradlin posted a 2012 clip of himself in his garage performing the Oscar Mayer Weiner song in stereotragic Holiday style—super slow, super slide-y, and with languid phrasing, all reductive and best used as a party stunt (I hesitate to mention the address, but here goes nothing: https://www.youtube.com/watch?v=HfH2ZdMrnN, but at your own risk). What it means for men to assume Holiday has everything to do with appropriation; a drag performer ironic as Joey Arias in the movie *Wigstock*, performing in the then-annual "Wigstock" drag festival in New York City celebrating drag performances and wigged culture as a queer response to

1969's Woodstock festival, performs a gorgeous vocal homage to Lady Day that is not founded upon indirect parody or satire, as the Christmas carol or meat-product jingles of Sedaris or Spradlin deliver. Arias is resplendent (in Geisha drag, avoiding any direct visual Holiday impression as s/he sings "Them There Eyes" with a high-stereotragic melodic scratch and wear). Thus Arias becomes a Holiday embodiment without dismissiveness but with humor that informs the performance as founded in a basic performative art that extends Holiday's legacy beyond reductive comedy or a series of eroding slurred phraseology. To absorb and extend the vocal legacy of Holiday as a male performer takes a more cohesive and visionary approach—one that the next male artist achieves as he assimilates Holiday's canon while paying his props and making his audience re-envision what they hear.

Strange Fruit, Multiplied

The genre-fluid neo soul-jazz artist José James has created a version of "Strange Fruit" that stands out not because his performance is homage, or mimics aspects of Holiday's vocal canon, but because James creates his own homage through innovative delivery of the song itself that not only captures the gravitas and power of the song in a technically-striking manner but also allows James the freedom to multi-track (and multi-task) his own voice with his band until he creates a chorus of vocalized pain, anger, and expressive outrage. As James starts the song, he sings a long note into the microphone, which is doubling as a recorder that responds to the touch of his foot. He continues several "takes" in this manner that then are played back and layered into one fused sound—sometimes elongated notes, sometimes utterances that depict the monosyllabic grief that sometimes accompanies the continual tragedy of lynching in any guise.

When James finally starts the song proper, his voice (backed by the slow-simmering, brilliant musicians comprising his band) has been transformed into a chorus of stunning beauty in the face of continued genocide. This use of technology—much like the use of the microphone itself in Holiday's time that allowed unprecedented vocal approaches, turning the table-to-table acoustics of Lady Day's earlier club performances into a forum that could amplify a whisper as much as a shout—creates a great example of a strange and bitter crop, indeed. In contrast, this "empowered" crop comes from an artist paying tribute on his own terms and continuing the genius of "Strange Fruit" as an example of stereotragic activism (by either James or Holiday) that will never diminish.

When a performer attempts to sound like Holiday, when is it homage, when is it a vocal collage of tics and rhythmic assumptions, and when—in the case of white performers, both of whom are male—does the performance veer into minstrelsy?

Billy's (Not Billie's) Holiday

What has to be seen not to be believed is the 1996 Australian musical film *Billy's Holiday*, directed by Richard Wherrett, written by Denis Whitburn, and starring the well-known Aussie performer Max Cullen in the titular role. The story is one of using a muse to find one's own voice—but with the most fundamental (and maybe worst) kind of appropriation, cultural or otherwise. Cullen can make neither his love life nor his artistic life work. Returning home one night after a failed gig with his jazz combo, he sees a shooting star in the sky … and wakes up sounding like Billie and singing Holiday standards. He then becomes a hit. An African Australian (I think) actress is filmed viewing Billy at different points in the film as he becomes an overnight success; she is always dressed in 1940s style and inhabits the frame peripherally, usually as a bystander at one of his venues. Worse, and tellingly, this meteoric Holiday surrogate is only filmed as lit from the mouth down and backlit to suggest her physical frame. In other words, she is all mouth (sound familiar?) and ostensibly exists to allow Billy with a "y" to channel her artistry. It is as ugly as it sounds. The imdb.com commenter ptb-8 stated under *'LADDIE' SINGS THE BLUES*:

> As a result there is now this curious movie that lacks the wow factor of seeing Max sing live in Billie's voice. It just doesn't make sense to make a film where the really really special thing about an actor's singing performance is not able to be convincing to a movie audience. Except that Cullen sounds like Macy Gray, Donald Duck, and a 4-year-old Holiday with a cold.

In keeping with the motif of Holiday as mouthpiece, in this case mainly a mouth throughout the entire film, it's noteworthy that the Australian film *Billy's Holiday* continues my "Beckettian" reference, in this case Holiday as only mouth equivocal with Beckett's short play and film entitled *Not I*, where the main "speaker" is only a red lipsticked mouth surrounded by pitch-black in the style of the beginning of *The Rocky Horror Picture Show*. Reducing Holiday to a mouthpiece to speak for our own agenda posits the worst kind of artistic larceny: a spiritual theft as much as an impersonation based on stitching mannerisms into a facsimile nowhere near the real thing, at worst a shapeless copy.

Zadie Smith (A-Side) Interview—Interlude

> DANTZIC: Were you listening to Billie Holiday's songs as you were writing? Were there any particular songs or performances that mirrored the emotional tenor

of the story for you? You're a singer, too. Does this help you understand the way she entered a song?

SMITH: A long time ago, I used to sing in old people's homes, and in bars sometimes, and I was often doing Billie impressions. You can replicate the phrasing but you can't come anywhere near that tension between delight and pain that she had [Leyshon].

The Odd Case of Miss Bonnie Pointer

Question: Who is the only performer to have displayed the influence of not only Holiday but also one of Holiday's stated influences (as stated in *Lady Sings the Blues*)? Answer: the youngest member of an American singing family considered by many to be vocal royalty and who helped bring back the Old Wave of pop music from 1972 to 1976, and more than just a footnote: Miss Bonnie Pointer. This kind of history lesson may not have permeated the minds of men on the dance floor sharing poppers, but nonetheless Bonnie Pointer created a few potent songs that instilled ecstasy in their listeners, on or off of the dance floor wherein Holiday's presence would become more than a spectral history lesson in dance floor nostalgia.

As one-fourth of her sibling group the Pointer Sisters, Bonnie, the youngest, was given songs to lead which clearly allowed her to showcase her vocal likenesses to Billie Holiday from the sophomore album the group recorded. "Black Coffee," an instant standard since Sarah Vaughan recorded it in 1948, features prominently on the Pointer Sisters' 1974 album *That's a Plenty*. "Black Coffee" is primarily piano and acoustic bass cushioning Bonnie's vocal, which alternates between short staccato bursts at the chorus ("Black … COF … FEE") and more liquid phrasing elsewhere: Overall, she is totally in control and totally enabling the jazz greats who influenced her. What's noteworthy is that Bonnie Pointer ends the song freely scat-singing—almost giving us an idea of what scat-singing (a very non–Holiday trademark) would have sounded like, or an approximation thereof, by Holiday herself.

It is also noteworthy that her sisters do not support her on this song, a testament to Bonnie's ability to go solo—which is indeed what happens by 1979. That year, Pointer emerged on a new label—Motown—and with an eponymous LP that featured another solo performance that shows how fully she felt comfortable in potentially eliciting comparisons to Lady Day, albeit this time in a more contemporary context.

This contemporaneous context—not a parody or a genre wherein Holiday reigns supreme (meaning jazz, of course)—is what differentiates Pointer from other Holiday tributes or stylistic comparison, for Pointer engages her Holiday vocalese in the setting of what is now thought of as a disco classic, one that also made the Top 40 of the American Billboard chart in 1979 as well. As currently as 2017, the following exchange appears on the YouTube page of "muzikman":

> Did she become possessed by a demon at the end of the song?
>   More like, it's a nod to Louis Armstrong…. Satchmo could scat like no other

Of a 3:30 song edited for Top 40 radio appeal and length, the last 30 seconds dedicated to a female artist who is Satchmo scat-singing and growling creates a referential and wonderful pop song, even for one that is now 39 years old. At the time, I recall thinking that Pointer's eponymous debut album, featuring three ballads where the timbre and phrasing we associate with Holiday were up front and elemental, was just a mimicry overall (which shows you how much an uppity 14-year-old cannot hear). The "Billie-esque" album tracks were part of a concerted effort to showcase Pointer as a stylist capable of eliciting comparisons and also perhaps earning credibility all through one gorgeous ballad track in the American disco era. The track in question, called "My Everything," is worth a listen on YouTube to fully get how a vocalist can feel at home in a Holiday groove and tone and still retain her identity as a performer. That Pointer felt free to embrace her Holiday similarities on her debut album becomes a sound example of unsung artistry through both direct and indirect vocal homage.

Credibility via Holiday might be one way to phrase Pointer's expertise both on the album tracks and the single, which peaked at #11 on the Billboard pop chart. It should be mentioned that the divine Satchmo vocalizations of the last 30 seconds of "Heaven" are much more prominently featured on the album version—there's a good two minutes of scat-singing there—and probably became the impetus for repeating the ear-happy aspect on the single release (and 12-inch single version, a longer version of the 45 and indeed a re-recording. It's noteworthy that Holiday is common to all these versions in different increments). In other words, here we have Pointer doing Billie doing Satchmo, all at once—a true musical and vocal mash-up at once. I can cite no other popular example of a Holiday "inspirationist" (though short and indirectly derivative of Holiday via Louis Armstrong, famously one of Holiday's favorite singers), until 1996's legendary debut of *Baduizm* by Miss Erykah Badu.

"The Billie Holiday thing"

Badu's debut brought with it inevitable comparisons between her and Holiday—track by sublime track of the LP resounded with Badu's highly original and very Lady Day-centric vocalizations, especially hear-able on her debut single "On and On" with its syncopated and languid refrain of "What a day, what a day…!" Badu, even through later singles such as "Bag Lady" or "Honey," still remains sounding like herself with elements of Holiday's vocalisms integrated seamlessly into each performance. In 1997, as her album and singles were ascending several Billboard charts, *New York Times* writer Natasha Stovall addressed Badu's comparisons by acknowledging the problem straight away:

> THE PUBLICIST FOR THE NEO-SOUL singer Erykah Badu, whose debut album, "Baduizm," and first single, "On and On," have been near the top of Billboard charts for a month, lays down one ground rule for an interviewer: "Erykah doesn't want to talk about the Billie Holiday thing."
>
> Critics for magazines from *Time* to *Rolling Stone* to *Vibe* have likened Ms. Badu's alternately sultry and clipped vocals to those of that legendary jazz singer. The comparison does not displease Ms. Badu, who changed her last name from Wright to reflect the sound of the scat-like riffs she sings. Billie Holiday, she says, is only one of her influences. Others include Marvin Gaye, Stevie Wonder and Chaka Khan.

With apologies to Ms. Badu and in the spirit of representing the whole artist and not just some reductive aspect that works for this analysis, I hear Chaka Khan in her phrasings and trills (especially, and not surprisingly) in Badu's live cover of "Stay" by Rufus and Chaka Khan and then through 2007's epic "I Want You" as well as Holiday's presence—all gorgeous artistry to be compared to, indeed. Badu, then, is the example of assimilating an influence as impossible to mimic as Holiday into one's own homage—to yourself and your active influences—as the mélange they actually are (as opposed to isolating the idea of what one legend represents and attempting to superimpose those superficial expectations upon an artist). It should be mentioned that Badu's tone has a sweet droll placement that conjures Billie at her best "it'll be alright but somebody may suffer" tone; it is tempting to imagine what Holiday would have had to say about Badu's exquisite 1997 dressing-down of that sketchy cad "Tyrone," a great live recording and mic-drop of a sustained read, indeed a modern-day spiritual cousin to Holiday's own politer, gently ironic ballad "Until the Real Thing Comes Along." I would argue that Badu is the real thing at any point in her career, wherein Holiday's presence enables her to achieve more than a citational status in music history—indeed, as her album trajectory has proven, Badu has forged new (neo-soul) ground that marries many genres and influences and always sounds like her.

To augment the examples of Bonnie Pointer and Erykah Badu, a short list of other artists who bring themselves to the Holiday table, finding their voices while having a phantasmagorical guide vocal from Lady Day in the background, would be (but is not limited to) Frank Sinatra, Tony Bennett, Nina Simone, Betty Carter, Carmen McCrae, Nancy Wilson, Dee Dee Bridgewater, Cassandra Wilson, Nnenna Freelon (particularly in her phrasing), Regina Belle (most notably in her signature ballad "So Many Tears" and other tracks from her debut album *All by Myself*) and Miki Howard (who created an entire homage album for Holiday in 1993) as well as the aforementioned Macy Gray, Jill Scott, Janelle Monae (especially on her *ArchAndroid* project) and José James, either sonically and directly aurally or indirectly through phrasing and a gentle rhythmic anarchy that says, *I am the beat.*

This Section Is Influenced by Geology

In attempting to review hallmarks of Holiday's celebrated vocal style as it developed through three distinct phases—young, mature, and geologic— and to compare it to certain performers (from, again, Diana Ross to David Sedaris to the drag artist Joey Arias and to the living legend Audra McDonald) ventriloquistic attempts to re-create a sound that seems impossible to capture except by mimicry, vocal quirk and affectation, this essay arrives at the following conclusion: that the geologic is the vocal delivery and sound that Holiday *appears* to be remembered for, as her voice depicts wear, abrasion, and unfathomable permanence—the style of a stereotragic geology at work, even in the stillest of moments. Scaffolding, exposure, and hi-fidelity musicianship as a convergence of centripetal forces solidified to show the scaffold and the bigger picture—these elements are most on display through Audra McDonald's performance, and may be the era we remember most if we don't dig enough to excavate the entire range of her three distinct vocal phases (ingénue Holiday, innovator Holiday, and stereotragic Lady Day as legend), wherein phrasing creates a sequence of gorgeous tremors, small, perhaps, but seismically delivered, the kind that would add up to open up, say, the San Andreas Fault. To hear this later geo-jazz-fusion, 1958's live recording of "Moanin' Low," performed for television for the Art Ford Jazz Party program, combines a younger Holiday aesthetic with who she was then, at the moment—a place Lady Day knew how to inhabit, the vocal coming from who she was then and there, an amalgamation of abrasive flow, shimmer, and a tenacious rough-rocked artistry rooted in feeling. Lori Burns states it best—indirectly emphasizing feeling versus the science of being merely a vocal impression—when she states,

> These moments in the Holiday canon create an impression of musical suspension or lyrical excursion; that is, she engages the strategy of melodic and rhythmic elasticity at moments when the text expands to admit a particularly subjective reflection. I would proffer that the expansion and elasticity of musical space and time is the hallmark of Holiday's musical signifyin(g), and it is owing to those qualities that her listeners are permitted the greater freedom of contemplation and interpretation. And that thought brings me back to my ultimate goal with this study, which was to demonstrate through analysis that the musical expression of Holiday's signifyin(g) practices is the product of her *feeling a style.*

On the subject of impersonating feeling in performance, Zadie Smith, voicing Holiday, has something to say (to borrow a catch-phrase from the drag artist Jasmine Masters, currently on Season 4 of *RuPaul's Drag Race All-Stars*):

> People ask: what's it like standing up there? It's like eating your own heart out. It's like there's nobody out there in the dark at all. All the downtown collectors and the white ladies in their own fancy furs love to talk about your phrasing—it's the fashion to talk about your phrasing—but what sounds like a revolution to others is simple common sense to you. [...] It's obvious to you that a voice has the same work to do, musically speaking, as the sax or the trumpet or the piano. A voice has got to feel its way in. Who the hell doesn't know that.

The brilliance of Holiday's vocal impact is the nuanced, swinging, rhythmically and improvisational sequenced containment of tone and timbre, departing from and returning to the rhythm of any song so that it becomes an elasticized event of singular musical response that sets new standards for jazz and vocal standards. The containment I hear embodies the contradictions of a two-sentence paragraph that appears early in Holiday's autobiography: "I was happy for a little bit. It couldn't last" (15). To acknowledge the transience of happiness in a song's length, suggesting that everything will be all right yet change, propels a Holiday performance and clarifies her sound to capture the reality of existence in its contradictions—literally or figuratively, demonstrated in a range of career recordings including "Laughing at Life," "My Man," "Glad to Be Unhappy," "Until the Real Thing Comes Along," the bittersweet "Mandy Is Two" and even "Gloomy Sunday." How to synthesize the tragic and the comic in a difficult life where existence is a daily threat, where the meaning of your talent is appropriated and reduced to just vocal tics?

The spectrum of fidelity to Holiday's dichotomous qualities voice has been lacking in performing Holiday or in creating homage, comic or otherwise. All comedy, all scratch, all hiccup spoken words and tonal elisions delivered behind the beat are excellent acknowledgments of how Holiday trained us to hear her superficially; our gig is to go deeper to where our souls touch and are touched by her incomparable and boundless artistry to deliver any song as only a musician who hears and notes the tragic and comic rhythmic measures of their soul can hope to perform.

Perhaps this is part of what legendary jazz producer John Hammond meant in a 1989 PBS documentary saying, when he first heard Aretha Franklin, "My God—that's the best voice I've heard since Billie Holiday" (*Aretha Franklin—Queen of Soul, Part 1*). What artists or impersonators aim for when practicing Holiday vocally is to voice the core of who we are, seismic, earthbound, sweet, gravelly, grave and celebratory at once—every scratch, every shimmer and quake—aims, finally, to transcend the stereophonic tragedy that limits a physical realm to the essence of its central, original music. In this sense Holiday may never be accurately mimicked beyond the tremors, the vibrato, the elisions and slides, the rhythm that steps back yet makes it to the next musical phrase nonetheless, as a body would when under geologic siege, reduced to the fact of its head alone, the political act divorced from the tone of its personal presence like a shaken, surrogate mouthpiece—the opposite of whatever we physically recognized and responded to when we first heard that voice, heard it change, modulate, and re-phrase in a late-night improvised set that we thought was a living rhythm.

I'll posit that Holiday's apparently tragic narrative may have caused us to hear for the vocal ruins as tragedy manifestations, just as we did for Aretha or even Whitney Houston at the end of their careers—a misplaced concern for the artist that created certain expectations in their vocal performances undergoing the inevitable change that voices go through in any career. James Baldwin brilliantly captured the causal way that a society of listeners may have misheard Holiday's voice as disembodied—that her vocal changes, i.e., "ruins," became displaced in a synecdochal way, representing with a "bland lack of concern" Holiday as a part for the whole embodied artist, just the apparatus of vocal chords, but not the support, the breathing apparatus, the lungs, the foundation, as well as the obvious and highly visible mouthpiece:

> We are altogether too quick to disclaim responsibility for the fate which overtakes—so often—so many gifted, driven, and erratic artists. Nobody pushed them to their deaths, we like to say. They jumped. Of course there is always some truth to this, but the pressures of the brutally indifferent world cannot be dismissed so speedily. Moreover, though we disclaim all responsibility for the failure of an artist, we are happy to take his success or survival as a flattering comment on ourselves. In fact, Billie was produced and destroyed by the same society. It had not the faintest intention of producing her and it did not intend to destroy her; but it has managed to do both with the same bland lack of concern [Baldwin].

To hear the artist completely, not reductively, with distinctive concern, I argue, is necessary to avoid keeping their overall trajectory from becoming stereotragic—hearing, and more accurately expecting—the ruin to supersede the living presence, not buried incrementally and trapped within the spectral detritus of their past—something that Beckett's Winnie from *Happy Days* might have appreciated but probably would hear as "rubbish" in more ways than one.

More Than a Feeling (Zadie Smith's B-Side)

Zadie Smith, again channeling Holiday in the *New Yorker* short story "Crazy He Calls Me," makes a curious comment on the part feeling plays in original interpretation—and how that is or is not elemental to this process:

> In the end, people don't want to hear about dogs and babies and feeling your way into a phrase, or eating your heart out—people want to hear about you as you appear in these songs. They never want to know about the surprise you feel in yourself, the sense of being directed by God, when something in the modulation of your throat leaps up, like a kid reaching for a rising balloon, except most kids miss while you catch it […]—landing on an incidental note, a perfect addition, one you never put in that phrase before, and never heard anyone else do, and yet you can hear at once that it is perfection. Perfection! It has the sound of something totally inevitable—it's better than Porter, it's better than Gershwin. In a moment you have written over their original versions finally and completely.

If we are to hear the sonic inevitability that Smith's Holiday exhorts, we nonetheless may need to keep in mind what John Hammond heard in his comparison of Aretha Franklin to Holiday; both artists came fully formed in terms of interpretative *sui generis* for any genre in which they performed. We know the real thing from a copy of it, in other words; if isolated vocal tics and mannerisms predicate the relaying of any vocalist as idiosyncratic and definitive as Holiday, we are left with the presumption that a mouthpiece can speak for the artist's entire body (in the sense of both their body of work and their literal total body, not just a singing head). We may pay the best homage to Holiday by keeping in mind what Whitney Houston said when interviewed for the PBS documentary on Aretha Franklin regarding her vocal qualities: "I can't even describe it—all I can say is I can FEEL it" (*Aretha Franklin—Queen of Soul, Part 1*)! Houston's comment indirectly yet nicely fulfills Holiday's earlier declaration from *Lady Sings the Blues*: "I don't think I'm singing. I feel like I'm playing a horn…. What comes out is what I feel"—and may be the most emotionally accurate way to hear how Holiday should be performed as tribute—as so much more than just a reductive, revolving tragedy, in stereo.

Embodied Soul

It's noteworthy that Amy Winehouse stated her influences as Dinah Washington, Sarah Vaughan, and Tony Bennett in the documentary *Amy* (2015); at the start of the film, the first time we hear Winehouse's voice is during a iPhone clip of her singing "Happy Birthday" and then Johnny Mercer's "Moon River" from when Winehouse was 16 as part of the National Youth Jazz Orchestra in 2000. In both instances, the timbre, while perhaps more akin to Dinah Washington's mellifluous belting, is still pure Holiday, with Farah Jasmine Griffin's description of Holiday's phrasing as "make it to the next bar without sweating" completely intact. Holiday thrives within a few bars of "Happy Birthday," whether it be through phrasing, lazy tempo, or elision between notes to create a fluid, original, totally reminiscent sound bite of an artist who may not cite Holiday literally but still creates a vocalized "citation" conjuring Holiday within the first three minutes of the documentary. Later, near the close of the film, Bennett himself says, in reference to Winehouse's struggles, "If she had lived, I would have said: slow down; you're too important.... Life teaches you, really how to live it … if you could live long enough."

The wise sound bite *"Life teaches you, really how to live it … if you live long enough"* suggests that if Winehouse could have only physically hung on, she might have found the surviving rhythm of her life as a result. This comment reinforces the stereotragic nature often assigned to Holiday; Winehouse, frequently cited as a Holiday vocal "mirror," is also often discussed in terms of the physical toll placed upon an artist struggling to synthesize their physical presences with their spiritual (or artistic) identities. Winehouse exudes a Holiday influence in an organic way, not as a conscious style choice, but as a rhythmical phrasing embodied in her voice's architectonics—the very foundation and seismic activity wherein rhythm, phonetical suppleness and timbre conjoin to make a sound that, in its placement, tone, and elasticity, have one forebear only—Billie Holiday. In the spirit of combining, *chez* Holiday, the physical realm of a fully embodied, corporeal voice with its spirited mind for good and not in imitative isolation of either realm, it's more than fitting, then, that the song Bennett and Winehouse were duetting on in the movie *Amy*— and one of the last songs Winehouse recorded—would naturally be that jazz vocalist's standard "plea" to synthesize the two elements of offered love itself, the very germane and applicable Lady Day classic "Body and Soul."

We owe it to Holiday to grow ourselves as we hear her at all stages of her incomparable career, to hear it together, from the piquant pertness of her early recordings to the divine gravitas of her later voice as we continue to foster her legacy as well as understand her better—and by *better* I mean completely and not reductively, not as a symbol for someone's worn idea of tragedy and addiction, not in reductive, facile expression, but as a union of body and soul. This union shows how to sustain a seamless, unmatched art that inexhaustibly moves humanity to understand mellifluously what it sounds like to be an African American artist who triumphs over adversity and appropriation to become resoundingly, applicably timeless *and* unified, all on her own terms.

Found in *The Complete Billie Holiday on Columbia 1933–1944*, Holiday's recording of "Having Myself a Time" exemplifies an early mission statement just under three minutes—allowing the listener to hear innovation in the guise of just being fully, resplendently, and musically herself. The lyrics are assertive and unapologetic—they answer to no one but the artist, wanting what she already has and having what she wants. The vocal matches this self-sufficiency in a swinging blend of form and content; Holiday is often a full beat behind the rhythm proper as she takes her time lyrically and rhythmically, telling us why she's having a time *herself*, without the need of anyone's interpretation. For these two and a half minutes, Holiday is enjoying life, nature, or singing, all without any fortune to speak of—the performance is a study in foot-tapping, soul-stirring reasons to make your own reality, as long as it's yours—resplendently, uniquely yours, in the moment and within the pulse of a small combo's groove.

The sonic truth is that at any point in her career, Holiday fully realized and embodied the idea of a compelling and larger sonic fidelity beyond tragedy and over and over again, as we push play and repeat on our devices, in the unique sound, phrasing, and timbre she owned every night at the mic and beyond. She created a new standard for the highest fidelity—but only to herself, having a time with time signatures, in front of or behind them, empowered beyond the limited realm of tragedy as long as singing will live for the record and beyond, to capture the singular changing tempo, dynamics and pitch of our listening lives.

WORKS CITED

Aretha Franklin—Queen of Soul, Part 1. 15 September 2015. Silvao Mazzello. 19 August 2018. https://www.youtube.com/watch?v=RKfkvbOP1sc&t=51s.

Baldwin, James. "On the Horizon: On Catfish Row." *Commentary*, September 1959. October 2018. https://www.commentarymagazine.com/articles/on-the-horizon-on-catfish-row/.

Beckett, Samuel. *Happy Days: A Play in Two Acts*. New York: Grove Press, 2013.

Burns, Lori. "Feeling the Style: Vocal Gesture and Musical Expression in Billie Holiday, Bessie Smith, and Louis Armstrong." *Music Theory Online: a Journal of the Society for Music Theory* 11, no. 3 (September 2005). 13 October 2018. http://www.mtosmt.org/issues/mto.05.11.3/mto.05.11.3.burns_frames.html.

Dove, Rita. "Canary." n.d. Poetry Foundation. https://www.poetryfoundation.org/poems/43359/canary.

Doyle, Sady. *Trainwreck*. Brooklyn: Melville House, 2016.

Griffin, Farah Jasmine. *In Search of Billie Holiday: If You Can't Be Free, Be a Mystery*. New York: Ballantine Books, 2001.

Hari, Johann. *Chasing the Scream*. London: Bloomsbury Circus, 2015.

Himes, Geoffrey. "What Makes Billie Holiday's Music So Powerful Today." *Smithsonian Magazine*, April 7, 2015. 2018. https://www.smithsonianmag.com/arts-culture/what-makes-billie-holiday-so-powerful-today-180954893/.

Holiday, Billie. *Lady Sings the Blues*. New York: Harlem Moon, Broadway Books, 1984.

Lane, Anthony. "Chatterbox." *The New Yorker*, 22 September 2014. 16 September 2018. https://www.newyorker.com/magazine/2014/09/29/chatterbox.

Leland, John. "Backstage With Billie Holiday." *New York Times*, 17 March 2017. 22 October 2018. https://lens.blogs.nytimes.com/2017/03/14/backstage-with-billie-holiday-jerry-dantzic/.

Leyshon, Cressida. This Week in Fiction: Zadie Smith on Inhabiting the World of Billie Holiday." *The New Yorker*, 27 February 2017. 24 July 2018. https://www.newyorker.com/books/page-turner/fiction-this-week-zadie-smith-2017-03-06.

"Moanin' Low." 1958. hoffmanjazz, https://www.youtube.com/watch?v=bb3mGYdohys.

Murray, Bill. *The Rolling Stone Interviews*. Ed. Jann Wenner. New York: Back Bay Books, 2007.

O'Hara, Frank. "The Day Lady Died." n.d. *The Poetry Foundation.* 10 August 2018. https://www.poetryfoundation.org/poems/42657/the-day-lady-died.
Primack, Bret. October 2018. http://www.ladyday.net/life/jaztimes.html.
ptb-8. "Billy's Holiday." 8 February 2006. imdb.com. 11 August 2018. https://www.imdb.com/title/tt0112509/.
Smith, Zadie. "Crazy They Call Me." *The New Yorker*, 6 March 2017. https://www.newyorker.com/magazine/2017/03/06/crazy-they-call-me.
Stovall, Natasha. "Just Don't Compare Her to Billie Holiday." *New York Times*, 6 April 1997. https://www.nytimes.com/1997/04/06/arts/just-don-t-compare-her-to-billie-holiday.html.
Szwed, John F. *Jazz 101.* New York: Hachette, 2000.

Billie Reverberates Her Blues

Advertising Love for Sale
That Costs More Than You Know

Tammie Jenkins

During a career spanning approximately 30 years, Holiday reigned as one of the premiere 20th-century blues singers. Initially performing covers of popular songs, Holiday began rearranging their musical accompaniment and adding her own lyrics, breathing new life into familiar works. The significance of her ability to appropriate a song in the context of sexuality, desire, and domestic violence enabled Holiday to draw on her lived experiences and embed them as autobiographical excerpts during her audio recordings and public performances. In essence, Holiday was her past, present, and public persona simultaneously, with substance abuse and physical violence serving as her only means of escape from the cruel reality that was her life, love, and eventually her death. Holiday's use of unstructured verses and situated discourses that blended spirituals, narrated ballads, and raw human emotions created a level of artistry that had not been previously recorded or publicly performed. Holiday possessed the talent to take a song, appropriate the words and attach to them new meanings while maintaining her unique capacity to tell a story with only her voice.

Employing Robert E. Stake's definition of case study "as the study of particularity and complexity of a single case, coming to understand its activity within important circumstances" (xi), I will analyze the vocal patterns (e.g., improvisation, syncopation, elongation) Holiday uses in her oral deliveries of these texts. Stake specializes in qualitative research methodologies such as narrative inquiry and case study, which provide researchers with alternative ways to collect and to interpret non-quantifiable data from multiple points of view. I use *Love for Sale* and *More Than You Know* as two distinct case studies documenting her deployment of language games, in her songs, to present views of sexuality, domestic violence, and feminism. For the purposes of this essay, I define language games as the use of lyrical repetition, signification (signifying), testimonial (testifying), improvisation, and street vernacular to rhythmically tell a story or to provide social critiques. I utilize public pedagogy as my conceptual framework, to excavate how Holiday's lyrics "negotiate space marked by historical, symbolic, and social mediations" in her public and recorded performances (Giroux 347). I use public pedagogy in conjunction with Stake's notion of case study, to explore the ways that Holiday uses *Love for Sale* and *More Than You Know* to articulate her lived experiences in ways that spoke directly to her detractors. Using narrative inquiry and narrative analysis as my qualitative research methodologies, I examine Holiday's songs as storied texts providing narratives of her lived experiences from multiple points of view. I analyze and interpret relevant verses containing encoded messages or other types of innuendo inviting listeners to interpret Holiday's meaning based on the ways she uses her natural bravado, accentuated vocalization, and breath pauses in both her recorded and public performances. Overall in this essay, I use the following guiding questions: What are the language games used by Holiday? In what ways does Holiday integrate elements of the Blues tradition into her oral delivery of her lyrics? What are the hidden messages or political undertones embedded in Holiday's songs?

Lady Lived Her Blues

The tradition of placing encoded messages or political undertones into a song is not unique to black-inspired musical genres such as spirituals, jazz, and the blues tradition; for such artists the integration of these discourses in their music was natural (Hobson 446). For decades, these individuals had used improvisation as an approach for embedding social rhetoric as well as semi-autobiographical narratives of lived experiences in their oral deliveries. The use of coded language and re-appropriated meanings were techniques often employed by early blues singers as a vehicle for politicization of their lyrics while situating their narratives in larger societal conversations. These performers relied on their voice, intonation, and ability to tell a story during their recorded and public performances. Exploring the use of storytelling by jazz and blues singers to situate their lived experiences in the context of larger cultural and social histories, Carolyn Bockner and Arthur Ellis found that these artists incorporated elements of nostalgia to lament their satisfaction or disdain through the use of multilayered vocalizations in their oral deliveries. For instance, Holiday penned the lyrics to "Don't Explain" featuring words articulated with "saltiness" (O'Meally 37) and yearning. Holiday stated in her ghostwritten autobiography *Lady Sings the Blues* that she was aware of Jimmy's relationship with Nina Mae, an English woman, he dated prior to their marriage (Holiday and Dufty 119). Although Jimmy denied the affair, he came home one night with lipstick on his clothes. Holiday stated she did not want an explanation and demanded that Jimmy take a bath immediately (Holiday and Dufty 119). From this incident, Holiday wrote "Don't Explain," which she performs with gut-wrenching angst and raw emotion expressing not only her disappointment, but also her willingness to accept Jimmy's infidelity.

By today's standards, Holiday was a truly innovative singer who used her lived experiences to express her excitement or discontentment with the status quo as well as her social realities. Perhaps unknowingly, Holiday possessed an innate ability to divest the meaning of words by integrating language games into her performances which made her lyrics relatable to audiences across intersections of race, gender, and class. Holiday drew on many of the language games that had become increasingly popular in blues and jazz music of the 1920s and 1930s, but Holiday added her own touch to make each use uniquely her own. Using wordplay, boasts, signifying, breathing cadences, lyrical symbolism, and repetition, Holiday was able to integrate her narratives of lived experiences in ways that were intersubjective and self-reflexive. In Holiday's audio recordings and public performances "through gestures and verbal manipulation [Holiday] reworked vacuous lines for new significance" (Leonard 156) which redefined the language being used and its associated meanings.

An example of this is Holiday's cover of Cole Porter's "Love for Sale." Both versions detail an unnamed female character advertising her services in hopes of securing a companion or two for the night. However, Porter's version has two additional verses which feature a prostitute waiting for the police patrol to clear the area before opening shop for the task of soliciting customers. Holiday eliminates the verses that provide the listener with the background regarding the time of day or the night this woman is open for business. Instead, Holiday sings of her love as "appetizing" and "young," sensually crooning as she compels her client to follow her and ascent behind her (Holiday 1945). Holiday ends the song as if the prostitute has made a sale, instructing or baiting the customer and extending him an invitation. The stairs lead the customer to the location that the prostitute uses to conduct her business.

Holiday's use of language games in her version of this song are implicitly stated; however, the undercurrents are apparent when listening to the audio of her 1954 recording. In the place of Porter's opening verse, Holiday incorporates a haunting musical interlude that acts as a prelude to the prostitute announcing her availability. While singing the words "love," "unspoiled," "soiled," and "sale," Holiday elongates these words by lingering on the final consonant sound in each. This serves to stress the significance Holiday has placed on them and perhaps illustrates her connecting these words to her lived experiences as a nine-year-old victim of rape and as a 14-year-old prostitute (Blackburn 15; Clarke 37). She also relies on the use of the word "love" as a substitute for words such as "sex," "affection," and "personal commodification." Holiday disconnects each from discourses of "love" and recontextualizes their meanings as separate entities.

Holiday performed "Love for Sale" in 1954 as a solo artist accompanied by a single instrument, a piano, which emphasizes the transition from love to commerce. The pianist, Oscar Peterson, played a series of single, lingering, and haunting notes before including multiple keys simultaneously. This repetitive piano riff is done three times; hence, setting the mood for listeners while laying a foundation for Holiday's oral delivery. Holiday begins her vocals with a naïve reflection showing that of a youthful inexperienced girl she sings "thrill" in a slight, high-pitched register. But Holiday concludes her musical rendition as an older woman who has acquired a wealth of knowledge over the course of her lifetime which is depicted in her deepened intonation as she sings the final line. Holiday sings the word "love" in a baritone-esque voice lingering on the "ov" sound before elongating the word "sale" phonetically stressing the "l" sound in "sale." However, a cover of "Love for Sale" performed by Simply Red's lead singer, Mick Hucknall, a capella during a live performance at the Monteux Jazz Festival in 2009, provides an alternative to Holiday's versions that includes Porter's original opening verses. Hucknall sings the opening verses from Porter's original composition slowly and sensually. The tempo changes when Hucknall sings the title line and continues throughout as he stresses the words "who," "supply," "price," and "paradise." Hucknall's vocalization changes as he deepens his voice for the word "love," and he elevates his intonations when singing "mill of " in which he shortens his pronunciation of "mill," but phonemically elongates the "l" sound in his pronunciation of "love." In contrast to Hucknall's performance of "Love for Sale," Holiday's version remains the most poignant. Holiday delivers the song's lyrics as a lament centered on the men that she encountered over her lifetime.

The term "mill" is often associated with the manufacturing of grain into flour as well as the chaotic movement of a large number of people or animals in public spaces. Typically, the word "mill" is absent in discourses of love and relationships; yet, Porter, Holiday, and other artists each elected to include the term in "Love for Sale" as a vehicle for articulating their view of male-female interactions. The "mill of love" is an expression of Holiday's thoughts and feelings regarding the ill-treatment that she often endured in her relationships beginning with her father, Clarence, and concluding with her last husband, Louis McKay, while signifying her longing for unconditional positive regard and affection. Holiday conceivably used her past relationships for inspiration with the oral delivery of these lyrics. The way Holiday sings about experiencing all kinds of love, except "true love" indicates a desire for unconditional love and highlights the failure Holiday has experienced in past relationships. For instance, an "old love" may refer to Louis McKay whom Holiday met at the age of 16 and developed quick feelings for only to become disappointed by his frequent extended absences until they reunited in the 1950s (Blackburn 276). The pair began dating in 1951, at which time McKay became Holiday's manager (Blackburn 276). During their marriage, McKay physically abused Holiday, stole money from her, as well as used Holiday's addiction to control every aspect of her life. At the time of Holiday's death, she and McKay were estranged and it was alleged that Holiday had begun divorce proceedings, but Holiday died without a will leaving McKay as her sole beneficiary of her estate (Blackburn 276).

While "mill of love" conceivably accentuates her relationships with Jimmy Monroe, John Simmons, and Joe Guy, each of whom Holiday rushed into the arms of for the wrong reasons with devastating results. Monroe, a trumpet player, was Clark Monroe's brother whom Holiday had also dated when she was younger. Jimmy was Holiday's first husband and is widely believed to have introduced her first to cocaine and later to heroin (O'Meally 15, 18). Monroe was a pimp who taught Holiday how to dress and conduct herself in public places. Although the two eventually married, Monroe continued his relationship with Nina Mae. His philandering and drug addiction contributed to the end of his marriage to Holiday. After the collapse of Holiday's marriage to Monroe and prior to her relationship with Joe Guy, Holiday dated John Simmons. This was during the time that Holiday began mainlining heroin (Clarke 223). Holiday left Monroe to begin a relationship with Joe Guy. Guy was a musician, who supplemented his income by selling drugs. During their relationship, Guy began supplying Holiday with heroin, a drug that he later became addicted to as well. Their relationship ended after two years, but the two remained friends with Guy serving Holiday's occasional road manager (Clarke 223).

Whereas "mill of love" in Holiday's "Love for Sale" is credibly indicative of her relationship with John Levy and later, Louis McKay each of whom were unfaithful, physically abusive, and used her name for their own financial gain. John Levy was a hustler who became Holiday's manager and paramour (O'Meally 15). McKay was a womanizer who supplied Holiday with drugs which he rationed to maintain control over her. McKay had a girlfriend on the west coast named Gloria. Like Levy, McKay benefited financially from Holiday by purchasing property in his name only, making investments, and managing her estate. Prior to Holiday's death and during their turbulent marriage, McKay fathered children with other women, but there are no definitive answers regarding whether or not Holiday had knowledge of McKay's other families. These events are reflected in Holiday's delivery of the song's lyrics, perhaps reflecting that she has experienced betrayal, abuse, and heartbreak in past relationships.

Love Returned Unrequited

Holiday spent most of her adult life in pursuit of lasting love. She encountered men who used her and broke her spirit which she reflects in her articulation of the lyrics: the words "true" and "love" are uttered with a sadness that shortens as Holiday sings "true" while elongating "love" with a tremble in her voice and intonation. In her lifetime, Holiday was a victim of two known sexual assaults during her prepubescent and preteen years. A second rape by an unknown assailant occurred when Holiday was 12. Although Holiday was not criminally prosecuted for the second sexual assault, she was emotionally and mentally arrested which sentenced her to a lifetime of abuses. Holiday's decision at the age of 14 to separate sex from love by prostituting compounded her inability to form positive attachments beyond sex or physical violence in which she was an instigating victim and perpetrator in both. Following her stint as a prostitute, Holiday began performing as a nightclub singer where she began encountering men such as Jimmy Monroe, John Simmons, Joe Guy, John Levy, and Louis McKay who would physically, emotionally, and mentally abuse Holiday under the guise of loving and/or caring for her.

A Voice of Her Own

Before I began studying Billie Holiday's music and artistry, I was convinced that the blues were about sadness, which the artist could only convey through the use of solemn music and sorrow-filled lyrics. Holiday's voice held an angst that her experiences enabled her to use as a form of artistic expression. Holiday drew upon knowledge she acquired from her time as a nightclub singer and touring with the likes of Count Basie, Artie Shaw, Benny Goodman, and others to list but a few to fine tune her artistry (Daubney 19; Griffin 18–19). Holiday also found inspiration from popular jazz singers of the day, which enabled her to use their vocal proficiencies to refine her own (Griffin 17; O'Meally 9). Holiday arrived in Harlem during the 1920s which coincided with the Jazz Age, the Harlem Renaissance, and the rise of blues music. This style of music enabled performers to incorporate elements of African oral tradition and enslavement, which included improvisation, call 'n' response, non-chronological storytelling, lyrical repetition, riffs, and restrain into their oral deliveries of a song's lyrics.

Using rhythmic elongation and wordplay, Holiday used her voice and intonations to dirty-up "the musical sound" in her oral deliveries by including "blends, growls, and rasps" which enabled her to perform songs that were intimate and conversational (Jones 20).Through strategic placement of her musical accompaniment, Holiday's heartfelt emotion and inner turmoil was accentuated by her natural "timbre" and "florid vibrato" (O'Meally 42), which enabled her to embed hidden messages or incorporate political undertones in her songs. For example, the song "More Than You Know" could be read as a story of Holiday's experiences with men from her father, Clarence, to her final love, Louis McKay. Holiday addressed discourses of abandonment and unrequited love; while professing to love the unnamed individual more than herself. Employing a style of singing that reflected the weight of her experience, Holiday set her narratives and their emotional elucidations into her layered life as a prostitute, a victim of sexual assaults and domestic violence, as well as a substance abuser whose condition permitted some of the men in her life to take physical, financial, and emotional advantage of her. Given her early history (abandonment, sexual abuse, domestic violence), one might wonder if that contributed to the many unfortunate decisions that Holiday made later in life. Holiday was a girl seemingly trapped in a woman's body without the resources or support necessary to reconcile these entities.

Finding Billie Holiday ... Losing Eleanora Fagan

Previously, scholars identified Holiday's recording of "Strange Fruit" as her singular protest song. However, Angela Y. Davis in *Blues Legacies and Black Feminism* examined Holiday's repertoire of popular songs in their entirety. Davis compared the themes of Holiday's music to those of Gertrude "Ma" Rainey and Bessie Smith as feminist music addressing the lives and experiences of black middle class women. Davis found that Holiday's songs like those of Rainey and Smith explored discourses of male-female relationships in terms of infidelity, domestic violence, abandonment, and sexuality. Similarly, Holiday's "Love for Sale" and "More Than You Know," subtly explored these discourses in ways that enabled her listeners to internalize the hidden transcripts embedded in the word choices and re-appropriated meanings contained in her lyrics. Hence, "[inspiring] marginalized voices to emerge from the historical world" (Hobson 448) including her own. Presently, scholars have noted that "she [often] lied to interviewers" (O'Meally 94) or purposefully omitted information perhaps to protect herself or out fear.

Holiday's modification of her autobiographical data has left researchers with many unanswered questions and a litany of partial truths that scholarship has only yet to excavate. Yet, there is a growing consensus suggesting that Holiday used her music to share her narratives of lived experiences with her audiences. Holiday's most noted endeavor came in 1935, when she performed in the "Saddest Tale," a song about domestic violence in Duke Ellington's *Symphony in Black: A Rhapsody of Negro Life*. This song's lyrics mirrored in many ways the physical violence that Holiday endured that was well-known to her, her perpetrator, as well as those in her inner circle. Holiday survived a lifetime of abuse (sexual, emotional, and physical) crammed into her short 44-year existence. Perhaps these experiences were instrumental in transforming Holiday from a woman of the streets to that of an icon, which she explores the song "More Than You Know." This is seemingly a love song in which Holiday expresses affection for another human being.

However, a close reading of the lyrics reveals a deeper underpinning, which expresses her role in driving this individual out of her life, while contradictorily longing for their return. She then qualifies the statement that should her lover ever become tired of her or their affair, she would not appear to grieve nearly as much as she shows. These feelings were part of her learned behavior, acquired during her formative years after being abandoned by both parents and left in the care of her aunt Eva Miller. Holiday had limited contact with her father, Clarence, and lived on and off with her mother, Sadie, for years, before moving into a place of her own. Her marriages to Jimmy Monroe and Louis McKay, as well as her relationships with Joe Guy, John Simmons, and John Levy, were compromised by their frequent womanizing, physical abuse, narcotics, and periodic absences. This is confirmed by her acknowledgment of such in her autobiography as well as documented interviews with Holiday's friends, conducted by Julia Blackburn, in 2005. The lyrical concern that her lover may grow tired of her might imply that Holiday was aware of her insecurities and the role they played in her adult relationships (romantic or platonic). By "tired" Holiday is referring to the weariness that her partner may feel after their continuous resistance or submission to the emotional whims of Holiday. Holiday expected more of her partners than many were able or willing to give her which contributed to Holiday initiating or searching for relationships in which she could expect to be abused or abandoned. This placed Holiday in the role of perpetual victim and self-created damsel in distress whose rescuer often entered her life with ulterior motives that Holiday may or may not have been aware of but welcomed with the expectation of abuse or abandonment.

On the other hand, "Love for Sale" a seemingly sensual song that innocently presents a prostitute drawing on her years of experiences to solicit a gentleman caller for the evening. What the underlying narratives of the lyrics infer is Holiday's re-appropriation of Cole Porter's words in ways that integrates her story into her oral delivery of the words and their re-appropriated meanings. I return to Holiday's omission of the first two stanzas of Porter's song, which details someone, imaginably the prostitute, whose narrative Holiday employs. Holiday's choice to remove the masculine aspect of the song's lyrics and replace it with only the female voice enabled her to introduce messages of empowerment, resiliency, and momentary freedom into her oral delivery. This unnamed orator describes the events which transpires as this lady of the evening waits in the shadows as a beat cop conducts his nightly rounds near the home female narrator uses for her business transactions. Instead, Holiday opted to begin her oral delivery with the words "Love for sale." This indicates to the listener that the policeman has completed his nightly check of the area and the path is cleared for her to solicit customers. It also signifies Holiday's removal of the masculine entity (the policeman) from her perception of womanhood and asserts the female voice into the conversation in ways that enable the prostitute to acquire agency.

As previously stated, she adds emphasis to the song's narratives through the song's command to follow her up the stairs, if the buyer wants to sample her goods. Her use of strategic silences during her singing "creates the illusion of sexual openness" (Hobson 444); while challenging her own objectification and agency as critical sites of struggle and subjugation in the larger society. The use of breath pauses enabled Holiday to open spaces between her lyrics, oral deliveries, and audience interpretations in ways that encouraged each to take action by engaging in socially imposed silences. This is evidenced by Holiday's oral delivery of these lyrics in which "the words [remain] Porter's, but the experiences [are] Holiday's alone" (Yaffe 156) allowed her to publicly articulate her lived experiences as a former prostitute. The embedding of hidden messages or political undertones has enabled artists such as Billie Holiday to use their lived experiences to stir the emotions of their audiences or listeners while permitting new meanings to emerge over time and space.

Conclusion: Posthumous Resonance

Billie Holiday was a songstress whose musical style was years ahead of her time. Even though her career only lasted three decades, Holiday remains one of the most recognizable singers of the 20th century. This essay employed "Love for Sale" and "More Than You Know" to examine Holiday's narratives of sexuality, domestic violence, and feminism entrenched in these songs' lyrics or implicitly stressed during her performances. Holiday used the words in these songs to retell her narratives of abandonment, sexual assault, prostitution, and other abuses in ways that re-contextualized her past as discourses of her present. The layers meaning Holiday embedded in her audio recordings and public performances of "Love for Sale" and "More Than You Know" are eternal reminders of a woman whose life was an open book set to music.

WORKS CITED

Blackburn, Julia. *With Billie: A New Look at the Unforgettable Lady Day*. New York: Pantheon Books, 2005.
Brockner, Carolyn, and Arthur P. Ellis. *Ethnographically Speaking: Autoethnography, Literature, and Aesthetics*. Walnut Creek, CA: AltaMira Press, 2001.
Clarke, Donald. *Wishing on the Moon: The Life and Times of Billie Holiday*. New York: Viking, 1994.
Daubney, Kate. "Songbird or Subversive? Instrumental Vocalisation Technique in the Songs of Billie Holiday." *Journal of Gender Studies*, vol. 11, no. 1, 2002, pp. 17–28.
Giroux, Henry A. "Public Pedagogy as Cultural Politics: Stuart Hall and the 'Crisis' of Culture." *Cultural Studies*, vol. 14, no. 2, 2000, 341–360.
Green, Meg. *Billie Holiday: A Biography*. Westport, CT: Greenwood Press, 2007.
Griffin, Farah Jasmine. *If You Can't Be Free, Be a Mystery: In Search of Billie Holiday*. New York: The Free Press, 2001.
Hobson, Janell. "Everybody's Protest Song: Music as Social Protest in the Performances of Marian Anderson and Billie Holiday." *Signs*, vol. 33, no. 2, 2008, pp. 443–448.
Holiday, Billie. "Love for Sale." *Billie Holiday Sings*, Cleft Records, 1945.
Holiday, Billie. "More Than You Know." Brunswick Records, 1939.
Holiday, Billie, and William Dufty. *Lady Sings the Blues*. Brooklyn: Harlem Moon, 1956.
Jenkins, Tammie. *A Case Study of Tracie Morris's Project Princess*. Ph.D. diss., Louisiana State University, 2013.
Jones, Stacy Holman. *Torch Singing: Performing Resistance and Desire from Billie Holiday to Edith Pilaf*. Walnut Creek, CA: AltMira Press, 2007.
Jung, Elan K. *Sexual Trauma: A Challenge Not Insanity*. Queensbury, NY: The Hudson Press, 2010.
Kilment, Bud. *Billie Holiday*. Los Angeles: Holloway House, 1990.
Lady Sings the Blues. Directed by Sidney J. Furie, performances by Diana Ross and Billy D. Williams. Paramount, 1972.
O'Meally, Robert. *Lady Day: The Many Faces of Billie Holiday*. New York: Arcade, 1991.
Porter, Cole. "Love for Sale." *The New Yorkers*, 1930.
Stake, Robert E. *The Art of Case Study Research*. Thousand Oaks, CA: Sage, 1995.
Swzed, John. *Billie Holiday: The Musician and the Myth*. New York: Penguin, 2015.
Yaffe, David. *Fascinating Rhythm: Reading Jazz in American Writing*. Princeton: Princeton University Press, 2005.

Lady Sings the Blues?

Tragedy, Autobiography and Reassessment

Anna Maria Barry

Since 2006, the BBC has periodically broadcast a documentary entitled *Queens of Heartache* (Nicholls). This film explores the lives and careers of five iconic female singers: Edith Piaf, Billie Holiday, Judy Garland, Maria Callas and Janis Joplin. The title of the film makes its hypothesis clear. These women, it suggests, can be collectively defined by the heartache they experienced. Despite the different genres, cultures and eras that these singers represent, they are shoved together in a box that is simply labeled "tragic." Billie Holiday's place within such a morbid milieu comes as no surprise. Even before her death at the age of 44, she was seen as a tragic figure. This was due to her troubled personal life that was blighted by well-documented struggles with addiction, poverty and racism. Holiday's music appeared to reflect these troubles, with songs that evoked loss, heartbreak and disappointment in an incredibly visceral way. Her premature death merely underscored this sense of tragedy, solidifying a reputation that has endured to this day. But despite these truths, the portrayal of Holiday as a tragic victim is unfair and arguably unfounded. It is a reductive characterization that robs her of her agency, threatening to eclipse her status as an artist, an innovator, a survivor, a writer and a vocal critic of social injustice. Furthermore, it is an idea that reflects a range of problematic ideas about Holiday as a black woman.

Why are we so inclined to see Billie Holiday as a tragic figure? What is at stake when we do this? Where might we look if we seek to challenge this idea? How should we remember her? These are the questions that this essay will try to answer. In order to do this, it will first turn its attention to *Lady Sings the Blues*. Holiday's autobiography of 1956 *presents us* with the voice of a woman who is no tragic victim. But this voice, we will see, has been overlooked, undermined, and called into question. I will offer a reading of this volume that allows us to locate a version of Billie Holiday that challenges the tragic narrative that has been woven around her. It is a reading that reveals the gulf between the identity she created for herself, and the one that has been created for her—largely by white men. We will see that the image these individuals have constructed owes much to prejudiced and patronizing ideas about her gender and race. The essay will then move on to consider Holiday in the context of other singers. As the aforementioned BBC documentary demonstrates, the urge to reduce female singers to one-dimensional figures is both widespread and persistent. However, a recent wave of recuperative efforts has started to reassess singers who have been patronized by posterity. Women including Nina Simone, Janis Joplin and Amy Winehouse have been afforded more intelligent and nuanced analyses than they had previously received. In this context, I will argue, Billie Holiday is surely due a radical reassessment. Happily, we will see that this appears to be on the horizon.

Lady Sings the Blues

Billie Holiday's autobiography was published in 1956. Its co-author was William Dufty, a white journalist who wrote for the *New York Post*. Dufty interviewed Holiday extensively, also relying on previously published interviews, news features and legal reports in order to piece together her life story (Szwed 22–26). The completed autobiography famously opens with two bombastic sentences: "Mom and Pop were just a couple of kids when they got married. He was eighteen, she was sixteen, and I was three" (Holiday and Dufty 3).[1] These opening lines suggest the direct, defiant and seemingly undiluted tone that characterizes the volume. Holiday recounts her life in a manner which seems to hold nothing back—she describes the abuse she suffered as a child, her work as a prostitute, her addictions and her incarcerations. Despite these difficult themes, Holiday tells her story with wry wit and humor, in a voice devoid of self-pity.

Since its publication, Holiday's autobiography has been derided, called into question and accused of not even being her own work. An examination of these responses reveals the extent to which her image has been shaped by ideas about gender and race, as well as attitudes towards jazz. John Szwed and Farah Jasmine Griffin describe reactions to *Lady Sings the Blues* in the black press, both discussing a review by literary critic J. Saunders Redding that appeared in the *Baltimore Afro-American* (Szwed 30; Griffin 48). Redding, they explain, found the "raw" language and sordid details of the book distasteful (Szwed 30)—it did not conform to the image of black middle-class respectability that his newspaper was invested in. Responses were also gendered. Griffin argues that, when reviews did praise the book, they "focused on Dufty's skill and talent" (Griffin 47). It is clear that Holiday's agency was elided, and credit was instead given to her white male co-author.

Scholars have drawn comparisons between the reception of *Lady Sings the Blues* and Ethel Waters' autobiography, *His Eye Is on the Sparrow*, which was published five years earlier (Waters and Samuels; Szwed 31–32; Griffin 47–48). The similarities between Holiday and Waters' volumes are significant: both are autobiographies of black women who sang, written in the same decade. Both subjects had been born into poverty and described their experiences with crime, addiction and sex. They both shared the same publisher, and each had a white male co-author. Their reception, however, could not have been more different; while Holiday was panned, Waters was praised. As Szwed explains, this is because Waters "cast her autobiography as [...] a conversion experience, a woman who found faith's triumphant rise from the ruins of her childhood, and was a credit to her race" (Szwed 32). In other words, Waters ultimately presented a favorable model of black womanhood.

Attitudes towards genre also had an impact on the reception of Holiday's autobiography. Szwed describes how jazz was no longer seen as popular music by 1956, instead occupying a more "rarefied place in the public's view"—a place guarded by "closet high modernists who wanted no mention of drugs, whorehouses, or lynching brought into discussions of the music" (Szwed 13–14). This led to a number of reviews that objected to Holiday's descriptions of the jazz world as she knew it. This world was perhaps best typified by her line "I guess I'm not the only one who heard their first good jazz in a whorehouse" (Holiday and Dufty 10). Many reviewers who attacked the book felt that such representations of the genre constituted "a betrayal of the whole cause of jazz" (Keepnews 112). *Lady Sings the Blues* clearly perpetuated ideas about jazz that its highbrow defenders wished to circumvent. However, the musical world that Holiday's autobiography described was nevertheless potent—many readers would have been attracted to salacious (and somewhat stereotypical) stories of sex, drugs and crime. Such themes, and their commercial appeal, could contribute to a reading of the text as sensationalized gossip rather than a serious piece of life-writing.

In the years that followed the publication of Billie Holiday's autobiography, its status became increasingly complicated. This was largely a result of the errors that biographers began to find in its pages, starting with its celebrated opening lines. Holiday's mother had given birth to her at the age of 19 rather than 13, while her father had been 17 and not 15, and the pair never married (Griffin 51). Holiday did not even report her birthplace correctly; she was born in Philadelphia, not Baltimore. These are just the first in a catalogue of inaccuracies that have been located in *Lady Sings the Blues*. Aside from such errors, the book has been accused of making false or exaggerated assertions about Holiday's musical achievements, including her claim to have participated in the writing of "Strange Fruit" (O'Meally 45).

The autobiography has also been criticized for its failure to tell the whole truth; Holiday did not explicitly disclose that her mother had also worked as a prostitute, for example (Nicholson 42).[2] These are not the only factors which have undermined the credibility of *Lady Sings the Blues*. Claims that the book was written solely for financial motives have been much repeated, with biographer Linda Kuehl typically stating that Holiday wrote the book "for money to support a drug habit" (qtd. in Szwed 14). The suggestion is that a commercial motive undermines the reliability of the text. Many have also argued that the volume was entirely Dufty's work, with some even claiming that Holiday could not read or write herself (Szwed 18–19). This somewhat patronizing (and gendered) view denies Holiday any agency. Griffin has rightly noted a double standard here; how, she asks, can those who claim the book was Dufty's work also accuse Holiday of lying (Griffin 46–47)?

It is clear that *Lady Sings the Blues* has had a complex reception. It has been criticized, questioned and dismissed. The autobiography, and Holiday herself, have been tangled in a web of agendas and assumptions relating to gender, race and genre. But is this fair? And is another reading possible? Dufty made no recordings of his conversations with Holiday, so we will never have a definitive understanding of the co-authors' respective roles in the production of *Lady Sings the Blues*. However, I believe it is worth considering what happens to our understanding of the text—and Holiday herself—when we credit her with agency. Szwed has recently done just this, in "an effort to see [Holiday's] authority restored" (Szwed 9). He explains that Dufty's key sources were interviews Holiday had given, arguing that "it was she who was at the source of at least some of the book's fabrications and misrememberings" (Szwed 8). It is within these fabrications and misrememberings that we might locate Holiday's agency.

Autobiography as Performance

Rather than constituting evidence of the unreliability of *Lady Sings the Blues*, its inaccuracies and omissions reveal much about the way in which Holiday wished to present herself—in fact, they can be even more revealing than "the truth." As Paul John Eakin has forcefully argued, all autobiographies are exercises in self-creation and should therefore be seen as works of subjective fiction rather than objective fact (Eakin). With this in mind, *Lady Sings the Blues* should be read as a creative construct that was designed to shape and negotiate Billie Holiday's identity. Judging it on its accuracy is beside the point. Christopher Wiley has made a similar observation in his study of 19th-century musical biography; he suggests that meaning often "hinges not so much on the factual information offered by authors as on the precise ways in which those details are expressed" (Wiley 162). Autobiographies therefore demand close and critical reading. We are required to read between the lines, asking why an author might have chosen to censor or manipulate the truth.

Here it is worth pausing to place *Lady Sings the Blues* within the broader historical context of performance and life-writing. Since at least the 19th century, autobiographies of performers (actors as well as singers) have been widely regarded with skepticism. This is mainly due to their "suspect reliability" and "self-promoting agendas" (Postlewait, "Theatre Autobiographies" 157). Those whose profession entails the performance of fictional identities through drama or song are not seen as reliable narrators. The idea that performers' autobiographies are little more than puffed up forms of publicity has meant that they are often denied serious critical attention (Postlewait, "Autobiography" 252). In this context, *Lady Sings the Blues* can be seen as part of a larger genre that has historically been somewhat misunderstood. As I have argued elsewhere in my work on opera singers' autobiographies of the 19th century, these texts might usefully be considered as another facet of performance—a performance of identity (Barry). Instead of judging them on their accuracy, we should interrogate them in order understand the image that a singer sought to project. Others have approached this understanding of *Lady Sings the Blues*; O'Meally has suggested we should read it as a "dream book" (O'Meally 21) that requires interpretation, whilst Griffin has argued that it represents a "performance of the Holiday persona" (Griffin 50). Just as we would not judge Holiday's vocal performance based on the objective truth of her lyrics, we should not judge her autobiography on the objective truth of its words.

Re-Reading Lady Sings the Blues

If we chose to give Holiday agency and read *Lady Sings the Blues* as a creative performance of identity, we'd find that the image she constructs for herself is entirely at odds with the tragic victim she is so often cast as. That is not to say that tragedy is absent. She describes growing up in poverty, being sexually abused and her many encounters with racism. She shares her experiences of prison, domestic abuse and addiction. However, she tackles each of these facets of her life with clear-sighted wit and defiance, in a manner that begs no pity. Take, for example, a passage in which she discusses being hit by her first husband Jimmy Monroe, around the time she started to take hard drugs with him: "Jimmy was no more the cause of my [addiction] than my mother was. That goes for any man I ever knew. I was as strong, if not stronger, than any of them. And when it's that way, you can't blame anybody but yourself" (Holiday and Dufty 120). Holiday is often characterized as an addict who suffered abuse at the hands of malevolent men. However, it is clear that she presents her experiences of addiction and domestic abuse in a very different way. She is at pains to emphasize her strength and free will— her dominance over men, even. As Szwed has recognized, "[Holiday] blames only herself for making bad choices and being too weak to resist drugs. Hers was not a victim's story" (Szwed 70).

In *Blues Legacies and Black Feminism*, Angela Y. Davis describes the blues tradition of "naming," which she traces back to the West African practice of "nommo" (Davis 33). This, she explains, is a traditional practice of naming problems and threats as a means of both sharing them with a wider community and exerting control over them. It is possible to read *Lady Sings the Blues* in this context. In its pages, Holiday describes (or "names") her struggles publicly in order to share them and take ownership of them. Indeed, she makes this desire explicit when she says of her autobiography: "I've raked up my past so I could bury it" (Holiday and Dufty 213). Read in this way, Holiday's autobiography becomes a defiant means of naming and claiming her troubles in order to exorcise them.

Furthermore, Holiday takes her troubles and turns them outward—she makes the personal political. *Lady Sings the Blues* is extremely socially and politically engaged. Within its pages, Holiday rages against racism, the injustices of America's contemporary drugs policy and its criminal justice system. Just one example is this extended critique:

> Imagine if the government chased sick people with diabetes, put a tax on insulin and drove it into the black market, told doctors they couldn't treat them, and then caught them, prosecuted them for not paying their taxes, and then sent them to jail. If we did that, everyone would know we were crazy. Yet we do practically the same thing every day in the week to sick people hooked on drugs. The jails are full and the problem is getting worse every day [Holiday and Dufty 153].

In this articulate passage and others like it, we find no victim. Instead, we are presented with a powerful woman's voice that calls to the 21st century. The themes Holiday discusses have the ability to connect and shed light on many of our most pressing contemporary concerns—from racism, police brutality and the criminal justice system, to sexual abuse, drugs policy and LGBTQIA+ rights.

The passage which is most revealing of the image that Holiday wished to project is one in which she meditates on her ability to sing the words "hunger" and "love" so powerfully:

> Maybe I remember what those words are all about. Maybe I'm proud enough to *want* to remember Baltimore and Welfare Island, the Catholic institution and the Jefferson

Market Court, the sheriff in front of our place in Harlem and the towns from coast to coast where I got my lumps and my scars [...]—every damn bit of it.

All the Cadillacs and minks in the world—and I've had a few—can't make it up or make me forget it [Holiday and Dufty 195].

This passage encapsulates the way in which Holiday paints her life as one of survival rather than tragedy. She feels no shame, she makes no apology, she asks for no pity—and she does so with wit and humor. She is no tragic victim, and certainly no "Queen of Heartache."

Women in Music

So why do we persist in seeing Billie Holiday as a tragic victim? In a recent meditation on the gendering of musical martyrdom, journalist Molly Beauchemin has argued: "Women who succeed in a big way upset convention, and we haven't yet figured out how to deal with that as a culture. When women succeed [...] we anticipate their downfall and pounce hard, relish the sillage of failure when we get a whiff." Though Beauchemin refers to Amy Winehouse here, her understanding can be equally applied to Billie Holiday.[3]

Critics, scholars and cultural commentators have frequently drawn comparisons between Holiday and Winehouse. A consideration of this parallel is illuminating, as it demonstrates that the urge to reduce women to gendered stereotypes is still strong. Both singers had powerful and original voices, and they shared many of the same struggles—addiction, domestic violence and run-ins with the law. Winehouse was vocal about her admiration for the elder singer, featuring a rendition of "There Is No Greater Love" on her debut album (Winehouse), and performing "Ain't Nobody's Business" at a Billie Holiday tribute concert in 2004 (Cummings). She even referenced the white gardenia that was Holiday's "signature trademark" (Greene 68), displaying a red flower prominently in her famous beehive. During the lives of both singers, the media relished their personal struggles with a morbid enthusiasm, pouncing on all of the sordid details. Perhaps the greatest similarity between the two singers, though, is their demise—both of course died prematurely due to drug and alcohol addiction. After the deaths of Holiday and Winehouse, the media continued (and continue) to pick at the scraps of their lives like vultures, casting them as tragic victims.

Paul Hearsum has studied coverage of Amy Winehouse's death in the British press, arguing that a number of tropes were repeatedly drawn upon by journalists—some framed her death as punishment for her transgressive behavior, whilst others attempted to suggest her posthumous "redemption" though her Jewish funeral, her musical legacy and the charity that was set up in her name (Hearsum). In other words, she was imagined in a variety of ways that were implicitly gendered—a 21st-century iteration of the Victorian "fallen woman."[4] Much like Holiday, Winehouse is predominantly seen as a tragic figure. In many ways this is not surprising—her premature death was unquestionably tragic. What is notable, however, is the way in which she has been so frequently compared to Billie Holiday. Daphne A. Brooks, for example, has called Winehouse "a caricatured Billie-Holiday-on heroin," going on to suggest that the younger singer "powerfully" invoked "the overdetermined *Lady Sings the Blues* construction of Holiday's mythically tragic iconicity" (Brooks 46, 49). This idea has been much repeated by critics and commentators, suggesting that Billie Holiday now functions as the archetype of the tragic female singer. Her example provides a blueprint that can be evoked as shorthand for other musical women whose lives have similar trajectories. This process of comparison is in itself gendered—Winehouse is imagined as another Holiday, and filed into the category of "troubled jazz star." This categorizing urge is nothing new—women in music have long been forced into stereotypical identities that fail to recognize their artistic and cultural contributions. This has been noted by Roy Shuker, who points out that female musicians "are seen in stereotypical terms: divas, rock chicks (e.g. Suzi Quatro, Janis Joplin), men-pleasing angels (Doris Day), victims (Billie Holiday) or problem personalities (Judy Garland)" (Shuker 146). It is no surprise that he cites Holiday as the archetypal victim.

Understood in this context, it is clear that Holiday's tragic image is just one manifestation of a bigger problem that seeks to exert control over women, forcing them to exist in the confines of stereotype and denying them autonomy, self-expression and artistic credit. This problem was all too evident in the aforementioned documentary *Queens of Heartache*, which ascribed a nickname to each of its subjects: Edith Piaf the "Urchin Queen," Billie Holiday the "Jazz Queen," and Maria Callas the "Drama Queen," for example. These ridiculous epithets are incredibly reductive, and again suggest the instinct to categories and, therefore, confine women. A documentary focusing on five random male singers with "sad" lives is, frankly, inconceivable. There are no "Kings of Heartache."

This (male) effort to contain women within the narrow confines of stereotype is also evident in *Lady Sings the Blues*. Though I have offered a reading of this autobiography that credits Holiday with agency, this was in some ways forced to exist within a structure that was imposed and controlled by men. William Dufty claimed that it was Holiday's second husband Louis McKay who first floated the idea of an autobiography, seeing an opportunity to "cash in on the confessional book vogue" (Blackburn 261). Holiday was initially averse to the idea. The book also had a male co-author, though (as we have seen) the extent to which he shaped the text remains up for debate. Szwed has described a rigorous editorial process, during which language was tweaked, the original ending was rewritten and (male) editors hacked away at sections of the text that made (male) lawyers nervous (Szwed 35–36). The title was even imposed by publishers—Holiday had wanted to call it *Bitter Crop* (Szwed 35). This direct reference to "Strange Fruit" suggests an intended foregrounding of socially-engaged themes, instead of emphasizing "the blues"—a title that hints at tragedy.

Holiday's account of her life story, then, was to some extent initiated, controlled and censored by men. Crucially, these men had a vested commercial interest in making her story as shocking and sensational as possible—Dufty described Holiday's struggle with addiction as the "gimmick" that would sell copies (Szwed 26). In other words, the autobiography was being steered towards a "tragic victim" narrative. As I have argued, this is not the image that Holiday herself sought to project. We must therefore read *Lady Sings the Blues* with an understanding of this control that was imposed upon her, whilst also seeing this editorial process as yet another example of the manipulation and appropriation of Holiday's image.

The release of *Lady Sings the Blues* in 1956 was celebrated with a concert at Carnegie Hall. Holiday's songs were interspersed with sections from her autobiography, read by critic Gilbert Millstein. How odd and incongruous it must have been to see her standing there silent, while her words (written in the first person, with heavy use of distinctive slang) were read by a white man. This concert serves as a metaphor for both *Lady Sings the Blues* and Holiday's image more broadly. Her life story, though her own, has been confined and controlled by the structure that was imposed upon it—largely by white men. Ideas about her gender and race, attitudes towards jazz, and an enduring desire to contain powerful women within stereotypes have all contributed to the creation of a caricatured Billie Holiday that has little basis in reality.

The (Photographic) Lens of Tragedy

Photography has also played a role in the creation of Holiday's tragic identity.[5] John Szwed has recently described the astonishing range of photographs that were taken of her, arguing that they seem to contain many different versions of the singer:

> Put fifty of sixty photos of her on a table and you will see a heavyset woman and a sylph in silk, an African American and an Asian, a saucy miss and a broken drunk, a perp in a mug shot and a smiling matron posing with a pet. In some pictures she's completely unrecognizable [Szwed 1].

Despite these diverse visual identities, the most famous and frequently reproduced images of Holiday tend to resonate with the idea of her as a tragic figure. A key example is William P. Gottlieb's iconic photograph of 1947, a frequently reproduced close-up of Holiday singing. In this portrait her eyes are closed and her head is tipped back, while her throat bulges full with the power of her voice. Benjamin Cawthra has suggested that this image is suggestive of Holiday's sadness, arguing that "if Billie Holiday is thought of as a tragic figure who nevertheless created beauty out of pain, Gottlieb's most reproduced photograph seems to affirm this" (Cawthra 89). Cawthra quotes Gottlieb himself, who said: "Her voice was filled with anguish [...] I caught this close-up of her in a way that you could really see the anguish that must have been coming out of her throat" (Cawthra 89). We might ask why both Cawthra and Gottlieb read this as a "tragic" image that suggests "pain" and "anguish." It could just as easily be interpreted as an image that suggests Holiday's vocal power, stage presence, or female sexuality. The reading of Gottlieb's photograph as indicative of anguish, however, demonstrates the persistent urge to view Holiday through the lens of tragedy. Indeed, Cawthra argues that, "as mythology, the photograph works as well as Holiday's ghost-written memoir in creating a tragic legend" (Cawthra 90). As this suggests, photographs of Holiday have been central to the creation of her troubled identity—perhaps as much as *Lady Sings the Blues* itself.

While we can contest a "tragic" interpretation of Gottlieb's photograph, other images of Holiday are far less ambiguous. If you type her name into Google Images, you are greeted with an array of well-known portraits—although she smiles in many of these, the "happy" photographs are more than matched by "sad" ones. In some she stares sternly, a picture of anger. In others she is mid-performance, with an expression that (as in Gottlieb's photograph) could be read as anguish. Then there are the famous prison mug shots that filled the tabloids during her lifetime, and the well-known photos taken in a recording studio towards the end of her life—in one she stares at the floor with a resigned expression, a drink in her hand. This is not the place to offer a full assessment of Billie Holiday iconography, but some key questions are pertinent to our purposes. To what extent did photography feed into the construction of Holiday as a tragic figure? How were these images circulated and perpetuated? Did the singer herself influence the creative direction of photo shoots? Has precedence been given to those photographs that conform to the idea of her as a sad figure? Do we only ascribe a "tragic" reading to these images retrospectively, now that we know how her story ended—or were they interpreted in the same way during her lifetime?

Billie Holiday in the 21st Century

Over the past five years there has been a great surge of interest in singers. Though "singer studies" is not yet established as a coherent academic field, increased attention has been paid to vocalists across a range of disciplines.[6] This work is contributing to a stronger understanding of singers as important cultural figures with the power to both influence and reflect the societies and cultures they come from. However, the majority of recent interest in singers has largely been located outside of the academic sphere and is evidenced by the extraordinarily wide range of documentaries, biopics, exhibitions, publications, and accolades that famous vocalists have latterly inspired. Examples include an acclaimed documentary about Kurt Cobain (Morgan), Bruce Springsteen's best-selling autobiography (Springsteen), Bob Dylan's receipt of the 2016 Nobel Prize for Literature, and the National Portrait Gallery's blockbuster exhibition *Michael Jackson: On the Wall* (London, 2018). As is clear from the range of these examples, the influence singers have exerted beyond the beyond the musical sphere is being recognized, with acknowledgments of their influence on the worlds of literature, art and fashion. Crucially, this new trend has not neglected women—in fact, much of the focus has been on female vocalists. Whilst efforts to celebrate female singers are overturning stereotypes and aiding a new understanding of important cultural figures, the (often male) urge to reduce women to tragic caricatures is still evident to some extent.

This renewed interest in singers is most evident in the field of film—and documentary film in particular. In 2014 *20 Feet from Stardom* (Neville) won the Academy Award for Best Documentary Feature. This film explores the lives of female backing singers including Darlene Love and Judith Hull. The following year documentaries on Amy Winehouse and Nina Simone won an Academy Award and Emmy Award respectively, whilst a critically acclaimed documentary on Janis Joplin was also released (Kapadia; Garbus; Berg).[7] Notably, the latter two films were directed by women. These documentaries concern themselves with more than a singer's music, instead offering nuanced analyses that attempt to peel back the layers of legend and interrogate what lies beneath. *Amy* functions as a study of celebrity and addiction, *What Happened, Miss Simone?* chronicles the singer's civil rights activism, and *Janis: Little Girl Blue* considers Joplin within a broad range of contexts including race, gender, addiction and the counterculture of the 1960s. More recently, two films about Whitney Houston have appeared: *Whitney: Can I Be Me* (Broomfield and Dolezal) in 2017 and *Whitney* (Macdonald) in 2018. The latter film's revelations about the sexual abuse Houston suffered as a child made headline news internationally (Mumford).

Although these documentaries acknowledge the tragedies and hardships that their subjects endured, they largely attempt to go deeper, recognizing the power of these women and the forces that shaped their careers. However, this is not to say that they are entirely unproblematic. Bronwyn Polaschek has argued forcefully that Asif Kapadia's *Amy* relies on the archetypal cultural narrative of the creative woman as a passive victim: Amy Winehouse is portrayed as deeply vulnerable, psychologically damaged by childhood experiences, susceptible to male influence, transparently autobiographical in her artistic work and propelled by a tragic life trajectory towards self-destruction [Polaschek 19].

She continues: "In contrast, Winehouse's complicated self-authored public persona is founded on excessive performativity, a close identification with her working-class origins and active resilience to contemporary neoliberal values of decorous femininity and self-control" (Polaschek 19). She concludes: "The documentary is dissonant with the public self that Amy Winehouse intended" (Polaschek 19). In other words, *Amy* ascribes a "tragedy narrative" to Winehouse, at the expense of her own agency. This mirrors the way in which Holiday's performance of self has been superseded by a narrative controlled by others—largely by men. The urge to reduce women to tragic stereotypes is clearly still strong.

This is not the place to offer a comprehensive assessment of the representation of female singers in contemporary documentary films. However, it would be pertinent to consider the role of documentaries in constructing gendered images of singers. Griffin argues that the 1972 BBC film *The Long Night of Lady Day* "posits white males as the primary voices of authority" (Griffin 111). We have already see that the BBC's more recent effort, *Queens of Heartache* (Nicholls), does little better. Although this latter documentary was made by a woman, it would also be worth exploring whether other films made by female directors (Garbus; Berg) generally resist the use of stereotypes better than those directed by men. Perhaps these are questions for feminist scholars of film.

We might also ask how documentaries about male singers differ from those that concern their female counterparts. *Montage of Heck* (Morgan) celebrates Kurt Cobain in a way that the aforementioned documentaries (about women) do not. Key events in his life are depicted through specially commissioned animated scenes, and the soundtrack features new versions of Nirvana songs, including "Smells Like Teen Spirit" performed by a children's choir. Cobain's life and art are therefore used as the basis for new art, and this both celebrates him and casts him in the role of inspirational originator. Although the film does deal with his mental health and addiction, it ends shortly before his death—we might compare this to the footage of Winehouse's body being removed from her house in *Amy* (Kapadia). Ultimately, Morgan's film consecrates Cobain as a genius rather than a tragic figure. We cannot so easily say the same of documentaries about female vocalists. It would also be pertinent to consider the mediums through which singers are celebrated. The aforementioned Michael Jackson exhibition examines his considerable influence on contemporary art, while the sell-out *David Bowie*

Is retrospective (Victoria and Albert Museum, 2013) toured the world for five years—it became the most visited exhibition in the Museum's long history (Nankervis). These men are hallowed and canonized by their presence in major international cultural canters. Where are the equivalent exhibitions on women?

It is clear that an intense and sustained interest in singers has been building. They are increasingly recognized as important cultural figures that are worthy of celebration and interrogation. Within this context, a reassessment of Billie Holiday is surely overdue. Happily, while this essay was being written, a new documentary on Holiday was announced. Based on the research of journalist Linda Kuhel, this is currently in pre-production (Grater). It can only be hoped that this will avoid regurgitating the "tragic victim" narrative that is so reductive. Perhaps one day a Billie Holiday exhibition will follow. The time is surely right.

"Crazy They Call Me"

In 2017, celebrated British novelist Zadie Smith was asked to write an introduction to a new book of photographs taken during Billie Holiday's run of shows at New Jersey's Sugar Hill in 1957. Smith (a former jazz singer) has explained that she wrestled with this task, struggling to find a voice that did justice to the woman whose own voice was so powerful (Leyshon). In the end she used what has been described as a type of "ventriloquism" (Muyumba), adopting Holiday's voice in an imagined second-person stream of consciousness. Smith's piece has subsequently been reprinted in both *The New Yorker* (Smith, "Crazy They Call Me") and a recent collection of her essays (Smith, *Feel Free*). It vividly evokes the distinctive voice of *Lady Sings the Blues*, exploring the gap between image and reality. Smith's Holiday is a singer who is defiant and scornful—vulnerable, yes, but also self-aware. She is hip to prejudice and wise to those who would use her.

The final paragraph of this piece is revealing. In it, Holiday rages at the way in which (male) journalists are never interested in her music, instead wanting to know "which man goes with which song" (Smith, "Crazy They Call Me"), or grilling her about addictions and convictions. They ask her about other artists, all of whom are also male: Louis Armstrong, Count Basie and Lester Young. This paragraph, then, serves as a metaphor for the problems that surround Holiday's legacy. Her story has been taken out of her hands, and written largely by men. In the stories they have told, other men loom large. Her musical talent not been given the level of recognition it deserves. Instead, the focus has always fallen on her struggles, not her victories. Her own voice is drowned out. Smith's powerful final lines reflect this silencing of Holiday's voice—a silencing that is imposed by the restrictions of her gender:

> Once, you almost said—to a sneaky fellow from the *Daily News*, who was inquiring—you almost turned to him and said *Motherfucker I AM* music. But a lady does not speak like that, however, and so you did not [Smith, "Crazy They Call Me"].

Although the fictional Holiday decides against giving this characteristically bombastic assertion of her talent, Smith ultimately hands her a microphone and allows her to do this. It is my hope that, in the 21st century, other writers, critics and scholars will do what Smith has done—interrogate the received truth about Billie Holiday, with an acute awareness of how sexism and racism have shaped this. I hope they will peel away the sadness and sensation, listening to her words and her music and exploring their meanings and implications. I hope they will give her back her voice. A voice that says: "I am no Queen of heartache. Motherfucker, I am music."

NOTES

1. This essay is dedicated to Will Gibson. Note that all quotations from *Lady Sings the Blues* are taken from the 2006 edition from this point onward.

2. However, as Farah Jasmine Griffin points out, this is strongly hinted at when Holiday shares an anecdote about "big red velvet hats" (Griffin 52).

3. The life and career of Winehouse paralleled that of Holiday in many ways. A study of the relationship between these two singers could tell us much about the evolving (or unevolving) construction of female musical identity.

4. For more of the gendered representation of Amy Winehouse in the British press, see Berkers and Eeckelaer.

5. For more on the important relationship between jazz and photography, see Cawthra; Pinson; Tanner.

6. Examples can be found in fields as diverse as French cultural studies (Looseley) and "prima donna studies" (Cowgill and Poriss), a sub-discipline of opera studies, concerned with the role of the female opera singer.

7. *What Happened, Miss Simone?* won the Primetime Emmy Award for Outstanding Documentary or Nonfiction Special, while *Amy* won the Academy Award for Best Documentary Feature.

WORKS CITED

Barry, Anna Maria. *The Dream of a Madman: Constructing the Male Opera Singer in Nineteenth-Century Britain.* Oxford: Oxford Brookes University, 2017.

Beauchemin, Molly. *Amy Winehouse, Kurt Cobain and the Gendering of Martyrdom.* 22 June 2015, https://pitchfork.com/thepitch/808-amy-winehouse-kurt-cobain-and-the-gendering-of-martyrdom/.

Berg, Amy, dir. *Janis: Little Girl Blue.* Disarming Films, Jigsaw Productions, 2015.

Berkers, Pauwke, and Merel Eeckelaer. "Rock and Roll or Rock and Fall? Gendered Framing of the Rock and Roll Lifestyles of Amy Winehouse and Pete Doherty in British Broadsheets." *Journal of Gender Studies,* vol. 23, no. 1, 2014, pp. 3–17.

Blackburn, Julia. *With Billie: A New Look at the Unforgettable Lady Day.* London: Jonathan Cape, 2005.

Brooks, Daphne A. "'This Voice Which Is Not One': Amy Winehouse Sings the Ballad of Sonic Blue(s)face Culture." *Women and Performance: A Journal,* vol. 20, no. 1, Mar. 2010, pp. 37–60.

Broomfield, Nick, and Rudi Dolezal, dirs. *Whitney: Can I Be Me.* Showtime, 2017.

Cawthra, Benjamin. *Blue Notes in Black and White: Photography and Jazz*. Chicago: University of Chicago Press, 2011.

Cowgill, Rachel, and Hilary Poriss, eds. *The Arts of the Prima Donna in the Long Nineteenth Century*. Oxford: Oxford University Press, 2012.

Cummings, Tim. "Billie & Me: Barbican Hall, London." *The Independent*, 8 Apr. 2004, https://www.independent.co.uk/arts-entertainment/music/reviews/billie-me-barbican-hall-london-55073.html.

Davis, Angela Y. *Blues Legacies and Black Feminism*. New York: Vintage, 1999.

Eakin, Paul John. *Fictions in Autobiography*. Princeton: Princeton University Press, 1985.

Garbus, Liz, dir. *What Happened, Miss Simone?* Eagle Rock Entertainment, 2015.

Grater, Tom. "Billie Holiday Documentary in the Works with James Erskine, Altitude (Exclusive)." *Screen Daily*, 6 Feb. 2018, https://www.screendaily.com/news/billie-holiday-documentary-in-the-works-with-james-erskine-altitude-exclusive/5126269.article.

Greene, Meg. *Billie Holiday: A Biography*. Westport, CT: Greenwood Press, 2007.

Griffin, Farah Jasmine. *In Search of Billie Holiday: If You Can't Be Free, Be a Mystery*. New York: Ballantine Books, 2001.

Hearsum, Paula. "A Musical Matter of Life and Death: The Morality of Mortality and the Coverage of Amy Winehouse's Death in the UK Press." *Mortality*, vol. 17, no. 2, May 2012, pp. 182–99.

Holiday, Billie, and William Dufty. *Lady Sings the Blues*. Brooklyn: Harlem Moon, 2006.

Kapadia, Asif, dir. *Amy*. A24, 015.

Keepnews, Orrin. "Lady Sings the Blues." *The Billie Holiday Companion: Seven Decades of Commentary*, edited by Leslie Gourse. New York: Schirmer, 1997, pp. 110–14.

Leyshon, Cressida. "This Week in Fiction: Zadie Smith on Inhabiting the World of Billie Holiday." *The New Yorker*, 27 Feb. 2017, https://www.newyorker.com/books/page-turner/fiction-this-week-zadie-smith-2017-03-06.

Looseley, David. *Edith Piaf: A Cultural History*. Liverpool: Liverpool University Press, 2015.

MacDonald, Kevin, dir. *Whitney*. Lisa Erspamer Entertainment, 2018.

Morgan, Brett, dir. *Cobain: Montage of Heck*. HBO Documentary Films, 2015.

Mumford, Gwilym. "Whitney Houston: Film Alleges Singer Sexually Abused as a Child by Dee Warwick." *The Guardian*, 17 May 2018, https://www.theguardian.com/film/2018/may/17/documentary-alleges-whitney-houston-was-sexually-abused-as-a-child.

Muyumba, Walton. "Zadie Smith's Brilliance Is on Display in 'Feel Free.'" *Los Angeles Times*, 7 Feb. 2018, http://www.latimes.com/books/jacketcopy/la-ca-jc-zadie-smith-20180207-story.html.

Nankervis, Troy. "David Bowie Exhibition Smashes All-Time Records." *Metro*, 9 Nov. 2016, http://metro.co.uk/2016/11/09/david-bowie-exhibition-smashes-all-time-records-6246946/.

Neville, Morgan, dir. *20 Feet from Stardom*. Gil Friesen Productions, 2013.

Nicholls, Jill, dir. *Queens of Heartache*. BBC2, 2006.

Nicholson, Stuart. *Billie Holiday*. Boston: Northeastern University Press, 1995.

O'Meally, Robert. *Lady Day: The Many Faces of Billie Holiday*. New York: Arcade, 1991.

Pinson, K. Heather. *The Jazz Image: Seeing Music through Herman Leonard's Photograph*. Jackson: University Press of Mississippi, 2010.

Polaschek, Bronwyn. "The Dissonant Personas of a Female Celebrity: Amy and the Public Self of Amy Winehouse." *Celebrity Studies*, vol. 9, no. 1, 2018, pp. 17–33.

Postlewait, Thomas. "Autobiography and Theatre History." *Interpreting the Theatrical Past: Essays in the Historiography of Performance*, edited by Thomas Postlewait and Bruce A. McCoachie. Iowa City: University of Iowa Press, 1989, pp. 248–72.

Postlewait, Thomas. "Theatre Autobiographies: Some Preliminary Concerns for the Historian." *Assaph C*, vol. 16, 2000, pp. 157–72.

Shuker, Roy. *Popular Music: The Key Concepts*. Abingdon: Routledge, 2017.

Smith, Zadie. "Crazy They Call Me." *The New Yorker*, 6 Mar. 2017, https://www.newyorker.com/magazine/2017/03/06/crazy-they-call-me.

Smith, Zadie. *Feel Free*. New York: Penguin, 2018.

Springsteen, Bruce. *Born to Run*. New York: Simon & Schuster, 2016.

Szwed, John. *Billie Holiday: The Musician and the Myth*. London: William Heinemann, 2015.

Tanner, Lee. *The Jazz Image: Masters of Jazz Photography*. New York: Abrams, 2006.

Waters, Ethel, and Charles Samuels. *His Eye Is on the Sparrow*. New York: Doubleday, 1951.

Wiley, Christopher. "'A Relic of an Age Still Capable of a Romantic Outlook': Musical Biography and The Master Musicians Series, 1899–1906." *Comparative Criticism: An Annual Journal*, vol. 25, Nov. 2003, pp. 161–202.

Winehouse, Amy. *Frank*. Island Records, 2003.

Merging Artists

The Legacy of Motown's Lady Sings the Blues

CLAUDIUS STEMMLER

In 1972 Paramount Studios released *Lady Sings the Blues*, a fictional biographical movie depicting the life of Billie Holiday. Loosely based on the identically titled biography written by Billie Holiday and William Dufty, the movie garnered five Academy Award nominations and established singer Diana Ross as a dramatic actress. Successful with audiences and receiving favorable reviews from film critics, the movie proved the economic viability of African American singers as the subject of biographical movies. Less pleased were writers on music who mostly considered the movie an inaccurate representation of Billie Holiday's life. Their disdain is perhaps rooted in the fact that "[p]eriod movies inevitably reflect more the period in which they're made than the period of their subject" (qtd. in Sanello XIII), as film critic Jack Matthews once wrote. This discrepancy might be considered further highlighted in biographical movies where audiences might expect adherence to a kind of factual truth based on the real life nature of their subject. In order to understand the appeal of *Lady Sings the Blues,* it might therefore be more sensible to look at the circumstances of the movie's production and release instead of its factual accuracy.

Billie Holiday as a Symbol of Authenticity

> "Billie Holiday's troubled story was Black America's story too." Donald Bogle ["Brown" 176]

When film scholar Donald Bogle equated the individual life of Billie Holiday to that of the general African American population, his statement implied that her life possesses a larger symbolic quality. Looking at the early 1970s he wrote that she "was treasured all the more by young Black America because mass White Americans still had not hooked onto her legend" ("Brown" 174). Bogle's assessments are noteworthy not merely for explaining why Holiday specifically appealed to the African American population but also for suggesting her symbolic appeal to encompass the population at large and not merely a specific segment. This broad appeal of Holiday can be seen reflected in the shared admiration for her by such otherwise politically divided individuals like Malcolm X and Berry Gordy. For Berry Gordy "[s]he sang from her soul, about her troubled life, coming from a place of both pain and purity" (73) while Malcolm X wrote that "Lady Day sang with the *soul* of Negroes from the centuries of sorrow and oppression" (220). It is in the differences and similarities between these two statements that the qualities of Billie Holiday as a symbol for the public, especially an African American public, can be seen. Both statements share the sentiment of Holiday as an artist of exceptional authenticity and suffering. But they differ in the fact that both men are also able to project their own personal beliefs on Holiday as a symbol.

While Gordy's assessment is in tune with the bootstrap mentality of an entrepreneur highlighting *her* as an individual, X's statement gives her a larger-than-life quality and understands her as a symbol of the historical oppression of African Americans. A further example for this projection of personal beliefs can be seen in singer Marvin Gaye stating that Holiday "turned herself inside out, all in the name of love" (Ritz, "Divided" 30) and that "[t]he hurt she felt was the hurt of all humanity" (Ritz, "Divided" 30). Retaining the larger-than-life quality of X's statement, Gaye replaces the African American specificity with general Christian savior imagery. In conclusion, Billie Holiday as a symbol is flexible enough to encompass many different belief systems around a shared core of African American authenticity.

The question of authenticity has always been of special importance to African Americans. The popular use of the term hereby revolves around Hegel's concept of being true to oneself (Varga and Guignon). This line of thought is usually combined with the belief that society forces the individual to decline parts of himself. While authenticity originally reflected the individual's relation to society, the term can be extrapolated by looking at the relations between larger groups inside a society, such as African Americans within a predominantly white society (Varga and Guignon). Specifically, there always have been advantages for African Americans who adapt to the preferences of the dominant culture.

In the 1970s, this question became even more important as the success of the Civil Rights Movement had led to rapid changes in African American culture. Some saw these changes as an assault on, or loss of an, authentic African American culture, and less integrated, more radical movements for

African American progress decried this assimilation (Japtok and Jenkins, "What" 28–30). This confirms the idea that "[q]uestions about authenticity tend to arise when culture is under assault" (Japtok and Jenkins, "Introduction" 1) and that "[t]he question of a clearly circumscribed notion of blackness, an authentic blackness, so to speak, is a political question" (Japtok and Jenkins, "What" 45). Throughout all this, Billie Holiday's combination of authenticity with a certain flexibility in terms of political interpretation made her an appealing symbol. This position was further helped by her death, which left her silent on contemporary issues and enabled others to interpret her beliefs according to their own beliefs and needs.

This perception of Billie Holiday's authenticity is rooted in her music as well as in her private life. As an artist, she is a jazz singer "wrapped in the blues" (Gaye qtd. in Ritz, "Divided" 30) and is thus connected to both musical genres considered the "allegedly, pure, authentic source of a pre–World War II African American culture" (Lüthe 6).[1] While she was a "successful cross-over star [she] managed to remain an 'authentic' black voice and figure" (Lüthe 188). This may be rooted in her singing containing recognizable vocal patterns, combined with the public perception of her private life. Because her private sufferings seemed to stem from the degradations of segregation, she publicly shared a general plight of the larger African American public. Her suffering further stands out because African American entertainers were comparably privileged in being able to ease their situation by adjusting to the needs of segregation and she didn't choose to do so. For doing this, entertainers like Louis Armstrong, Hattie McDaniel, or Stepin Fetchit suffered a setback as symbolic figures in the 1960s and 1970s. Their earlier stereotypical performances in movies, once perhaps perceived as making the best out of the opportunities offered, were now making them "'villains,' 'betrayers,' nothing more than toms and handkerchief heads" (Bogle, "Toms" XXI).[2] In comparison, this made Holiday's star shine even brighter. Furthermore, thanks to her literary autobiography, Holiday's life story remained accessible even after her death. The book's factual inaccuracies (Ritz, "Introduction" XII) do not take away from its revelation of an emotional, symbolic truth about Holiday. Interestingly, these inaccuracies coupled with accusations that she only wrote the book for it to be made into a movie (Ritz, "Introduction" XII), suggests that she might have aimed at or at least been supportive of making herself a symbolic figure.

The United States and the Rise of Motown

The 1960s were a decade of massive change for the African American community. Not only did economic and educational opportunities previously denied become accessible but there was also a new higher visibility of African

Americans in popular culture (Lüthe 15). One such element of higher visibility was the music of Motown and its roster of artists including the Temptations, Marvin Gaye, and the Supremes with their lead singer Diana Ross. Berry Gordy, the owner of Motown, had always aimed at reaching white, as well as black, audiences (George, "Where" 86). He achieved this by being "highly aware of the meaning of inscriptions of blackness to his performers" (Lüthe 21) and renegotiating public ideas of "blackness" in order to appeal to white audiences. Thus, in the early 1960s Motown often hid their artists being black (Lüthe 69–70) before their music's rising popularity made this strategy impossible.[3] Motown then invented new "black masculine and feminine types that strikingly diverged [from] traditional cultural representations" (Lüthe 70). These new types could either be seen as the "first step into a post-racial age in American popular culture" (Lüthe 5), the representation of a growing black middle class (Lüthe 2) or as "whiting-up" (Lüthe 39), a counter-act to the earlier white performances of blackness in minstrel shows.[4] Ideologically, this integrating strategy made Motown a musical counterpart to the civil rights movement led by Dr. Martin Luther King.[5] This kinship was also reflected musically as Motown tended to incorporate more stylistic traits of African American music genres in their output in synchronization with the civil rights movement's success and visibility (Lüthe 58). This closeness to the civil rights movement became problematic for Motown when, after the assassination of Dr. King in 1968, the civil rights movement's progress seemed to stall. More radical ideologies for African American progress garnered support and the black middle class, including Motown, was criticized as having "accepted unconditionally the values of the white bourgeois world" (E. Franklin Frazier qtd. in Japtok and Jenkins, "What" 26). Thus, Motown's cultural authenticity as African American was questioned (Lüthe 205). Instead of a unified corporate answer, this development led to the end of Motown's classical period and the following years marked a diversification in terms of artist images and musical output (Lüthe 205). While some artists like Marvin Gaye embraced this new freedom by making concept albums touching on subjects previously off limits, for others, like Diana Ross, this change seemed to create an uncertainty about the future direction of her career. Similar to her earlier solo albums the movie version of *Lady Sings the Blues* can be seen as Motown and Diana Ross experimenting with different images for her. More specifically, they tried to harness the symbolic qualities of Billie Holiday in order to advance Ross' career.

Motown's Lady Sings the Blues

The movie version of *Lady Sings the Blues* was a cooperation between Paramount Pictures and Motown. Gordy's strong personal interest in the project can be seen in Motown supplying further funding after the movie exceeded its budget and Paramount threatened to shut down production (George, "Where" 218). Not only was Gordy able to secure his personal choices of lead actors (Gordy 314) but he also seemed to act "as Ross' *de facto* director, to the consternation of director Sidney J. Furie" (George, "Where" 218).

In the early 1970s not just Diana Ross but Motown generally had an image problem because its successful strategy of reaching out to white audiences (Lüthe 2) was now being questioned (Lüthe 23). *Lady Sings the Blues* can be seen as a reversal of this strategy which Motown employed earlier to become part of mainstream white American culture. To achieve that, Gordy had pushed for the Supremes to be able to sing the so-called standard "You're Nobody 'Til Somebody Loves You" on national TV (Lüthe 107; Gordy 209) and thus going from "African American singers" to just "American singers." With *Lady Sings the Blues*, he not only let Ross play the "authentic" Billie Holiday, but also strengthened a connection between Motown and an established African American musical legacy as embodied by the assortment of jazz standards Ross gets to perform. On another level, this also strengthens a connection between Motown and African American culture which was generally accepted as "authentic." For Motown, a successful company eschewing middle class values, the movie therefore can be seen as a reaffirming statement that the company's position in terms of economy and class does not detract from its own African American authenticity.

Billie and Louis

The movie's depiction of Billie Holiday is a continuation of the image of black femininity constructed in the musical output of Motown's female groups. One of Gordy's proclaimed goals for the movie was to honor Billie Holiday (Gordy 310). He did so by making her "a bourgeois lady" (Bogle, "Brown" 174), and the protagonist of "the screen's first full-fledged black romantic melodrama" (Bogle, "Toms" 245). Her sexuality is depicted in a rather chaste fashion, something especially evident when compared to the number of sexual relationships Billie Holiday herself named in her autobiography. While the movie shows Holiday being raped and working as a prostitute, both elements are kept brief and neither are the sexual acts depicted nor their psychological effects reflected upon.[6] Instead, Holiday almost immediately meets and falls in love with "a dream prince charming in the form of Billy Dee Williams as Louis McKay" (Bogle, "Toms" 245). While there is some slightly raunchy banter between them, this relationship moves the fictional Holiday closer to middle class ideals and distances her from the hypersexual female African American stereotype of the Jezebel (Lüthe 28).

In comparable fashion, the film's Louis McKay is a continuation of the male image previously constructed in the music of Motown's male groups. In songs like the Temptations' "Ain't Too Proud to Beg" or the Four Tops' "Baby I Need Your Loving," the male lead singer's lyrics show him as weak and suffering because of the state of his romantic relationship (Lüthe 117–118). Besides vocabulary like "needing" or "begging," both songs share the male singer reflecting on failing supposed standards of masculinity. In both cases, the male part is shown lacking agency and therefore willingly submitting himself to his female addressee who appears in control of the relationship's future. Again, this averts a presentation of African American hypersexuality like the long-standing stereotype of "the buck" (Bogle, "Toms" 13–14). The buck combined "the myth of the Negro's high-powered sexuality" (Bogle, "Toms" 13–14) with the racist imagination of "an animalism innate in the Negro male" (Bogle, "Toms" 14). As the cinematic embodiment of a white fear of male African American sexuality, the buck mythos fittingly originated in D.W. Griffith's *Birth of a Nation* (Bogle, "Toms" 13) with white actors performing as black characters. In the years before *Lady Sings the Blues* blaxploitation movies like *Sweet Sweetback's Baadasssss Song* and *Shaft* picked up on this stereotype to create a "new-style defiant buck hero" (Bogle, "Toms" 234). While confident and assertive, these characters were rather unappealing to middle class, as well as romantic, aesthetics. The Louis McKay of *Lady Sings the Blues* stands in stark opposition to these characters. Almost from the beginning, he appears deeply devoted to Holiday, treats her pleasantly, and later is shown to keenly suffer trying to steer her away from drug addiction. At the same time, the movie also shows him sexually yearning for Holiday thereby evading the forced chaste nature of earlier African American performances in romantic parts like Harry Belafonte in *Bright Road* and *Carmen Jones* (Bogle, "Toms" 190). Both the depictions of Louis McKay and Billie Holiday can be seen as offering positive black images as counterpoint to those shown in the then popular blaxploitation movies.

Furthermore, the movie depicts Billie Holiday as economically moving up into the middle class. While she starts out poor in rural Baltimore, she then moves to New York City and begins an economic upward movement. Her geographical movement echoes that of many African Americans in the early decades of the 20th century (Mauk/Oakland, 95) while her economic ascension mirrors the more recent new possibilities of African Americans in the aftermath of the Civil Rights Movement. While obtaining status symbols and engaging in conspicuous consumption, the film's protagonist always retains her authenticity by the virtue of being Billie Holiday. Besides being depicted with luxury items the actual Billie Holiday also owned, she is shown keeping a comparable middle class apartment furnished with goods appearing of European heritage like a painting of a topless woman. Together with Billie and Louis' first date in an Italian restaurant, this connects the economic upward movement to the enjoyment of cultural goods of European heritage. Financially, this upward movement seems very much supported by Billie Holiday going on tour with an entirely white band. By making the "unquestionable authentic" Billie Holiday a trailblazer for such behavior the movie seems to legitimize Motown's strategy of reaching out to white audiences and marks the conspicuous consumption of the black middle class as authentic.

By making her part of a classic cinematic romantic relationship and showing her engaging in conspicuous consumption the movie's version of Billie Holiday becomes a symbol of middle class values and ideals. At the same time, she remains authentic by the virtue of the individual she is based on. Similar to the musical output of Motown, the film version of *Lady Sings the Blues* attempted to merge markers of African American authenticity with those typical for middle class values. The movie's success then confirmed that there was an audience for the image of blackness being encompassed herein.

The Music of Lady Sings the Blues

The soundtrack of *Lady Sings the Blues* consists of two large, distinctly different elements. First, there is a non-diegetic score composed by Michel Legrand. This music underscores the movie in typical fashion most notably through the repeated use of a love theme for the relationship between Billie Holiday and Louis McKay. What is of greater interest here is the other element: an assortment of songs often performed inside or played as part of the diegetic world. With some exceptions, these are songs existing in well-known recorded performances by Holiday herself. The first song played in the movie is "Tain't Nobody's Bizness If I Do" in a version performed by Blinky Williams. This song first appears as a record to which the young Billie Holiday devotedly listens to. This early scene is the movie's only hint at African American musical history preceding Holiday and influencing her work. For that, the song can be considered well chosen as it not only exists in a recorded version by Holiday herself but also by Bessie Smith, who Donald Bogle called "the last of a specific type, the dark diva firmly entrenched in the black community" ("Brown" 32) and who was also a great idol of Holiday herself (Bogle, "Brown" 66). Additionally, the song's lyrics present a strong and independent woman, and its placement in the movie's beginning suggests it as a starting point for the characterization of Holiday herself. Another noticeable exception are two songs briefly performed later in the narration by white singers. When contrasted with the movie's Billie Holiday their lighthearted singing seems to lack emotional depth. As these singers are picked ahead of Billie for a radio broadcast, this highlights the stark disadvantages and barriers African Americans had to overcome.

Throughout the movie, Diana Ross performs the Billie Holiday songs by appropriating Holiday's singing style while staying in her usual vocal range. When it became public that Ross was intended to play Holiday, one major criticism was that her voice "didn't have the shading or depth of Lady Day's" (Bogle, "Brown" 176). Her singing performance could have proven critical for the movie's reception but positive reviews by film critics (Bogle, "Brown" 176) and Motown singer Marvin Gaye citing *Lady Sings the Blues* as proof for Ross' qualities as a singer (Ritz, "Divided" 171) suggest that she succeeded. Most of the songs either begin or end in a diegetic performance by Ross after or before they accompany a montage sequence. But with the notable exception of the soundtrack's single "Good Morning Heartache" most songs appear heavily truncated. This way, the musical placement can almost be seen as an appetizer for the commercial soundtrack release.[7] Many of the songs are also used in a musical-like fashion, their lyrics reflecting the narrative events. For example, a brief separation of Billie and Louis results in her singing "Lover Man (Oh, Where Can You Be?)" and her seeing the body of a hanged black man leads into a performance of "Strange Fruit." As a whole, this use of music shows the importance the music itself has for the movie's narration and style. While Billie Holiday's symbolic qualities might exceed her musical oeuvre, they are still rooted in the music itself—and the movie reflects this.

Diana Ross as Billie Holiday

Before the release of *Lady Sings the Blues*, the public image of Supremes lead singer Diana Ross stood in stark contrast to that of Billie Holiday. Because of her role in the Supremes break-up she was "often thought of as the selfish, superficial, overly ambitious sister" (Bogle, "Brown" 176). In previous years the Supremes were part of the creation and construction of a new image of black femininity (Lüthe 193), but this new image was now at risk to fall out of favor with the public. This uncertainty about the direction of her public image is reflected on the covers of Ross' first three solo albums. On her self-titled debut (1970), she is depicted "as a poor, boyish child" (Lüthe 184), the cover of the sophomore *Everything Is Everything* (1970) seems comparably close to her former glamorous image as a Supreme, and the third album *Surrender* (1971) shows her with a huge Afro appropriating black power imagery (Lüthe 185).

But this flexibility in adapting to the economic needs of her career had become a flaw. As a symbol of African American success aligned to the Civil Rights Movement she was, often implicitly, charged with lacking authenticity.

Even though it was another career move, portraying Billie Holiday allowed Ross "to reclaim an authentic black female body [...] and to crossover into the Hollywood movie business" (Lüthe 188). The wish of merging actor and role is made explicit in the movie's advertising tagline and opening credits which state: "Diana Ross is Billie Holiday."[8] The movie's opening scene shows Holiday/Ross dressed in fine clothes escorted by police, changed into prisoners' attire and then put into a padded cell. This opening sequence presents Ross in a new way, stripping her of layers of glamor and thereby suggesting a new authenticity underneath. The scene ends with the camera moving into a close-up of her face, her eyes staring into empty space before the scene dissolves in a way to signal the following scene to be a flashback. In the next scene, Holiday is a teenager and from then on the narration continues chronologically up unto the opening sequence and further on. This detachment of the opening sequence from the following narration hints at its purpose of showing a "new" Ross. From then on, the audience witnesses the young black teenager becoming a star, mirroring Holiday's as well as Ross' life (George, "Where" 218). While not ignoring Holiday's fall, the movie chooses to delegate it to the sidelines by closing with her triumphant Carnegie Hall concert and only faded in newspaper articles informing about the following tragic events leading up to her early death. For her performance, Diana Ross received a Golden Globe award, an Academy Award nomination and was positively singled out in many of the movie's reviews (Bogle, "Brown" 176–180). Bogle called it "a splendidly developed star performance in the classic sense" ("Toms" 246) in that while "one never forgets one is watching Diana Ross" ("Toms" 246) the performance remains believable in itself.

Appealing to White Audiences

By depicting the fictional Holiday touring with a white band, *Lady Sings the Blues* depicts her as a trailblazer in terms of reaching out to white audiences. Doing this, the filmmakers seem to legitimize Motown's own reaching out to white audiences by suggesting themselves following Holiday's footsteps. The movie itself can also be seen as reaching out by offering images of racial harmony in front of the diegetic background of segregation. This is done by making an anonymous group of whites in the South the movie's only racist perpetrators while other, more individualized, white characters treat the system of segregation with ridicule and disdain. Furthermore, with the exception of drug-addicted musician Harry (Paul Hampton), the white characters always seem to have Billie's best interests at heart. White persons of authority like nightclub owner Jerry (Sid Melton) don't seem to mind being joked about by their black employees and Louis and Billie have their first date in an Italian restaurant with none of the white customers are bothered by their presence. In the movie's fictional version of the United States, segregation only seems to really exist in the South. Combined with the white characters' disregard for segregation, this gives the impression that racism was disliked by the general white population of the United States but forced unto the whole country by a racist minority in the South. Instead of historical accuracy the movie's depiction seems to hereby project a post-racial vision of harmony unto the past. This depiction also lessens the impact of systematic racism on Billie's personal sufferings. While there are poignant moments like her use of make-up to lighten her face, the movie more strongly focuses on the demands of her career and the following drug addiction as the main causes of her suffering.[9] Not only highlighting personal responsibility instead of the social conditions, this depiction also aligns the movie with middle class notions of femininity. Not only is Billie shown as suffering throughout her career she is also presented as happy while staying at home after having decided to quit working. When a need to perform then makes her resume her career, she again steps into a self-destructive cycle. Following historic precedent, this can also be read as the filmmakers' warning female audiences about leaving behind the domestic sphere.

In order to further appeal to white audiences, the movie distances African American characters from white society who could be perceived as threatening. Moving beyond Billie and Louis, many other African American characters adhere more closely to established stereotypes. When depicted as living in closer proximity to white society, these characters tend to be shown as non-threatening. This is the case with Billie's mother (Virginia Capers), who is a classical soft-mannered "mammy" (Bogle, "Toms" 9) working in a white household. Alternatively, a stereotype like the hypersexual buck, originally based on white anxieties about black sexuality, is turned into comic relief. The would-be customer of Billie as a prostitute, Big Ben (Scatman Crothers) initially appears as a hypersexual man entering her room, stating that he is "something else under them sheets." Completely self-absorbed, he continues to talk about his sexual prowess while she disregards him and leaves. The scene ends with him standing outside the house in his undergarments yelling after her, which marks him as more comical than threatening. Different from this, threatening African American characters like Billie's rapist (Harry Caesar), drug dealer Hawk (Robert L. Gordy), and the two hoods beating up Billie's confidant Piano Man (Richard Pryor) are never shown in contact with white American characters. Instead they seem to populate a dangerous world detached from white society, further giving reasons to righteous African American characters to escape from there.

Despite *Lady Sings the Blues* being used to reaffirm the cultural authenticity of the African American personnel involved, this does not mean that the filmmakers did not try to appeal to white audiences too. Specifically, the movie appeals to white audiences by distancing threatening African Americans from them and designating a subgroup of whites as the cause of racial conflict. This can be seen as a white-washing of U.S. history by denying the acceptance segregation enjoyed throughout mainstream white society in all parts of the United States.[10] In this case, Motown's economic interests seemed to trump a closer allegiance with the ideology of Dr. Martin Luther King. While Dr. King was partly critical of the role of white liberals for African American advancement (93–101) Motown's *Lady Sings the Blues* woos them as potential audience.

Merging Artists as a Form of Cultural Continuity

Previous sections illustrated the way Motown and Diana Ross tried to harness Billie Holiday to reclaim their African American authenticity from a point of economic motivation. But, whether intentionally or not, this also made *Lady Sings the Blues* a blueprint on how to create a kind of continuity in African American cultural history. Seen as an homage by the then contemporary successful generation of African American artists to their predecessors *Lady Sings the Blues* creates a direct link between these generations.

Since then, there have been other performances by African American artists creating such intergenerational cultural continuity. There was, for example, Beyoncé Knowles playing a fictionalized version of Diana Ross in *Dreamgirls* (2006) and Etta James in *Cadillac Records* (2006) or Jennifer Hudson playing a fictionalized version of Supremes member Florence Ballard alongside Knowles in *Dreamgirls*. By linking the performer and the performed, these performances can be seen as serving several functions. On one level the casting of Knowles to play the Diana Ross–like Deena Jones works as a commentary on the similarities between the different singer's careers.[11] Additionally, the role allows Knowles to affirm her cultural authenticity by appearing as part of a larger ensemble of African American actors. The same effect holds true for Jennifer Hudson performing as the Florence Ballard–like Effie in the movie. Hudson first became more widely known after appearing on *American Idol*, a casting show explicitly dedicated to the artificial creation of popular artists. As the musical version of *Dreamgirls* already established Ballard as the "authentic" Supreme (Lüthe 109), the character is well suited to grant Hudson an authenticity contrary to her first appearing in a distinctly artificial TV format. Aside from these career advantages the performances by Knowles and Hudson, just as Ross' several decades earlier, create continuity between different generation of artists by making the contemporary artists appear as torchbearers of the artists as which they perform. For Ross and Knowles, for example, the otherwise superficial similarities between their careers are getting a more distinctive embodiment through Knowles' performance. If the differences between their musical output made us previously not connect them, Knowles' performance definitely opens up the question if Destiny's Child and Knowles are another generation's equivalent to Diana Ross and the Supremes.

This effect of cultural continuity is further pronounced by the fact that the apprehension of the earlier singer often does not end with the movie performance itself. Thus, already Diana Ross made Billie Holiday songs part of her live program following her performance in *Lady Sings the Blues*[12] just as Beyoncé Knowles has incorporated Etta James signature song "At Last" in her performances after *Cadillac Records*. Another example for this is actor-singer Jamie Foxx who followed up on his performance as Ray Charles in *Ray* (2004) with a Charles-styled feature on the Kanye West track "Gold Digger." In the song's intro Foxx appropriates Charles singing style before the sampled voice of Charles himself is used. Furthermore, the song's video shows Foxx frequently singing synchronized to Charles' sampled voice and thereby recalls Foxx's earlier movie performance. In all these cases, playing the part of an earlier artist appeared to makes the artist feel more at ease or having a legit claim in apprehending the earlier singer's material. The artists therefore appear to confirm their own art to exist in a greater continuous cultural whole.

When looking beyond these performances, it is especially noteworthy that there is no similar tendency within biographical movies of white American singers. In such movies, the subject is usually embodied by an established actor, typically without any distinctive musical pedigree. These different approaches to casting might be seen as the result of the different cultural significance musicians possess for "their" respective communities. While white American singers often become significant artists by consciously placing themselves as outsiders to "their" community's cultural mainstream,[13] successful African American musicians are often located firmly inside their community but outside the white U.S. mainstream.[14] Thereby, these casting choices regarding African American singers create continuity between generations while confirming that all participating artists (parties) belong to larger authentic African American culture, despite the many changes each generation encompasses.

Conclusion

Lady Sings the Blues is a project that sprang from Motown's expansion into the movie industry while simultaneously having to adjust to a changing political and cultural climate. Taking advantage of Billie Holiday's ongoing popularity as a symbol of authenticity, the movie revitalized and enlarged her as a symbolic figure. As presented in the movie, this new symbolic Billie is further removed from the actual individual's life and more closely aligned with ideological middle class values such as conspicuous consumption or romantic courtships which were already present in Motown's musical output.

The movie's influence can be seen as two-fold. On the one hand, it likely helped and still helps keeping Billie Holiday present as a popular symbol. Through broadcasts and home releases the movie might be one of the easiest access points in terms of interest in Billie Holiday. Although, like with other historical individuals made popular by movies, this comes at the price of the movie's interpretation overshadowing less dramatized, fact-based accounts. On the other hand, the artistic choices made in the movie and its commercial success have made it a blueprint for following biographical pictures of African American singers. Here, the film's critical and commercial success have made it a blueprint on how to create cultural continuity between generations of artists while remaining economically viable. The casting of Diana Ross, which might have been a simple career move on part of the interested parties, created a connection between the performer and the biographical subject existing beyond the film itself. Since then, this feat has been reproduced in other biographical pictures of African American singers and thereby created a network of cultural connectivity between different generations of African American artists.

NOTES

1. While in contrary Motown is often seen as having perfected the adjustment of African American musical output in order to appeal to white audiences.

2. In Armstrong's case his "coon" performances might even be seen as tainting his great musical biography. They could be seen as a reason why no attempt at a biographical movie has yet been made.

3. For example, not depicting the artists themselves on the record covers (Lüthe 69–70). Most striking perhaps the single release of Mary Wells' "You Beat Me to the Punch" which shows only a white woman while putting the singer's name in quotation (Lüthe 80).

4. Just like the "blacking-up" of minstrel shows to understand Motown's representations as "whiting-up" only functions supported by a racist belief in delineating behavioral patterns along racial lines.

5. This ideological connection was further extended as Motown released public speeches of Dr. King on a sublabel specifically established for that reason (George, "Where" 62).

6. Which would have been another possible, more psychologically intimate, angle for a biographical movie. This would allow to connect Holiday's later problems to earlier sufferings. It is unsurprising that the moviemakers didn't pursue this as they didn't seem to interested be in Holiday's fall, practically ending the movie with her staging a triumphant comeback.

7. Curiously, the soundtrack release is an odd one, not delivering full Diana Ross performances of the Billie Holiday songs. Instead, many tracks seem to be directly lifted from the movie's audio track even including sound effects and dialogue. By including many dialogue

scenes and brief musical performances the soundtrack reaches double album length while only having a small number of songs performed in complete versions.

8. Perhaps inspired by the tagline "Sean Connery IS James Bond" used for *You Only Live Twice* (Chapman 108).

9. This is also reflected in Ross' preparation for the role. In her memoirs she very much dwells on Holiday's drug addiction and suggests it to have been the cause of Holiday's pain and problems (165–166).

10. As for example the enthusiastic response to *The Birth of a Nation* by President Woodrow Wilson testifies (Bogle, "Toms" 10).

11. Similar to Diana Ross, Knowles' role as lead singer of Destiny's Child and her successful transformation into a solo artist gave the perception of her being the main cause when the group broke up in 2006.

12. For example, her album *Live at Caesars Palace* includes a *Lady Sings the Blues* medley.

13. For example, by apprehending African American musical forms.

14. The mainstream middle class society often only embraces them in hindsight.

WORKS CITED

Bogle, Donald. *Brown Sugar*. New York: Da Capo, 1980.
Bogle, Donald. *Toms, Coons, Mulattoes, Mammies, and Bucks: An Interpretative History of Blacks in American Films*, new 3d ed. Oxford: Roundhouse, 1994.
Chapman, James. *Licence to Thrill: A Cultural History of the James Bond Films*, 2d ed. London: I.B. Tauris, 2007.
George, Nelson. *The Death of Rhythm & Blues*. New York: Plume, 1988.
George, Nelson. *Where Did Our Love Go? The Rise & Fall of the Motown Sound*. London: Omnibus, 2003.
Gordy, Berry. *To Be Loved: The Music, the Magic, the Memories of Motown: An Autobiography*. New York: Warner Books, 1994.
Japtok, Martin, and Jerry Rafiki Jenkins. Introduction. *Authentic Blackness/"Real" Blackness: Essays on the Meaning of Blackness in Literature and Culture*, edited by Martin Japtok and Jerry Rafiki Jenkins. Black Studies & Critical Thinking 26. New York: Peter Lang, 2011, pp. 1–6.
Japtok, Martin, and Jerry Rafiki Jenkins. "What Does It Mean to Be 'Really' Black? A Selective History of Authentic Blackness." *Authentic Blackness/"Real" Blackness: Essays on the Meaning of Blackness in Literature and Culture*, edited by Martin Japtok and Jerry Rafiki Jenkins. Black Studies & Critical Thinking. New York: Peter Lang, 2011, pp. 7–51.
King, Martin Luther. *Where Do We Go from Here: Chaos or Community?* Boston: Beacon Press, 2010.
Lüthe, Martin. *Color-Line and Crossing-Over: Motown and Performance of Blackness in 1960s American Culture*. Culture in America in Transition 3. Trier: Wissenschaftlicher Verlag Trier, 2011.
Malcolm X. *The Autobiography of Malcolm X*, Penguin Classics ed. New York: Penguin, 2001.
Mauk, David, and John Oakland. *American Civilization: An Introduction*, 5th ed. London: Routledge, 2009.
Ritz, David. *Divided Soul: The Life of Marvin Gaye*. New York: Da Capo Press, 1991.
Ross, Diana. *Secrets of a Sparrow*. London: Headline Book, 1993.
Sanello, Frank. *Reel v. Real: How Hollywood Turns Fact into Fiction*. Lanham, MD: Taylor Trade, 2003.
Varga, Somogy, and Charles Guignon. "Authenticity." *The Stanford Encyclopedia of Philosophy*, Summer 2016 ed., edited by Edward N. Zalta. https://plato.stanford.edu/archives/sum 2016/entries/authenticity/, accessed 7 March 2017.

FILMOGRAPHY

Carpenter, John, dir. *Elvis*. Dick Clark Productions, American Broadcasting Company (ABC), 1979.

Condon, Bill, dir. *Dreamgirls*. Paramount Pictures, Dreamworks Pictures, 2006.
Furie, Sidney J., dir. *Lady Sings the Blues*. Paramount Pictures, Jobete Music Company, Motown Productions, Weston Associates, Furie Productions, 1972.
Gilbert, Lewis, dir. *You Only Live Twice*. United Artists, Eon Productions, 1967.
Gordy, Berry, dir. *Mahogany*. Paramount Pictures, Jobete Film Corporation, 1975.
Griffith, David W., dir. *The Birth of a Nation*. David W. Griffith Corporation, Epock Producing Corporation, 1915.
Hackford, Taylor, dir. *Ray*. Universal Studios, Bristol Day Productions, Anvil Films, Baldwin Entertainment, Unchain My Heart Louisiana, 2004.
Mangold, James, dir. *Walk the Line*. Fox 2000 Pictures, Tree Line Film, Konrad Pictures, Catfish Productions, Mars Media Beteiligungs, Twentieth Century–Fox Film Corporation, 2005.
Martin, Darnell, dir. *Cadillac Records*. Sony Music Film, Parkwood Pictures, LightWave Entertainment, 2008.
Mayer. Gerald, dir. *Bright Road*. MGM, 1953.
Parks, Gordon, dir. *Shaft*. MGM, Shaft Productions, 1971.
Preminger, Otto, dir. *Carmen Jones*. Carlyle Productions, Twentieth Century–Fox Film Corporation, 1954.
Van Peebles, Melvin, dir. *Sweet Sweetback's Baadasssss Song*. Cinemation Industries, Yeah, 1971.

Songs

Beyoncé. "At Last." *Cadillac Records*, Columbia, 2008.
Blinky Williams. "Taint Nobody's Bigness If I Do." *Lady Sings the Blues*, Motown Record Company, 1972.
Diana Ross. "Good Morning Heartache." *Lady Sings the Blues*, Motown Record Company, 1972.
Diana Ross. "Lover Man (Oh, Where Can You Be?)." *Lady Sings the Blues*, Motown Record Company, 1972.
Diana Ross. "Strange Fruit." *Lady Sings the Blues*, Motown Record Company, 1972.
The Four Tops. *Baby I Need Your Loving*. Motown Record Company, 1964.
Kanye West and Jamie Foxx. "Gold Digger." *Late Registration*, Roc-A-Fella Records, 2005.
Mary Wells. *You Beat Me to the Punch*. Motown Record Company, 1962.
The Temptations. *Ain't Too Proud to Beg*. Motown Record Company, 1966.

"Owning" Billie Holiday in Several Representative Jazz Poems

WILLIAM LEVINE

How could an analysis of several representative poems on Billie Holiday help to intervene in current arguments on cultural appropriation? Postromantic lyric poetry has generally tended to oppose its language, voices, and forms to the types of commercial economies that are all too likely to exploit Holiday's suffering for the purposes of entertainment and preserve a standing order of class-based, racial, and gender exploitation. More specifically, lyric poems about jazz artists are characteristically empathetic towards the musicians they take as their subject for eulogies, elegies, and other forms of tribute. This class of poetry can be said to establish an alternative economy, one that assigns a singular value to artistic accomplishment and musicians as a catalyst for personal insight and interpersonal identifications that are opposed to the values of mass culture or even markers of aesthetic taste that can prove to be empty by comparison. As futile as it is to determine authentic sincerity from the poetic text alone, the depiction of genuinely-earned appreciation trumps crass appropriation.

When poets emblematize the struggles and suffering of such jazz artists as Billie Holiday, they may indeed be appropriating lives and stories from another culture they have no inherent claim upon for their personal or professional benefit. The restrictions upon direct quotations from the poems to be discussed in this essay are a reminder of copyright laws that grant property rights to all authors, whether poets or the purveyors of pulp fiction. Yet the most culturally-sensitive poems that cross possibly asymmetrical cultural boundaries also respond to the challenge of reflecting upon and justify their representations of the jazz artist. Following some recent discussions about cultural appropriation in fiction and the fine arts, I will argue that the poems offer some reciprocating recognition, if only in aesthetic terms, and clearly cannot be said to exploit the culture that they draw upon or perpetuate the oppression of a less empowered class in their efforts to represent Billie's life and art fairly and in good faith (Gulches and Holmes; Michaels).

Without romanticizing or privileging lyrical poetry about jazz artists as a special mode of discourse, the following discussion of nine poems that respond to Billie Holiday's art and life, each one reprinted in two prominent jazz poetry anthologies, will assert that their representations of the singer differ significantly from typical mass-cultural reductions of her life. Despite some problems common to any artistic medium representing her pain or victimization, Holiday's life and work are not invoked for titillation or other forms of self-indulgent entertainment. Several of the poems openly critique reductive accounts that hinge on sensationalizing her drug abuse, acts of prostitution, victimization by men, criminality, self-destructive celebrity, and other troubling facets of her life that could easily manipulate a mass cultural audience. As the poet Terrance Hayes dismissively remarks of one such interpretation, Diana Ross' starring performance in the 1972 film *Lady Sings the Blues,* "You know the story" (Young 230). In response to this one-dimensional portrayal, Hayes, like several other authors of "Billie poems," constructs a lyrical episode that forges a more genuinely earned connection to her life and better represents her legacy so that a sympathetic reader will also see this difference.

To be quite blunt, this essay will ask, "Who owns Billie?" A more tactful way of posing this question may be "Who has the authority to represent her, and whatever field of cultural signification her life may signify, in their poetry?" The question presumes that all the poems guard against exploitative co-optations and, at the very least, attempt to return some alternative value to their representations in exchange for their "use" of Billie. But does any poet have a stronger claim to represent her on the basis of racial, gender, or other experiential affinities? Of all the poems to be discussed, only Rita Dove's "Canary" (1989) which, as I shall argue, openly confronts the problems of representing an already-commoditized Holiday that almost all the other poets recognize to a lesser degree, is written by an African American woman. Without examining each poem, no one could even begin to decide whether Dove has a better, more intuitive grasp of Billie's life and its reception than Terrance Hayes or Cyrus Cassell's, both black males, or, for that matter, any other poet, regardless of race or gender. Taken to an absurd extreme that would have to exhaust every possible par textual and contextual factor, concerns over appropriation would have to clear a poet of all possible grounds of transgression for writing about but not belonging to any exploitable category to which Holiday belonged, not just race and gender. What about jazz musicianship, drug use, imprisonment, illegitimacy, bisexuality, or prostitution? Some boundaries must be set regarding the poet's claim to write about an "other" besides empathy and appreciation, and the readings that follow will identify a set of "Billie poets" as the unacknowledged legislators of fair appropriation. Of course, the representations of Billie in each poem can vary from very compressed references and metaphoric allusions to fully developed elegiac tributes. Such poetic uses are a far cry from "telling someone else's story" for personal gain, to appease private guilt (Banks 90), or in a manner of paternalistic condescension. An overview of each poem allows for an understanding of how it constructs and argues for an "alternative economy" that resists succumbing to exploitative treatments of Holiday.

As for the formal means by which poets "claim" Billie, a spontaneous moment in their childhood that has introduced the now-mature poetic speaker to her voice on record may initiate a unique type of "crisis poem": that is, a recollection of a difficult moment or phase in early life that converged with the speaker's first impression of Holiday's voice, which has lingered in memory and possibly catalyzed a later resolution of the childhood crisis. On the other hand, a poetic reflection on her misrepresentations could direct the speaker towards a more insightful portrait. How Billie fits into a "poetic economy" may thus run the gamut from a seemingly naïve, naturally intuitive moment to a fairly sophisticated consideration of respectful boundaries for cultural appropriation. The poems under discussion fall across a spectrum that includes various degrees and convergences of naïve and reflective approaches. A poem about listening to Billie as a child and identifying with her in an innocent, unreflective way can be written only from the perspective of an adult who has reflected on how this formative emotional connection with the singer has been earned. A poem that critiques a false or misguided use of Holiday typically arrives at a resolution that approaches sincere empathy, arising from apparently spontaneous feelings that have been freed from a network of culturally-degrading or reductive significations. The authority of the poet to "use" Billie ultimately turns on the validation and representation of a private lyrical moment, one that is earned by the speaker's biographical experience corresponding to the singer's powers of expression. All the poems in the ensuing discussion distance themselves from the types of economy that have no legitimate claim to "owning" Holiday, but questions of how openly or convincingly they construct and contemplate their appropriation remain to be addressed.

Why does "The Day Lady Died" (1964; Young 237) set a template for later tributes to Billie, even those that do not approach its unconventional manner? It is what Frank O'Hara himself called an "I do this, I do that" lunchtime poem (Siskel). The speaker registers the seemingly idle, trivial events of an afternoon spent eating lunch and shopping for his friends until the very final lines, when the news that Billie has died forces him to recall a sublime memory of her live singing. The most obvious answer would be that it places Billie's voice beyond any ordinary economy, its transactions, and the consumption of its products. The work that the speaker has to do to register his appreciation involves surrendering various kinds of cultural props and common appetites in order to reactivate his memory of living in her moment and in a sense humble himself before her.

The poem openly dramatizes the speaker's immersion in a vacuous cultural economy, a mixture of high-cultural choices and plebeian, street-level needs, which the memory of Holiday and the shock of realizing her death outweigh and exceed. The ultimately trivial shopping trip and other acts of consumption precede the news of her death, and the register of banal events threatens to overwhelm the entire poem before the brief, poignant moment of the closing recollection; however, many interpretations have looked for foreshadowing, calculated ironic reversals, or other signs of coherence between the pedestrian activities and the closing memory (Corcoran 146–49). Literally an arresting, breathtaking moment for the speaker, the memory of Holiday's singing demands that the speaker step outside the comfortable realm of his literary tastes and their attendant class values, as well as his ordinary needs and habits on this day. Billie's whispering delivery of her lines at the Five Spot resembles an out-of-body experience for the audience and speaker. This epiphanic moment undermines the earlier account of his "quandariness" when shopping for presents for his friends, withdrawing funds from the bank, deciding on a purchase of high literature, eating a burger and drinking a malted, looking for French cigarettes, recording names and places that seem to mark his time and map his urban route without any apparent meaning. The speaker's complacency is disrupted upon seeing her image and the news of her death on the front page of the *New York Post*. The tabloid newspaper's headline story is by definition a mass-cultural reduction of her life that demands the speaker's personal supplementation through his memory and shared private experience. In the poem's resolution, he virtually relives a moment when Holiday not only took his and every other club patron's breath away, as if intimating mortality, but also halted his visit to the men's room and thus arrested yet another ordinary life routine. Entering the late-career Billie's world leaves the speaker hovering between life and death not long before the shadow of death actually fell.

Whether or not one says O'Hara "appropriates" a jazz singer from another race, gender, and cultural field for the sake of accruing poetic capital, "The Day Lady Died" remains a template for later elegies and tribute poems, insofar as the text of the poem takes the speaker outside a world of materialist economic reductions in order to appreciate a voice and by extension a life that also sought such freedom. Her life and music become a roadmap for a speaker's quest to escape futility or insignificance. This unconventional elegy's formal means of establishing authenticity earns its crowning resolution precisely because it does not offer platitudes or blank praise in the manner of a traditional poetic remembrance (Carroll 160). Billie's power speaks through an indefinable negative space. She enters the poem's narrative only in its final lines and is not even mentioned by name, except in the title's riddling pun (in the inversion of Lady Day to "The Day Lady Died"). She is mostly present by contrast with what is absent or only minimally suggested in the poem, and not as a pre-categorized form of taste like the speaker's purchases on his shopping trip; she thus rises above an ordinary market of cultural appropriation (Ross 66). The evocative quality of her whispering delivery and economy of phrasing also converges with the aesthetic ideals of contemporary lyric poets (O'Meally 33). Whether or not any poems following O'Hara's template are just as convincing, they continue to dramatize a speaker's connection to Billie as if just the hint of her voice inspires awe like an oracle that privately reminds poets of their calling. It is an irrepressibly mimetic reaction, despite the differences between musical and verbal media.

Also furnishing a model for poems that seek to free Billie and her most empathetic listeners from the forces of commodification, Rita Dove casts her poem "Canary" (Young 239) not so much as a personal economic transaction with Holiday's power as a set of lyrical, yet critical insights on her place in a system of mass-cultural appropriation. The impenetrable mysteries of her selfhood and self-invention are opposed to the titillating, suffering character that becomes commodified in a consumer culture that markets even the image of an inscrutable woman as ripe for others' appropriation (McStay). The poem exposes the popularizations that would make Holiday's story both a cautionary tale like the canary in the coal mine and an exemplary myth of the "woman under siege" who justifies and serves to glorify more pedestrian cases of female suffering in passionate romantic relationships.

Dove's image of Holiday more closely approaches the singing caged bird of Paul Lawrence Dunbar's 1899 poem "Sympathy" (Griffin 156–59). From the very first lines, Dove's lyric plainly asserts that Billie will always be misrepresented and misunderstood, that her voice and persona conveyed both darkness and light, decrepitude and elegance as if trying to present a balanced picture, even of the negative space around the artist, pre-appropriation or mythologization. The poem does not openly identify who appropriates Billie's story to perpetuate the myth of the "woman under siege," and it may be difficult to draw a sharp line between contemporary tabloid press accounts of her life and the image she and her collaborator William Dufty constructed for interviews and in *Lady Sings the Blues*. As she says in her own words about her time during the war in the 52nd Street nightclubs, "I had the white gowns and the white shoes. And every night they'd bring me the white gardenias and the white junk" (133). But the poem's memorable final line, "If you can't be free, be a mystery," ambiguous as it is, offers at least some buyback of agency and identity, not just for Billie, and the addressee "you" could very well be a surrogate for Dove in the very act of writing such a poem (Clausen 13) or any woman subjected to a romanticized and ultimately disabling myth of being "under siege."

Self-invention of one's private, impenetrable life, here configured as the shadowy or burnt qualities of Billie's voice and possibly even her drug use (Baker 577), is conflated with narcissism, personal adornment, metaphorical cooking, peak performance, and finally "ownership" of her image in an openly disorienting, parenthetically enclosed second stanza. This self-constructed but inevitably re-appropriated image nonetheless serves a pre-emptive defense against the inevitable sacrifice of women's agency and normalization of suffering under an all-consuming myth of romantic passion. That would be the fate of simply being objectified in someone else's exploitative love story, whereas self-mythologization, if only through some common bond of poetic and musical self-fashioning, may be at best only a defensive mask and pre-emptive claim for a limited, irreducible selfhood, but remains the first step towards undermining mass-cultural reduction.

Consider too the way that George Barlow's poem "In My Father's House" (1981; Feinstein and Komunyakaa 7–8) places a besieged Holiday at the center of its precarious alternative economy. As a tribute to a father who carves out what limited time he has available to write and play jazz before leaving home for a humdrum daily job, this remembrance rightfully celebrates these stolen moments of creativity, perhaps the best legacy he provides for his young son who would become a poet. The cathartic effect of early-morning musical expression extends to and transforms the typically dull morning commute in the poem's resolution so that car horns and surrounding industrial noises sound like orchestrated instruments.

But even if the father could overcome the blues on the days when he acts on his musical impulses, an earlier stanza that speculates on the content of his dreams, presumably the source of his inspiration, ends on an unresolved note, a surrealistic image of "pretty Billie/eating gardenias with a needle/ singing the blues away." This compressed reference and its pun on the word "needle" lead to an ambiguous sense of how far an alternative economy of freedom can reach. The image combines beauty and mortality, flourishing inspiration with frittering decay, an autonomous spirit with self-destructive drug addictions, and possibly a transmogrified image of how the self-consuming expression in Billie's voice is preserved through a record player's needle. In this depiction, she stands both inside and outside the system that would devour her, as does the father, who, thanks in part to this cautionary nightmare, is inoculated from self-destructive harm and rejuvenated by the poem's end. While the poem may not openly state the terms of fair use for its representation of Holiday, the father, a "black Beethoven" is claiming limited artistic freedom that otherwise would have been consumed by his job at the Alameda Naval Base, literally an arm of the military-industrial complex and its function in an economy that steals time, energy, and the ability to sustain and pass on an Afrocentric cultural legacy.

Yet another brief, but central reference to Holiday's place in both exploitative and redemptive economies of value guides Robert Wrigley's "Torch Songs" (1986; Feinstein and Komunyakaa 242). In a poem that celebrates this genre by reconciling artistic contrivance with the authenticity of the feelings that the best performances of such songs deliver, one particular stanza stands out because it poses two key rhetorical questions. The questions might seem at first to call into doubt the artistic illusions, artifices, ruses, and insular sources of inspiration that, if the listener typically suspends disbelief, allow full therapeutic appreciation of a woman singer's persistent torch-bearing for her lost love. Wrigley, however, seems to slant his questions from the very start so that the well-concealed artistic mechanisms behind the ostensible drama of such songs are justified by their final effect on the listener.

The speaker first asks whether Billie addresses her songs as much to a lost lover as to her greatest influence, Bessie Smith, who is also said to have been singing to Billie. The second question asks whether it makes any difference that the male composers of Tin Pan Alley wrote the words for women to sing and make real. In both cases, the poem's sweeping democratic vision of these "national anthems of longing" validates both artistic liberties. It justifies the reciprocating artistic relationships that perpetuate the genre's popularity.

The poem's relentlessly optimistic tribute to a uniquely American art form that delivers stories of painful romantic loss homeopathically may, however, too easily suppress a reader's urge to ask further questions about the two major rhetorical questions. Namely, what sort of agency, if any, do women torch singers have under a regime of male songwriters who construct the singer's persona and literally feed her their stories? And couldn't the relationship between Billie and Bessie, the only marker of any racial difference in the entire poem, be claimed as uniquely female and African American? Perhaps ironically designated as "Smith" and "Holiday," as if they are common factory workers who take part in one stage of a larger national enterprise, they are nonetheless singled out for special attention, but are they any more than just another pair of contributors to a cultural treasure that belongs to all citizens? This is not to say that the poem deliberately masks the racial, class, and gender stratification that is inherent in a collective artistic enterprise, one that arguably rises above mere economic exploitation in its most enduring productions. Indeed, the intertwined rhetorical questions may be the most tactful possible means of addressing such illusions of equality, even in the process of encouraging such illusions.

Celebrating a collective, homogenizing national enterprise may demand guarding against the risk of nearly erasing the cultural differences and imbalances of power among its contributors. By contrast, a single-focus tribute to the power of Billie's voice may need to check a tendency to privately symbolize her value and may insufficiently differentiate between the speaker's projections and the broader cultural meanings attributed the singer. Whether or not an inspired, highly personal reaction to Billie on record is considered a form of appropriation, the very title of Lisel Mueller's poem "January Afternoon, with Billie Holiday" clearly hinges on a trope of companionship between listener and singer. Mueller presents her euphoric, expansive tribute as a reciprocating gift economy with its own boom-and-bust cycle. In response to the tonal variety and multiple identities of Billie's voice, the speaker's mimetic urge for unbounded freedom and desire is restricted only by the crush of inevitable disappointment and other forms of constraint, loosely configured as the singer's foreknowledge of a sobering "tomorrow," a prescient understanding of life's limitations. For instance, the very first metaphors for her voice compare it to chalk, parchment, and oil, a range of tactile images that double as figures for artistic media or even forms of instruction and historical preservation. With its governing metaphor of Billie's voice as shifting winter morning sunlight, the first stanza effects a transition from a hint of racialized violence to healing and nurturing: the low sunrays that shoot out through tree branches resemble knives stuck through "compliant" black bodies, but through a certain reflective modulation, the "light" of her voice is identified with diluted milk and age-old wisdom for poor people.

This complex metaphor is the only marker of race in the poem, with the remainder of the text essentially mapping the speaker's absorption and translation of Billie's voice into a private verbal performance, characterized by its rapidly shifting imagistic and metaphoric impressions. The speaker's impressions of Billie's voice register a shape-shifting, life-affirming plenitude and unbounded desire that continue to rise and expand even as her articulation is said to "scrape" against the innocent romantic lyrics she sings, as if about to hit a wall and ultimately meet some form of rejection. A briefly quoted phrase from the song "Cheek to Cheek" anchors the poem's speaker's rhapsodic impressions of Billie's voice in an unbounded, omnidirectional human desire for freedom and unending love, configured as an urge for unconstrained space and heavenly airiness in the face of mortal limitations and pain. As Angela Davis has noted, Billie's interpretations transformed what were often just sentimentally manufactured Tin Pan Alley lyrics through allegorical recoding in her need to resist limiting racial and gender categorizations (165–72).

Mueller's poem touches only briefly on the markedly political implications of Holiday's resistance to human and societal constraints. More subtly, maybe even more broadly, it poses an inevitable economic crash that must follow an effusive boom cycle of seemingly endless reciprocating tributes to the singer's generosity. The poem thus checks and dismantles its own idealism, its insistent trope of unbounded companionship on a winter afternoon. Ironically, the "bust" cycle is prompted by the very same voice that triggered the speaker's contagious rhapsody. "Tomorrow" with its erasure of short-lived freedoms—what Holiday is said paradoxically to remember in her singing—is what short-circuits the gift-giving economy that informs the lyric.

Like some of the other "Billie poems" that move beyond lyrical privacy and allow her recorded voice to mediate turbulent moments in racial history, the Afrocentric "folk culture" and its daily travails of survival that she addresses are what validate the alternative economy of Cyrus Cassells' poem "Strange Fruit" (1983; Feinstein and Komunyakaa 30–31). The speaker considers how the song the poem is named after haunted him as a child and remained with him as he continued to learn about the tragic suffering and lynching of African Americans. The solitary childhood memory of Holiday's voice triggers a feeling of distress that comes to signify an entire race's historical burden of fear and humiliation. For Cassells, Holiday's recording of "Strange Fruit" acts homeopathically as he gains his first intimation of a collective racial death and a corresponding impulse to mourn. The song frightens him well before he understands the systemic repercussions of lynching. Only in the lyric's brief resolution does the adult speaker, listening again to "Strange Fruit," arrive at a point where he is better equipped to respond to his childhood fright and sadness. In that moment he recognizes the root cause of lynching in the fears of the oppressors and imagines a world on the brink of uttering "that one word" that would end the cycle of actual murders and internalized walking deaths among generations of African Americans.

The exposure to fear and tragedy in childhood is what finally leads the speaker to complete the circle and entertain the possibility that racialized fear will die among both victims and persecutors. The speaker has learned to inoculate himself against such fear and envision a utopian horizon. The poem describes a therapeutic or cathartic "use of Billie" in its pathology of an internalized legacy of racial suffering. By mapping his experiential path of developing tragic self-awareness, the speaker justifies his representation of her as a catalyst for his intensified feelings and a herald of his unfolding comprehension of his trauma—for example, when he personally identifies with Emmett Till. But how does this earnest personal testimony to Billie's powers stand against any established economy that limits her full value? The answer may lie in the poem's first lines, which quote and begin to embellish upon the lyrics of the song whose title it borrows. After registering the apprehensions that the words and music instilled in the young speaker, the poem elaborates on the central metaphor of the song: victims of lynching who hang from trees are indeed a "strange and bitter crop," a perversion and corruption of the natural cycle of life and regeneration typical of a harvest bloom.

Translating the song into a confessional lyric, the poem reclaims the Abel Meeropol (writing as "Lewis Allan") poem (1937) and song (1939) for the victims and those who may live to see the end of victimization. The composer, who reacted to a photograph of a lynching in Marion, Indiana, in 1930, is never mentioned, in a way perpetuating the longstanding misattribution of the song to Billie herself (Szwed 160–63). One may only speculate that the poem's quiet contemporary lyric idiom transforms and redirects the rough agitprop cabaret style of the song lyrics, with their blunt mnemonic rhymes, irregular meter, and acrimoniously ironic contrasts, towards a regenerated poetic realm of racial ownership and agency in seeking justice. Such a redirection, moreover, would parallel the two distinct audience reactions when Billie performed the song first for the Greenwich Village crowd at Café Society, made up mostly of white liberals, and later sang it uptown at the Apollo Theater for those who had come north during the Great Migration and their children. Whereas guilt-ridden silence and awe prevailed at the club (Nicholson 113), two thousand people were said to be sighing in unison at the theater (Jack Schiffman, son of the Apollo's owner, qtd. in Margolick 99). Though Meeropol's lyric was considered too controversial to be deemed economically viable by Columbia Records and Holiday initially had trouble adapting to the first "we" song she had ever performed, she left her indelible stamp on the song and "owned it" in cultural memory. In response, Cassells' poem continues on the path that Billie had taken uptown decades earlier by personalizing the speaker's connection to the protest song, reshaping it in the process, and restoring its ownership to those with the strongest claim to have felt and internalized the fear of lynching, both the literal and institutionalized kinds, all their lives.

Adapting, supplementing, personalizing, and rewriting parts of Billie's songs in a contemporary poetic idiom should meet adequate standards of reciprocation, recognition, empathy and understanding of the source culture. The poet and editor Kevin Young seemed to be aware of the intertextual play between Billie's most poetic song lyrics and contemporary verse responses to this material when he included the lyrics to "Strange Fruit" and "God Bless the Child" along with his selection of poems about Billie in the final section of his jazz poetry anthology. Although it is anthologized in the Feinstein and Komunyakaa anthology and not Young's, Claire Collett's "Midsummer" (1989; 37) retains some slightly muted echoes of "Strange Fruit" in its account of listening to Billie at a young age. The speaker hears the tragic foreboding as well as the possibilities for guidance and resiliency in her voice. Unlike Cassells' poem, Collett openly dramatizes the misguided consumption of Holiday's voice to which she opposes her developmental insight. The speaker, a young English girl, quietly observes her father, either divorced or widowed, play his Jack Teagarden and Billie records loudly while drinking, smoking, and engaging in an imaginary argument with his absent wife: the records make up the soundtrack to a regressive phase of his life. The use of Billie as a reference point in the poem among a cluster of self-destructive activities may suggest an elegy for a father en route to his ultimate demise, but the speaker also reflects on her need for an independent future. At risk of being drowned and silenced in her father's sorrow and neglect, she has an entirely different, private takeaway from hearing Billie's voice, which both correlates with and rises above this depressing scene. Closely attentive to the voice, she paints it as both "cool" and "bitter," "thick," yet shrouded in darkness. The ambivalent tone of the closing lines implies that the speaker finds guidance as well as sorrow in Holiday's voice, which seems more tangible, fully present to the young speaker's senses, and intuitively understood during hard times than when the father hears her only to mask and retreat from his immediate reality. The speaker's final image of Holiday responds to her previous focus on the steady beam of light across the field from her house. Her voice literalizes and fulfills an earlier metaphorical wish for a light at the end of the tunnel.

The world of "Strange Fruit" enters the poem only in the speaker's tactfully minimal allusions to the song's landscape. Collett attributes the song's contrasting impressions of seeming innocence and the brutal violence that infects it to Billie's voice itself rather than the lynching fields and thus defuses any possibilities of imbalanced, asymmetrical, or self-serving appropriation. It's the experiential wisdom of Holiday's voice rather than an unwarranted parallel between parental negligence and lynching that fuels this subtle adaptation of the song and the artist's performance.

By contrast, an attempt to "claim" Billie on the basis of a well-anchored familial or communal "folk" line of descent is almost the entire point of Terrance Hayes' "Lady Sings the Blues" (1999; Young 229). The title signals a poem that will contrast the misrepresentations of the 1972 Diana Ross film with the authentic testimony of the young speaker's mother, a plausible scenario no matter how fictionalized the story may be. (Hayes would have been only one-year-old when the film was first released.) She watches the film with her young son, who says he is "old enough to know *Heartache*," whether this refers only to the song "Good Morning Heartache" or, more broadly, to the difference between genuine and artificial expression. The poem moves past the commonplace observations that Diana Ross isn't as evocative a singer as

Holiday and that the star remains improbably attractive even as she portrays episodes of drug and alcohol abuse, imprisonment, and other scenes of Holiday's advancing decrepitude. These initial criticisms are only the start of the speaker's efforts to dispel the attractions of the film's slow-building illusions, even as Ross is oddly said to "dispel" a song note as if it's a note of uncertainty about her authenticity. The extended conceit of Diana Ross as a singing flower suggests a falsely comforting hothouse motif that places the film viewer literally and figuratively in the dark. Even though the speaker skeptically reflects on this experience from an adult's perspective, it's not until the resolution that the film's illusions are completely punctured. After the boy and his mother exit the theater, she tells him that the Diana Ross does not sound like Billie, and he hears her humming "Good Morning Heartache," presumably in response to the loss of the boy's father.

This familial scene, not the film scenes, briefly and conclusively establishes a "folk" inheritance of her cultural significance. What might be called a sympathetic hum testifies to the power of the mother's having witnessed and absorbed the voice and feeling of Holiday. The poem affirms an alternative economy that depends on the activation of cultural memory. Billie's performance of songs like "Heartache" continues to speak to the mother. The act of writing such a poem also attests to the value of a legacy, the inheritance of the truth about Billie against mass-cultural reductions, and in its way bonds the mother, remembered as "my lady," and child in an affirmative familial moment despite the loss of the father. Given that the film depicts Billie's decline as an overfamiliar story that the star presence merely sanitizes or prettifies, the question of how to justly represent Billie's pain, though, seems to be answered only by the mother's humming, as if the cathartic effect of hearing and echoing Holiday is also a way of channeling the singer's pain, of sharing, confronting, and releasing the communal burdens to which she gave voice.

The final poem to be discussed will also serve quite fittingly as the conclusion to this essay. Perhaps the last word on appropriations of Billie, Tony Hoagland's "Poem in Which I Make the Mistake of Comparing Billie Holiday to a Cosmic Washerwoman" (2003; Young 231) depicts an actual dialogue that he had with Terrance Hayes over the cultural and racial meanings of Billie's voice (Hoagland). The self-deprecating title seems to present the author as a politically incorrect white poet, caught in the act of uttering an insensitive, indecorous, stereotyped metaphor. Yet the nearly apologetic inclusion of this extended comparison, made as dignified as it can be and freed from some of the comic interracial misunderstandings and idealizing excesses that precede it, is what resolves the poem's tension between a utopian, post-racial future and the American legacy of a tragic racialized past. After Hayes criticizes Hoagland for at first too readily essentializing Holiday as "the black soul" and symbolizing the night that surrounds them as African American, the speaker first arrives at a quiet, private thought about her voice's resemblance to water washing the shore of a lake, which he enlarges upon in the final stanzas. After imagining, along with Hayes, visions of artistic glory rising from the squalor of ghetto neighborhoods and the eventual birth of a redeeming figure who will redefine African American ownership of the American literary canon, Hoagland returns his focus to the indelible stains of our nation's past rather than the utopian future. It is here that his impressions of Holiday's voice and song matter are far more racially sensitive than the title suggests. Hoagland's elaborate, privately contemplated metaphor describes her singing as a futile attempt to wash the sorrow from the dark, sad song he and Hayes are hearing on the car radio, to submerge its very words in water only to find that it is like a sheet with an irremovable stain. If the final lines imply that Hayes' mere presence in the passenger's seat inhibits Hoagland from giving voice to this or any other metaphor that could be taken the wrong way and directs him instead just to listen to Billie, the poem still seems to share the same manner of resolution as O'Hara's elegy: her voice takes his otherwise fatuous breath away and arrests the ordinary course of life. The path to this resolution is further complicated by the speaker's need to rein in his excessive claims to understanding the historical suffering and prospects for liberation of another race. Yet his deference to Hayes paradoxically opens up the door to better dialogue about asymmetrical cross-racial exchanges that revolve around the uses of Holiday, even if such dialogue must properly begin in silent appreciation and the prospect of ongoing self-correction by the appropriating author.

WORKS CITED

Baker, Houston A., Jr. Review of *Grace Notes* by Rita Dove. *Black American Literature Forum*, vol. 24, no. 3, 1990, pp. 574–577. *JSTOR*, doi:10.2307/3041752.

Banks, Russell. "Review: The Myth of Billie Holiday." Review of *Lady Day: The Many Faces of Billie Holiday* by Robert O'Meally. *Transition*, no. 57, 1992, pp. 88–93. *JSTOR*, doi: 10.2307/2935157.

Carroll, Paul. *The Poem in Its Skin*. Chicago: Follett, 1968.

Clausen, Jan. "Still Inverting History." Review of several volumes of women's poetry, including *Grace Notes* by Rita Dove. *The Women's Review of Books*, vol. 7, no. 10/11, 1990, pp. 12–13. *JSTOR*, doi: 10.2307/4020806.

Corcoran, Neil. *Poetry and Responsibility*. Liverpool: Liverpool University Press, 2014.

Davis, Angela Y. *Blues Legacies and Black Feminism: Gertrude "Ma" Rainey, Bessie Smith, and Billie Holiday*. New York: Pantheon, 1998

Feinstein, Sascha, and Yusef Komunyakaa, eds. *The Jazz Poetry Anthology*. Bloomington: Indiana University Press, 1991.

Galchen, Rivka, and Anna Holmes. "What Distinguishes Cultural Exchange from Cultural Appropriation?" *New York Times*, 8 June 2017. www.nytimes.com/2017/06/08/books/review/bookends-cultural-appropriation.html.

Griffin, Farah Jasmine. *If You Can't be Free, Be a Mystery*. New York: The Free Press, 2001.

Hoagland, Tony. "Dialogue Partner in 'Cosmic Washerwoman' Poem?" Received by William Levine, 30 May 2017.

Holiday, Billie, with William Dufty. *Lady Sings the Blues*. 1956. New York: Harlem Moon, 2006.

Margolick, David. *Strange Fruit: Billie Holiday, Cafe Society and an Early Cry for Civil Rights*. Philadelphia: Running Press, 2000.

McStay, Chantal. "Rita Dove's 'Canary.'" *The Paris Review*, 17 July 2014. www.theparisreview.org/blog/2014/07/17/rita-doves-canary.

Michaels, Walter Benn. "The Myth of 'Cultural Appropriation': Even Our Own Stories Don't Belong to Us." *The Chronicle of Higher Education*, 2 July 2017. www-chronicle-com.ezproxy.mtsu.edu/article/The-Myth-of-Cultural/240464.

Nicholson, Stuart. *Billie Holiday*. Boston: Northeastern University Press, 1995.

O'Meally, Robert. *Lady Day: The Many Faces of Billie Holiday*. New York: Da Capo, 2000.

Ross, Andrew. *No Respect: Intellectuals and Popular Culture*. New York: Routledge, 1989.

Siskel, Callie. "It's Cooking." *Poetry Foundation*, 9 July 2014. www.poetryfoundation.org/articles/70133/its-cooking.

Szwed, John. *Billie Holiday: The Musician and the Myth*. New York: Viking, 2015.

Young, Kevin, ed. *Jazz Poems*. New York: Alfred A. Knopf, 2006.

Brigitte Loves Billie

Channeling Holiday in Domino *(1988)*

Fernando Gabriel Pagnoni Berns

The shift from the 1980s to the 1990s sees the slow construction of two new feminist paradigms: postfeminism, which advocates the status quo through the "power girl" mindset, and third wave feminism, which developed a political theory that embraced differences and contradictions that constitute women's identities. Neither paradigm prevails upon the other (Gamble 42). Popular culture negotiated with this new social and cultural context, filled with uncertainty about the concrete role of women at the end of second wave feminism. Hollywood channeled this lack of clear direction with the return of the *femme fatale* in the 1990s, together with a global market in softcore erotica for women (Jennings 305).

As a complex illustration of the era, Italy produces *Domino*, directed by feminist author Ivana Massetti (1988), a story with Brigitte Nielsen leading an international cast. The storyline revolves around Domino (Nielsen), a very successful but worn-out director of videos, who, having lost the capacity to love, searches any path possible trying to find something that can drive her to any sense of real identity and agency. She is only sure of something: that she will find answers about herself if she can successfully channel Billie Holiday's persona, the woman who, according to Domino, had "bared her soul" in each performance. With this goal in mind, Domino wants to produce Holiday videos, obsessed as she is with the singer. Through a reclamation of Holiday's proto-feminist persona, the character of Domino (and the decade as a whole) wants to find authenticity in a world dominated by womanhood depicted through images emptied of any real content.

In equal parts softcore porn film, music video (in the mid–80s when music videos were novel for some) and experimental film, *Domino* asks about what happens with women at the end of feminism. The film is dominated by two women: Nielsen and Holiday. It seems a contradiction. These two women cannot be more different. At the time of the film, Nielsen was recently divorced from Sylvester Stallone. Nielsen's exploits (modeling, music, film, posing nude for *Playboy*) were well-covered in the entertainment media and the world press in the 1980s. Nielsen starred in many B-films that asked her to appear scantily dressed and was widely known for her "hypermasculine" performance of femininity (Funnell 206). She was open-minded, brassy and known as a woman with attitude. For some, she was an attention-seeker. It can be argued, however, that a decade so burned out with feminist radicalism saw any woman with desires of agency as harsh and abrasive. Brigitte Nielsen's star persona follows, in some ways, Billie Holiday's life. By the time Holiday was working the after-hours club circuit with a regular routine, Billie was also noted by a brassy attitude: "Club owners, customers, and many of the other singers thought that Billie was arrogant, allegedly prompting some of the girls mockingly to call her 'Lady Day,' one explanation of how Billie acquired her famous moniker" (Greene 17). Further, as "she became more famous, her brushes with the law became more frequent" (Ibid). She could be scandalous in her age, like any opinionated woman fighting for a place in a world seemingly dominated by men.

Nielsen's star persona, heavily associated with her partner and eventual husband Sylvester Stallone and the glossy femininity of her *Playboy* magazine appearances, shapes any reflection about performance and the real persona, ideas that tend to go in opposite directions. In this regard, if Holiday's face "was the idea of change, the possibility of hope" (Tulloch 101) she can be that again, but now, for the postfeminist 1990s.

The Backlash of Feminism in the 1980s

Domino is a film that engages with the politics of female performance and the role of women in the mid–80s. The film was dedicated to a figure of female empowerment (Billie Holiday) and it was held by a feminist director. In this context, it is important to make a brief sketch of the state of feminism at the late 1980s and the uncertain times ahead to understand the complex ideas and images framing *Domino*.

Second wave feminism was also a collective that continued, and opposed, in some ways, the traditional feminism of the first wave. While second wave feminism was "timid" in its goals (a reform of the condition of women in the interior of society), second wave feminists proposed the movement of "women's liberation" as collective and revolutionary. Its founding moments in the 1960s can be found in Betty Friedan's book *The Feminine Mystique* (1965) and the foundation of NOW (National Organization for Women) in

1966, founded by Friedan herself, an institution that sought to bring women into full participation in America. Together with NOW came the Women's Liberation Movement in America, which originates in left-wing movements such as the fight for civil rights led by African Americans, anti–Vietnam War and student movements of the 1960s. Rather than reformist goals, second wave feminists asked for a process of "consciousness-raising" that could transform what is experienced as personal into political terms, with the recognition that "the personal is political" and "that male power is exercised and reinforced through 'personal' institutions such as marriage, child-rearing and sexual practices" (Thornham 26).

As the decade progressed, some felt that women were going too far in their claims, even going to the point of essaying forms of female separatism in self-sufficient strong female-only communities apart from common "patriarchal" life (Pilcher and Whelehan 141). In the last years of the 1970s, a time in which the countercultural movements shifted towards disillusionment and hedonism, and in the first years of the 1980s, dominated by the neoliberal politics of President Ronald Reagan, feminism in general suffered a severe backlash at the hands of media and institutions that blamed many social illnesses on the "exaggerated" claims of feminism. Together with this backlash came internal differences within the feminist collective itself, which helped to take second wave feminism to its end (Thornham 35).

Through the 1980s, this ideological backlash presented feminism as passé, since women mostly achieved, supposedly, what they wanted. Slowly but progressively, the word *feminism* was turned into a "bad word." By the last years of the 1980s, "feminism was dead, or so the media had repeatedly claimed" (Okoomian 208). Either because the goals were achieved (women as equals to men) or because feminist objectives were considered too radical, a feminist might have been deemed obsolete to the public agenda.

Second wave feminism was followed not by one collective, but two, in the 1990s: third wave feminism and postfeminism, not two complementary movements but, in fact, oppositional to each other. While third wave—the term "third" indicating continuity—celebrates multiculturalism and difference (the main difference with second wave feminism), postfeminism marks an end—the prefix "post" indicating "superseding" (Pilcher and Whelehan 107) to traditional forms of feminism.

The most influential definition of postfeminism is given by Susan Faludi, who in her *Backlash: The Undeclared War Against Women* (1991) portrays postfeminism as a reaction against the ground gained by second wave feminism. Gamble states that for Faludi, the paradigm of postfeminism "is the backlash," and "its triumph lies in its ability to define itself as an ironic, pseudo-intellectual critique on the feminist movement, rather than an overtly hostile response to it" (Gamble 38). Faludi refers to the 1980s as "the backlash decade" during which an "undeclared war" was waged against feminism. The media not only told women that their struggle for equal rights had been won, but also that they were paying a bleak price in broken relationships, solitary lives and bitterness since there were no child nor husband to give them company. Hollywood joined the backlash in the late 1980s and 1990s, with the return of the *femme fatale* who came back from the past (classical cinema) to reiterate the popular image of powerful women as sick and dangerous. Films such as *Fatal Attraction* (Adrian Lyne, 1987), *Basic Instinct* (Paul Verhoeven, 1992), *Poison Ivy* (Katt Shea, 1992), *The Body of Evidence* (Uli Edel, 1993), and *Disclosure* (Barry Levinson, 1994), among many others, used the trope of the destructive woman as a warning about the dangers of female radicalism (Lindop 44).

The coming of the erotic thriller in the 1990s came with the resurgence (after the 1970s) of the softcore erotica (and *Domino* easily sits within this subgenre)—productions with stars like Shannon Tweed or Monique Parent in different grades of undress. By definition, softcore pornography involves depictions of nudity and simulated sexual conduct, but it is not as explicit as hardcore pornography. This subgenre was linked to feminism since the former was, supposedly, made not just for men but for women as well. Glossy and sanitized, with qualities of made-for-TV movie, these films, unlike hardcore, were not marketed just for VHS but were screened in cable TV (at late time slots) in the 1990s. As one view of women's traditional lack of interest in erotica has been given as their desire for plot, narrative and character-led pieces (Williams 261), these films were heavy in both, plot and characterization.[1]

Domino is a companion piece to the erotic thriller and softcore erotica of the era. The film uses in many scenes the chiaroscuro of the traditional film noir. Softcore erotica put women center stage, but their acts of agency within the narratives were made only at surface-level, as their "empowerment" is sustained merely in sex. Looking at female nakedness can become coded in terms of spectacle, subjugation, and violence. In traditional cinema, the sexualized human body is female, and Brigitte Nielsen's nakedness cannot easily escape sexual desire even if the film speaks about female subjectivity. This is perpetuated by Domino, whose sexualized outfits and behavior—she smokes constantly, plays with sex, and looks mostly cold and distant—mark her as a *femme fatale*.

On the other hand, *Domino* fits softcore with the recurrent use of Nielsen's naked body and the recurrence to highly stylized sex scenes. For example, there is a long scene in which Domino masturbates, her hand touching her genitals (albeit covered in transparent fabrics) in close shot. Softcore, the erotic thriller and *Domino* came in a time in which the two new paradigms of feminism were yet to be born, and the future of the feminist collective was uncertain. In this sense, the film oscillates between (yet to be born) postfeminism and "sluttiness" as a rhetorical tool for empowerment and positive negotiation of female active sexuality and the (yet to be born) third wave, with its recuperation of feminist possibilities for political work. Both *Domino* (the film) and Domino (the main lead) struggles to find their place in a time mostly free from concrete politics of feminism. Where to go when there is no feminism?

It is particularly interesting, in this sense, that the film tries to get some answers using the Billie Holiday persona and legacy. Biographers insist in the fact that Holiday rejected to being reduced to an object, be it as a black person or woman of color. What the film takes from the legacy of Holiday is her capacity to fashion herself so her stage persona, her identity to be consumed by audiences, can match her subjectivity and need for empowerment. Rather than being some concept of "Africaness," Holiday created a larger-than-life identity that were both, easy to sell and, at the same time, a representation of her vulnerable heart. Behind the surface of stylized sadness, was a woman struggling with real, palpable grief.

The character of Domino tries to channel Billie as a method for finding identity and agency in a world framed by ambiguity and empty visuality. Especially interesting to her will be Holiday's resistance to stereotyping and her determination to find her own voice in a revulsive world. With traditional feminism dead, and no new paradigm to replace it (yet), Domino struggles, as we will see in the next section, to find her own voice, ethos and passion in a depoliticized time.

Domino: *Finding the Feminine Voice Via Billie Holiday*

Massetti never was shy about her goals at the moment of directing *Domino*. She wanted to make a feminist film: "My first movie, *Domino*, and her quest to bridge love and sexuality, was a cry to give value to a woman's sexual discovery as part of her journey as a woman" ("Exclusive"). Massetti addresses the fact that she wants to marry two spheres considered as mutually excluding: sex and love. While sex runs the risk of being exploited by media, love remains, to some extent, an intimate form of subjectivity, foreign to consumption. It can be argued that Massetti tries to blends together postfeminism and forms of identity outside the sphere of sex, with love as a common ground between postfeminism and third wave. Agency is important to the notion that individuals can contribute to changes in society and, in this scenario, Domino wants to act rather than just react. Rather than been consumed by the gaze of men, she wants to love, she directs her emotions actively towards someone who deserves her feelings and passion. Domino uses her beautiful body to find sex, but sex does not really fulfill her anymore. The film eroticizes Nielsen's performance, but asks from audiences more than simple voyeurism and excitation. As Massetti states, "Domino's heart and body didn't function. She was numb, I'd say now" ("Exclusive UK Interview"). There is an incompatibility between the politics of the body and how it is represented (as an erotic object to-be-looked-at) and Domino's agency, and the film oscillates between these two points of view.

The sexual explorations of the female lead, who is constantly changing male partners and appearing in different stages of undress, coded Domino as postfeminist. Postfeminism is at ease in a media-saturated world, where mediated images of pre-fabricated "girl power" and free sexuality prevail as the ultimate goal for women. In postmodernity, "girl power's brash glamour is paired with laddishness in a period where girls must act like boys to get ahead" as the British musical group Spice Girls teaches us (Carson 95). At the center of the ideal of girl power lies an immensely profitable fashion and beauty industry, and as the basis of girl power is the pleasure that came with the creation of self-aware identities of femininity. Female identity and images of empowerment are, then, commodities to buy and discard. Furthermore, postfeminism seems obsessed with youth, girlhood (no matter the real age), sex and image. Even more, the word "slut" has had a particular role in the iconography of postfeminism (Evans 79).

"Slut" disrupts the traditional image of the "good girl," inviting women to engage with their sexual freedom. The problem resides in the ways in which media depicts this sexual freedom: the "sluttish" attitudes run the risk of responding, mostly, more to male fantasies than female empowerment. The negotiation of identities is given only through the capitalist market, as women—especially young women—are invited to adopt self-fulfillment through "slutty" attitudes—acts of sexual empowerment that mostly masks the subordination of women to men's desires—and glittering, glossy images of strong women which are only surface-level and apolitical. As Cris Mayo points out, there are pro-sex feminists who too easily presumed that sexual freedom translated into freedom in general (137). Female mobilization of the term "slut" is particularly interesting in the context of the late 1980s and first years of the 1990s, with the coming of softcore and the return of the *femme fatale*.

In this scenario of nascent postfeminism, Domino embodies "girl power": she is sexually active, successful, and wears fabulous clothes. Further, her constant change of wigs indicates a woman trying and later discarding identities, as if her "self" were malleable and commoditized. This instability of her subjectivity, however, also points to a woman looking for a voice and identity of her own within a world of pure surface, in which sex, like that projected in softcore, runs the risk of becoming a spectacle for men rather than empowerment for women.

Massetti recognized the contradictory destiny of *Domino*: "the censorship didn't like that freedom. They hated that she was living her sexuality in such a free way. So they decided to take the film out of the circuit. They censored it. They gave it the equivalent of an X rating, so the film never had its rightful public." This misunderstanding "was brutal for me. I felt betrayed and at the same time I felt that I had failed" ("Exclusive UK Interview"). This "failure" marks how easily visual depictions of female sexuality can shift from being a tool for women's empowerment to pornography fabricated to excite male viewers. The film begins with a close shot of a digitalized image of Domino's heart, who is enduring a routine medical check-up. Her doctor says her heart is in very good condition. Domino, in turn, replies that she has never seen her heart before, a way of highlighting her alienation regarding her feelings and her role in this new world without clear direction regarding the role of women. The title's credits that follow roll upon the semi-naked silhouette of Nielsen's body (slowly dressing up in an androgynous way, with coat, man's hat and pants, while smoking a cigar). She is interviewed in the fictional late-night TV show "Body and Soul." The show's title refers to the dyad body/soul, as two mutually excluding spheres, one representing sex and the other, love.

There is also a reference to Holiday's legacy in a double way. First, because "Body and Soul" remains a jazz standard, with hundreds of versions performed and recorded by dozens of artists, including Ella Fitzgerald, Annette Hanshaw, Etta James, Sarah Vaughan and Frank Sinatra. Second, *Body and Soul* was the title of a studio album made by Holiday, released in 1957, which contains a rendition of this song. There is a possible third, more obscure meaning, since Holiday, in her memories, remembers how her grandmother talked to her about her past as a slave woman and the way in which she felt "owned body and soul by a white man" (Kliment 26). Choosing this particular title for the fictional TV show, Massetti makes a double meaning. In one hand, she refers to the legacy of Holiday. On the other hand, the director points to the situation of feminists (and Domino) in the 1980s. The dichotomous discussion regarding feminist politics in the late 1980s can be (brutally) simplified in terms of *body* or *soul*. *Body*, because postfeminists declared themselves in charge of their own sexuality, sustaining new positive politics in sex where the term "slut" lost its pejorative meaning to become a reaction toward conservative views on female agency, and *soul*, as third wave feminist were worried that "sexual freedom" supplanted politics and "freedom" in general.

Domino is clearly postfeminist, but she is also looking for something else, something that she cannot put her finger on (perhaps because it was not yet created). The fictional interview highlights the feeling of numbness over-coming Domino. The voice of the invisible male interviewer (a hint to the power of patriarchy to remain oppressive and invisible while women must answer for their actions) interrogates Domino: he states that women should be pretty and capable of expressing their inner feelings (again, body and soul). When he asks Domino if she can do that (express herself), she rejects any concrete answers, favoring rather an ambiguous "any woman can do that," avoiding the personal "I." The answer emphasizes the troubles that Domino has to express her inner Self, and thus her need to find someone who can do that for her. In this sense, Billie Holiday will lend a voice to Domino. Through the interview, Domino admits feelings of doubt and contradictions framing her life.

The male voice sounds slightly triumphant when she "admits" feelings of insecurity, almost an admission of some kind of culpability, an addressing of weakness. She retorts that everyone "feels that way. Don't you?" but the male voice, charged with pride, denies such a feeling. Facing him (who remains out of frame) directly, Domino simply states:

DOMINO: We are different.
MALE INTERVIEWER: You and I?
DOMINO: No. Men and women.
MALE INTERVIEWER: (laughs). That is so ambiguous!

This brief exchange of words reveals that Domino is struggling to find not only her own voice, but that of women in general. The era had replaced female voice with the image of (naked) empowered women enjoying sex as the main act of liberation, as substitute to feminism. Domino engages in this freedom, but this kind of liberty is not enough to her. The male voice asks her to "admit" (another hint to some female "guilt") how good-looking she is. Clearly, he tries to objectify her into a role of passive object to-be-looked-at, situation that the film itself will, contradictorily, emphasize through nude scenes. The question "Are you married?" pops out next, pointing the patri-archal need of putting women under the institution of marriage as the right thing to do, an act of oppression, as previously mentioned, denounced by some second wave feminists. She, gorgeous and seductive but dressed in mas-culine garbs, is powerful but interrogated by male powers, embodies the con-tradictions of an era riffed with uncertainties regarding the future of feminism. Holiday herself, like Domino/Nielsen, could be considered slightly masculine, a "female dandy": "Her ability to flit between masculine lines and hyper-feminine guise, puts her on an equal footing with the black male dandy" (Tulloch 126). Thus, all three women (Nielsen, Domino, Holiday) cannot be reduced to fixed notions of femininity or style. These women nego-tiate with the contradictions inherent in eras that want to put women in center stage, all the spotlights upon them, only to be the passive objects of male appropriation; all the above, of course, disguised as "empowerment."

The interview reveals that Domino is almost obsessed with Holiday. Domino explains that she is doing a video about the singer, whom she admires because Holiday "was always in love"; here, a real admission of weakness. Domino feels no love. She is empty, the embodiment of sex without feelings, of postfeminism without politics except that of sexuality. To Domino, love stands for passion and fulfillment, for voice and agency, rather than just sexuality. It is clear that Domino does not see in Holiday a woman who was permanently love-struck: she admires the capacity of Holiday of beings always open, "readable"—"baring her soul," as she says, for the people around her, an attitude that Domino seems to secretly envy. As Domino states, Holiday opened herself in each song, in each performance. Domino, in turn, fears the vulnerability that comes with openness, her real weakness, her "secret." Holiday's openness makes the singer strong, rather than weak. Domino sees in Holiday a feminist icon capable of teaching women how to get in touch with their inner voice, agency and sense of Self, even if filtered through the politics of aesthetics and stage performance. The vulnerability that Holiday expressed through her musical stage performances—she sounded just like a woman crying—contrasted with her more assertive persona, a woman prone to keep her "guards up" (Greene 34).

The parallels between Domino and Holiday become clear throughout the film. Biographer Meg Greene states that Eleanora (Holiday's real name) "did not want to be pushed around, subject to the whims of others. She began to develop a tougher, harder view of life, the world, and men. Resolving never to endure rejection from a man, Eleanora had a series of brief relationships and broke up with her boyfriends before they had the chance to break up with her" (9). The description fits Domino as well. Massetti does a subtle parallelism between the figures of Domino and Holiday: both must learn how to lower their guard and let love (and lovers) within their lives without renouncing any inch of their will.

To add another layer of complexity to the film, the scene of Domino's interview cut to a wide shot of Domino watching the show in a TV screen; she is resting on a swimming pool, completely naked except a soaked white bikini bottom. Nielsen's "perfect" silicone breasts and trim figure are a striking contrast with her words about female vulnerability: this is a clear example of body and soul as an unresolved dichotomy, as incompatible issues. This reinforces the argument that if women want to get political (and "the personal is political"), they should leave behind any sexualized image of themselves, always susceptible of shifting into male fantasies while passing as "female empowerment." In the juxtaposition of contradictory images (a glamorous naked Domino watching herself talking about her vulnerable self), the film predates (by some years) the birth of the disparate and contradictory ideological points of views sustained by postfeminism and third wave feminism.

There is a striking parallel between Holiday and *Domino*: the complex interlinking of performativity and authenticity. Performance was an important issue in Holiday's life: it "enabled Billie to distinguish herself from other torch singers. She did not wear her emotions on her sleeve; instead, she revealed herself gradually as the song unfolded. Hers was a carefully crafted and sophisticated performance [...]. This carefully woven tapestry of life and music was the origin of the persona that audiences came to identify with Billie" (Greene 31). Her rendition of "Strange Fruit" at the Café Society, for example, is evoked this way: "the room was completely blacked out, service stopped [...]. Everything was dark except for a little pin spot in her face. That was it." The objective was to contrast the silvery hue of her tears against the complete darkness: "The tears never interfered with her voice, but the tears would come and just knock everybody in that house" (qtd. in Tulloch 100). Tears were present each night, a channeling of an inner, authentic sadness that made her art into an act: "Holiday's acting abilities gathered together the complexity of meaning and shaped it into searing emotional intensity through lack of pretense" (Krasner 143). As she gained experience in her career, Holiday began to tidy up herself to construct a stage persona. Through the 1930s, "she marceled her hair, a popular hairstyle that involved using a curling iron to impress the hair with deep, regular waves. She powdered her face, which also featured highly arched and penciled eyebrows, and carefully applied lipstick" (Greene 40). Her clothing changed as well, becoming more personal and urban. Rather than the typical satin dresses, she favored "long gowns, accented by pearl necklaces draped around her neck and hoop earrings" (Ibid).

In drag and performance, realness is not "to be alike" or realistic but "conscious presentations of an illusion" (Han 147), a dramaturgy that projects an identity but is, at the same time, an elaborate and larger-than-life artifice. Drag hinges on the external visibility of an inner persona, life experience, fakeness and authenticity, all cohabiting in the same time through an artistic act. Holiday, as a woman, was never really involved in drag, but her performances were articulated to perform the real, a concealed truth of sadness that Billie exhibited, as acting, in her shows. Performance was a way to channel her inner self. She "creates senses of sadness or solitude that are strangely *impersonal*" (Schleifer 176) in the sense that these feelings, part of Holiday's inner Self, were re-enacted in each performance, in any stage appearance through what might be called a performative identity of vulnerability. Holiday was *real* mostly (and maybe only) in front of an audience (White 177): this is the aspect that Domino tries to reclaim for herself. Performance is a suitable vehicle to present, through the safety of fakeness, a true Self. Behind the safety of a fake appearance, people can say real things about themselves to the world.

Domino revolves around performance and authenticity. Massetti stated that she was not interested in realism, but in symbols and metaphors ("Exclusive"). The sets of the film are fake-looking, the corners covered always in darkness with windows framing frozen shadowy figures, mannequins rather than humans. All the performances are highly theatrical, and the spatial/temporal setting suggests art-decó (a reference to the 1930s, a time of glory for Billie Holiday) with futuristic elements (such as transparent elevators or sliding doors in apartments). Domino changes her wig in each scene, and the *mise-en-scène*, as mentioned, calls back to the noir films of the 1950s rather than the hyperrealism of the 1980s.

Sex and romanticism, desire and intimacy were important for both Domino and Holiday. Both have their troubles with romance, Domino ditching men who wants her only for her looks; Billie with ostensibly bad luck in relationships. After the interview, Domino comes to her house, where she finds that an admirer has sent her a man of plastic as a gift: a black mannequin. The mannequin will be one of the two men with whom she engages in a weird kind of "romantic relationship." She will love the plastic man, especially his capacity of hear her without judging her, what allows her to open up her feelings to "him." She takes him for rides in her car, and sits him at the dinner table; the man of plastic the perfect match for a woman fearing loneliness but incapable of expressing her vulnerability.

Her vulnerability, however, is expressed not through Domino's voice, but Billie Holiday's music. Two songs from the repertoire of Holiday are part of the film's soundtrack: "You Don't Know What Love Is" and "For Heaven's Sake" (the latter rolling on at the final credits). The former plays when Domino slowly dresses up the mannequin, constructing it (him?) as her male partner. She even gives it an "adequate" name: Don Juan. The lyrics work as in ironic contrast with the scene. The song speaks about undying love, while the scene depicts a woman getting company from a piece of plastic. Domino will later say, "his heart is not made of plastic, but real." Don Juan can neither live nor die. There is another man in Domino's life, a stalker who calls her regularly, letting her know that he is watching her from the safety of distance. Unlike other men in Domino's life, the stalker *really knows* Domino. He knows that she feels alone, defeated and tired. He wants to hear what she has to say. She finds in this faceless admirer another person—besides the mannequin— to whom she can open up. It is clear that Domino can only open her feelings with men who are not really there, safeguarding her ego from the pains of real, face-to-face relationships. Domino only can talk of her feeling with anonymous men or through evoking Holiday, her muse, in music videos.

On May 2, 1929, Holiday, still named Eleanora, was arrested on charges of prostitution (Greene 15), so it is no coincidence that Domino finds in an African American prostitute (Joy Garrison) the perfect performer to channel Holiday in her videos. Prostitution belongs to the world of illusory appearances: the fetish assumes the illusion (appearance) of an authentic experience (sex) while remaining fake, just performance (the lack of pleasure). Finally, Domino finds her perfect Holiday, a woman who had blended together surface and authenticity, body and soul. Within a world of glossy erotica emptied of politics of femininity, there is a brief glimpse of authenticity, of real femininity: real pain, sorrow and agency, filtered through stylized performance and glamour. Behind a world of mediated images of femininity, a spark of authenticity still survives, even if in the recreation of an icon of the past who has come to recuperate feminism or, at least, the female voice from empty visuality and hollow performance.

Holiday, as a ghost from the past, is the one who fleshed out Domino's subjectivity and stand for her, a sister who has come from time ago to help another sister in distress. *Domino* ends with a video recreating a performance of Holiday. Domino is seen directing the video. After the scene, Domino tells "Billie" that she has decided to direct another video, one in which she can re-enact not the voice of a star from the past, but many of the events surrounding her. Now, the re-enacting of herself, of her own voice. Holiday has showed her the path; now, Domino can follow. Even if the film gives no answer about the future of feminism, it gives Domino the power to get behind the scenes and give cinematic form to her fears, desires and contradictions. She has the agency to do so now.

Conclusion

Domino cannot answer to the politics of postfeminism and third wave since both branches were still nascent at the moment of the film's production. Thus, the film is ambivalent in the depiction of women within film and in real life. Massetti admits that she would do things different now, maybe downplaying the erotic aspects that take *Domino* close to softcore, itself a subgenre ambivalent about the role that women play within this universe of sexual fantasy.

Domino herself is part of the artificial world that the film denounces: she is, like Don Juan, pure artifice. A figure made of plastic, perfectly embodied in Brigitte Nielsen's star persona. Her plight is her desire to find something real within this universe in which women are slowly turned into "powerful" sexualized images, propagated by two of the new (old, in fact) visual narratives of the late 1980s and first years of the 1990s: softcore erotica and the erotic thriller led by *femmes fatale*.

The legacy of Billie Holiday is not just that of a woman strong enough to make her own path. Many stars have done that. The presence of Holiday helps Domino to understand that body (sexual desire, visuality and the politics of postfeminism) and soul (agency and third wave feminism) can be reconciled. Holiday, through her performances and songs, through fake and real tears, created a character that is ready to be accepted and consumed by audiences. This performative ritual, it can be argued, follows the dictates of contemporary postfeminism and its sense of sensuality, glamour and empowerment. Holiday's exterior persona, however, was just the embodiment of a woman bravely fighting loneliness, racism, chauvinism and poverty. Glamorous but rude, vulnerable and invulnerable, sensual and cold, authentic and fake, feminine and androgynous, empowered and disempowered, Holiday and Domino both bridge the irreconcilability of post feminism's' sluttish attitude with the preoccupations on freedom and female agency of third wave feminism within a context of death and rebirth of a feminism born from backlash.

Domino, then, has the glossy surface of a *Playboy* magazine and the heart of *The Feminine Mystique* beating within. The film can be seen now as a cultural artifact illustrating an era framed by uncertainty about the potential end of feminism. In this sense, it is no coincidence that Massetti recurs to the figure of Billie Holiday as a potential bridge between two eras capable of given some stability and hope for the future.

NOTE

1. Some examples of soft erotica can be found in *The Affair* (Danny Taylor, 1995), *Electra* (Julian Grant, 1996) or *The First 9½ Weeks* (Alex Wright, 1998).

WORKS CITED

Carson, Fiona. "Feminism and the Body." *The Routledge Companion to Feminism and Post-feminism,* edited by Sarah Gamble. London: Routledge, 2006, pp. 94–102.

Evans, Elizabeth. *The Politics of Third Wave Feminisms: Neoliberalism, Intersectionality, and the State in Britain and the US.* Basingstoke: Palgrave Macmillan, 2015.

"Exclusive UK Interview 2016 Ivana Massetti." http://www.thenewcurrent.co.uk/tnc-interview-2016-ivana-massetti.

Faludi, Susan. *Backlash: The Undeclared War Against American Women.* New York: Random House, 2006.

Funnell, Lisa. "Negotiating Shifts in Feminism: The 'Bad' Girls of James Bond." *Women on Screen: Feminism and Femininity in Visual Culture,* edited by Melanie Waters. Basingstoke: Palgrave Macmillan, 2016, pp. 199–212.

Gamble, Sarah. "Postfeminism." *The Routledge Companion to Feminism and Postfeminism,* edited by Sarah Gamble. London: Routledge, 2006, pp. 36–45.

Greene, Meg. *Billie Holiday: A Biography.* Westport, CT: Greenwood, 2007.

Henry, Astrid. *Not My Mother's Sister: Generational Conflict and Third-Wave Feminism.* Bloomington: Indiana University Press, 2004.

Kliment, Bud. *Billie Holiday: Singer.* Los Angeles: Melrose Square, 1990.

Krasner, David. *An Actor's Craft: The Art and Technique of Acting.* New York: Palgrave Macmillan, 2012.

Kuhn, Annette. *The Power of the Image: Essays on Representation and Sexuality.* London: Routledge, 2005.

Lindop, Samantha. *Postfeminism and the Fatale Figure in Neo-Noir Cinema*. Basingstoke: Palgrave Macmillan, 2015.

Mayo, Cris. *Disputing the Subject of Sex: Sexuality and Public School Controversies*. Lanham, MD: Rowman & Littlefield, 2004.

Okoomian, Janice. "Third Wave Feminists: The Ongoing Movement for Women's Right." *Women's Rights: People and Perspectives: People and Perspectives*, edited by Crista DeLuzio. Santa Barbara: ABC CLIO, 2010, pp. 207–224.

Pilcher, Jane, and Imelda Whelehan. *Key Concepts in Gender Studies*. London: Sage, 2017.

Schleifer, Ronald. *Modernism and Popular Music*. Cambridge: Cambridge University Press, 2011.

Thornham, Sue. "Second Wave Feminism." *The Routledge Companion to Feminism and Postfeminism*, edited by Sarah Gamble. London: Routledge, 2006, pp. 25–35.

Tulloch, Carol. *The Birth of Cool: Style Narratives of the African Diaspora*. London: Bloomsbury, 2016.

White, John. *Billie Holiday: Her Life and Times*. London: Omnibus, 2012.

Williams, Linda. *The Erotic Thriller in Contemporary Cinema*. Bloomsbury: Indiana University Press, 2005.

Winter, Han. *Geisha of a Different Kind: Race and Sexuality in Gaysian America*. New York: New York University Press, 2005.

Seeing Is Believing?

Reading Billie Holiday Through Photography

MATTHEW DUFFUS

Though her voice is unmistakable, little about Billie Holiday, the individual, can be viewed similarly. Even the titles of books about her address this issue—*In Search of Billie Holiday: If You Can't Be Free, Be a Mystery*, by Farah Jasmine Griffin; *Lady Day: The Many Faces of Billie Holiday*, by Robert G. O'Meally; and *Billie Holiday: The Musician and the Myth*, by John Szwed, to name just three. In some ways, the more one reads about her, the less one knows for certain. This is only exacerbated by Holiday's own factually-questionable autobiography, *Lady Sings the Blues*, and the multitude of ways she has been interpreted by writers over the years. These challenges led me to the photographic record, for, as Szwed explains, Holiday was "one of the most photographed black women of her time" (71). But even the photographs fail to offer a definitive identity: "[p]ut fifty or sixty photos of her on a table and you will see a heavyset woman and a sylph in silk, an African American and an Asian, a saucy miss and a broken drunk, a perp in a mug shot and a smiling matron posing with a pet. In some pictures she's completely unrecognizable" (1). While these individual photographs seem to complicate rather than clarify her image, a recently-released collection of photographs taken by Jerry Dantzic, published as *Billie Holiday at Sugar Hill*, might provide an answer to this quandary; the sheer quantity of the more than a hundred of images seems to provide the "context" art critic and novelist John Berger sees as being essential to "situat[ing] the printed photograph so that it acquires something of the surprising conclusiveness of that which *was* and *is*" (*About Looking* 64, 65). In other words, Dantzic's work may provide viewers with a clearer, more comprehensive view of Holiday ("that which *was*") than has previously been available in the photographic, and perhaps even the written, record.

The multiplicity of identities noted by writers such as Szwed shouldn't come entirely as a surprise, as Berger writes in "Appearances" that "[a]ll photographs are ambiguous" (58). Viewed singly, or even together, as Szwed mentions above, photographs often lack the context that would allow them to cohere into a definitive portrait. Their ambiguity is exacerbated by the varying degrees of skill that viewers bring to the study of such objects. In *On Photography*, Susan Sontag also comments on photography's elusiveness but points to how this ambiguity contributes to the image's power: "[a]ny photograph has multiple meanings; indeed, to see something in the form of a photograph is to encounter a potential object of fascination" (23).

Fascination is an apt word for what happens when one looks at a photograph of Holiday; such images may not always correspond with the reality of who she was, but they certainly capture the viewer's attention. To understand what happens when we look at photographs of Holiday and the role such representations play in coming to grips with her life story, one must begin with a brief survey of critical theory about the art form, both in relationship to jazz specifically and to photography in general, before considering noteworthy photographs of the singer herself. Doing so will provide a language with which to analyze photographs of Holiday and an understanding of how photography has contributed to the mythology of jazz and Holiday. Finally, while these individual photographs seem to complicate rather than clarify her image, a recently-released collection of photographs taken by Jerry Dantzic, published as *Billie Holiday at Sugar Hill*, might provide an answer to this quandary; the sheer quantity of the more than a hundred pages of images seems to provide the "context" Berger sees as being essential to "situat[ing] the printed photograph so that it acquires something of the surprising conclusiveness of that which *was* and *is*" (*About* 64, 65). In other words, Dantzic's work may provide viewers with a clearer, more comprehensive view of Holiday ("that which *was*") than has previously been available in the photographic, and perhaps even the written, record.

Recent years have seen an increase in writings about the role photographic representation plays in our understanding and appreciation of jazz. One such critic, Benjamin Cawthra, writes in *Blue Notes in Black and White* that "[p]hotographs show the story [of jazz], but they also shape it in ways that not only document but mythologize" (7). One need only consider the collaboration between photographer William Claxton and trumpet player Chet Baker for an example of just such a mythologizing. The images of a young Baker in the studio, as captured by Claxton, reinforce the "James Dean of jazz" mythos that surrounded him, just as the photographs of a drug-ravaged Baker, decades later, are Exhibit A in documenting the ill effects of drug abuse on jazz musicians.[1] While photographs of Holiday do not depict the same stark changes, her mythic stature is still enhanced by the photographic record. For instance, who can forget Gottlieb's close-up of Holiday, mid-song, from 1948, with her head thrown back, mouth open, and bare neck showing the effort that went into her singing? Or the numerous black-and-white photographs of her with a bright, white gardenia behind her ear? Many significant jazz musicians, like Holiday and Baker, are known to us as much for their distinctive representations as for their music. The fact that these representations vary, over the years and from photograph to photograph, only makes them more alluring.

K. Heather Pinson also focuses on jazz photography as myth-making in her book on noted photographer Herman Leonard, *The Jazz Image*. In discussing the connection between Roland Barthes' work on mythology and her own ideas about jazz, she writes, "the myth presents the musician as an individual, one capable of genius, and presents the musician as hero" (61). Thinking about Holiday, in particular, one cannot help noticing the sheer number of photographs that feature her alone, or at the center of the frame, relegating her fellow musicians to a supporting role. In this way, she becomes the "genius" Pinson refers to, someone who transcends the contributions of her sidemen, not someone who works together with them, as is required to make truly great music. No matter the emphasis placed on individual soloing and improvising, making a lasting jazz album necessitates a close, some might say nearly telepathic, connection among the musicians. Pinson quotes Ronald Radano: "*Jazz* is first and foremost a story of heroes" (61, emphasis in the original). The work of photographers like Leonard, Gottlieb, and Claxton helps to reinforce this, as do many of the photographs of Holiday in performance, which position Holiday as the lone hero, in Radano's parlance. This is a common strategy when depicting singers but seems particularly striking when juxtaposed against Holiday's output, which often features her instrumental counterparts almost as much as Lady Day.

Photographer Lee Tanner emphasizes the link between jazz and photography in his preface to *The Jazz Image* with a quotation from *New York Times* writer Barry Singer: "[n]o music has been more adored by the camera. Something about the faces in jazz, and the ephemeral improvised moment, have infatuated photographers ... inspiring viewfinder variations as eloquent as the most transcendent jazz solos" (13, ellipsis in the original). While Singer may overstate the case for jazz photography, the reference to "transcendent jazz solos" connects the improvisatory aspects of jazz and photography in a way that hearkens back to the theories of Roland Barthes, one of the leading theorists on photography. One need only think of the way the television camera, in a different medium admittedly, lingered on the interplay between Holiday's reactions and Lester Young's soloing on the 1957's *The Sound of Jazz* performance of "Fine and Mellow." Even Ken Burns, noted documentarian and creator of PBS' ten-part series *Jazz*, highlighted this as one of the seminal moments of the time.

I would now like to turn to some of Barthes' theories, as expressed in his seminal work *Camera Lucida*, that will help elucidate what attracts us to photographs of Holiday. In discussing what separates indifferent reactions to photographs from ones that grab the viewer's attention, Barthes writes, "suddenly a specific photograph reaches me; it animates me, and I animate it. So that is how I must name the attraction which makes it exist: an *animation*. The photograph itself is in no way animated (I do not believe in 'lifelike' photographs), but it animates me: this is what creates every adventure" (20, emphasis in the original). Here, Barthes refers to the stimulation one feels when looking at an interesting, arresting, or—though he might quarrel with such a term—revealing image. When looking at such photographs, the viewer places himself in the picture, or makes an associative leap from this photograph to something in his own life; this is the photograph's *studium*, the "application to a thing, taste for something, a kind of general, enthusiastic commitment, of course, but without special acuity" (26). Many photographs elicit such "general, enthusiastic commitment" due to their overall composition and subject matter. This does not mean that they hold a special, or unique, place in the viewer's memory, as they are "without special acuity" or the type of fascination Sontag referred to in *On Photography*. Transcending the *studium*, however, is the "element which rises from the scene, shoots out of it like an arrow, and pierces me" (26). This is the *punctum*, the "accident which pricks me (but also bruises me, is poignant to me)" (27). Only those photographs that hold that special attraction for the viewer can be said to contain a *punctum*. As such, "[t]he *studium* is of the order of liking, not of loving; it mobilizes a half desire, a demi-volition; it is the same sort of vague, slippery, irresponsible interest one takes in the people, the entertainments, the books, the clothes one finds 'all right'" (27). In other words, a photograph that contains only a *studium* may lead a viewer to give it a second glance, but only those with *punctum* will "animate" viewers to remember them long after one has turned away from the image. My aim, later in this essay, is to focus on those Holiday photographs that contain such a *punctum*, those rare photographs that have risen above the "all right" and become part of the lore surrounding her.

One cannot talk about photographs as though they are created in a void, without reference to the photographers who capture the images. As Barthes writes, "the great portrait photographers are great mythologists" (34), just as Cawthra and Pinson assert, decades later, in their respective work on jazz photography in particular. According to this idea, photographers like Herman Leonard and William Gottlieb elicit a *punctum* through a "'second sight' [that] does not consist in 'seeing' but in being there" (47). In this way, even the greats are at the mercy of the happy accident, one that "does not necessarily attest to the photographer's art; it says only that the photographer was there, or else, still more simply, that he could not *not* photograph the partial object [the detail that becomes the *punctum*] at the same time as the total object" (47). Barthes means that photographers cannot plan for the presence of a *punctum*; instead, they are at the mercy of what they see in the viewfinder, which ends up being what they reproduce for the viewer in their photography. For me, the "partial object" or *punctum* is evident in Holiday's relaxed-seeming crossed hands in Charles Peterson's photograph from the "Strange Fruit" recording session but is not evident in Charles Willoughby's 1951 Tiffany Club photograph. In that photograph, I see the Holiday who is so often the inscrutable subject in other photographs, *pace* Szwed, but the image is merely "all right," as it adds nothing new to my understanding of its subject. I will come back to this distinction between *studium* and *punctum*, and to other of Barthes' ideas, when I turn to specific Holiday photographs, in detail. First, however, I want to consider Berger's thoughts on photography as they relate to my focus on Holiday.

Like Barthes' *punctum*, Berger finds that "[a] photograph is effective when the chosen moment which it records contains a *quantum of truth* which is generally applicable, which is as revealing about what is absent from the photograph as about what is present in it. [...] It may be found in an expression, an action, a juxtaposition, a visual ambiguity, a configuration" (*Understanding a Photograph* 26, emphasis added). This "quantum of truth" is similar to Barthes' *punctum* in the sense that it is what separates great photos from those that are "all right." Of course, it is up to individual viewers to discern this truth. Therefore, Berger considers photography to be "the process of rendering observation self-conscious," because the effectiveness of a photograph can never be "independent of the spectator" (25, 26). Both the photographer and viewer are involved in this "process" as the photographer has "*decided that seeing this is worth recording*" (25, emphasis in the original) while the spectator must learn "to read photographs as one learns to read footprints or cardiograms" (26). In giving the photographer greater volition in choosing what to photograph, Berger departs from Barthes. He believes that the photographer sets the "quantum of truth" before the spectator, but that it is up to the spectator to see it. The degrees to which various spectators learn to see explains the differing reactions people have to the same photograph. According to Berger, "[f]or the man with a Polyfoto of his girl in his pocket, the quantum of truth in an 'impersonal' photograph must still depend on the general categories already in the spectator's mind" (26). These "general categories" of what makes for great art allow some photographs to achieve this "quantum of truth," but they are not universal. They are better understood through repeat viewing, when one pays close attention to more and more photographs. While this does not demand the academic study of photography, it does depend on the presence of an active observer who is self-conscious in scrutinizing her reaction to a photograph.

According to Berger, the challenge of learning to read photographs lies in the fact that "because the photographs carry no certain meaning in themselves [...] they lend themselves to any use" (49). A photograph that one viewer finds moving may end up, under different circumstances, seeming kitschy or overly-sentimental when appended to an inspirational or motivational poster. Part of the reason for this is that "[a]ll photographs have been taken out of a continuity. If the event is a public event, this continuity is history; if it is personal, the continuity, which has been broken, is a life story. [...] Discontinuity always produces ambiguity" (58). This is doubly true for photographs of a public personage, like Holiday, whose images are quite often public events, for jazz enthusiasts, as well as personal events for the singer and her fellow musicians. While one may pay special attention to Peterson's photograph, mentioned earlier, because it documents the recording of the now-iconic "Strange Fruit," viewers can only assume that that recording session carried weight for Holiday's own life story as well. In *Lady Sings the Blues*, her autobiography, Holiday equates singing "Strange Fruit" with her father's death, in Dallas, Texas, where he was refused treatment in several hospitals due to racial prejudice (95, 77). Significantly, Dantzic's thorough documentation of Holiday over the course of several months, as depicted in *Billie Holiday at Sugar Hill*, which I will consider later, may provide the missing link, the "continuity of history." Rather than merely capturing Holiday during one public or personal event, Dantzic sought to capture Holiday in all aspects of life, thereby providing viewers greater access to the singer than we have ever had.

Turning to Holiday's photographic record, I'd like to focus on four key images: Peterson's 1939 photograph of Holiday recording "Strange Fruit"; Gjon Mili's shot of Holiday with drummer Cozy Cole at a jam session in Mili's New York studio, from 1943; and the aforementioned Gottlieb and Leonard photographs, from 1948 and 1949, respectively. Significant both for their artistry and their influence on the Holiday mythos, these images span the ten-year period when she rose to prominence and were all taken while she was performing. I offer these four images of Holiday as ones that support the Holiday legend—in keeping with so many of the above critics' references to photography and mythology—rather than coalescing into a definitive portrait of the singer. Later, when I discuss Jerry Dantzic's *Billie Holiday at Sugar Hill*, I will concentrate on candid, private shots of the singer, as well.

For starters, the first photograph, taken by Charles Peterson, blends the public and private as it was taken during a recording session, a typically musician-only event that the public is invited into thanks to Peterson's photography. As readers learn from Cawthra's *Blue Notes in Black and White*, Peterson came from a musically-inclined, vaudevillian background which made him particularly well-suited to capturing musicians in performance.

Thanks to the tutelage of Edward Steichen and Clarence White, he transitioned to photography in the mid–1930s, photographing jazz musicians for publications such as *Saturday Evening Post, Town and Country,* and, most significantly, *Life* (Cawthra 34–35). Peterson's most notable photograph from the Commodore Records "Strange Fruit" recording session captures Holiday in mid-song, eyes closed, head tilted back and to the right in a way that highlights her face and neck perfectly thanks to Peterson's lighting. She is backed by four musicians—two saxophonists, a trumpeter, and a bass player—with the upper register of a piano visible to the extreme left of the image, balancing the microphone and stand at the opposite side of the photograph. Even with all of this to take in, Holiday is the main attraction. The viewer's eye is drawn to her face, flower-print dress, and favored fur coat, an interesting juxtaposition, to use Berger's term, with the lyrics of "Strange Fruit," which memorialize African Americans lynched by hanging throughout the Jim Crow era. Capturing the recording of this iconic song is clearly the "public event," but for this viewer, the photograph transcends this event in its artfulness.

Knowing the context surrounding the image is helpful, but Holiday could have been recording a commercial jingle and the image would still linger in the mind, whether due to the intensity of all five people in the picture or the photograph's *punctum,* the special quality that allows one photograph to rise above the mundane and become truly memorable, which I find in Holiday's crossed hands, just below waist-level. Two rings and a bracelet are visible in the photograph, and, thanks to the angle of the light, her left thumb casts a shadow over her right wrist. There is an innocence to this pose that that belies the typically-scandalous aspect of Holiday's reputation, visual or otherwise. Perhaps we are seeing the singer in her preferred environment, the place where she can relax and be at peace. Perhaps, knowing the context, she has lost herself in the lyrics to this powerful ballad and considered her own experiences with racism. Like all photographs, the meaning of this image is ambiguous, as Berger writes, but I believe it is impossible to look at this photograph and think it is merely "all right." In short, its artfulness makes it linger in the mind, just as its context marks it as a significant event in Holiday's career, as "Strange Fruit" would become one of her seminal recordings.

This recording is not without controversy, however. According to Farah Jasmine Griffin, author of *In Search of Billie Holiday: If You Can't Be Free, Be a Mystery,* "critics and biographers, especially white men, have claimed that she was too stupid to know what she was singing when she first performed and recorded the song" (130). In recent decades, writers and musicians such as Griffin, Angela Davis, Ntozake Shange, Cassandra Wilson, and Abbey Lincoln have sought to reclaim Holiday by "restor[ing] her to her complexity, her gifts and her courage in the face of powerful claims to the contrary" (131). The image captured by Peterson may not clarify how we should view Holiday's feelings about "Strange Fruit," but it is significant both as a documentation of this key moment as well as for its ambiguity, which matches writers' initial fraught reaction to Holiday's involvement in the song and its recording. As we have come to understand Holiday's (as stated by Griffins) "complexity, her gifts and her courage" (131), the photograph takes on new meaning. It is no longer merely a shot of a singer performing in a studio; as we understand more about Holiday's views on race, we can view it as a strong statement for equality and a condemnation of brutality.

By the time of Gjon Mili's organized jam session/photo shoot in 1943, Holiday had recorded both "Strange Fruit" and "God Bless the Child"; the two songs she is most associated with, and she would soon sign with Decca, for whom she would record one of her biggest hits, "Lover Man," the following year. Writing about the background of Mili's jam session photographs, which captured Duke Ellington, Holiday, and Mary Lou Williams, to name just three, Cawthra states, "Mili's loft studio turned into the site of one of jazz's most famous jam sessions. When the images appeared in *Life* in October 1943, the country got a dramatic new look at some of the most significant African American musicians in jazz photographed in a flattering style" (47). Like many jam sessions, this one went on almost until the sun came up, and the music "emerge[d] as something fresh and unforgettable" (48). Significantly, this jam session was interracial at a time when black and white musicians rarely shared the bandstand, and it is worth nothing that the audience, as well, was interracial (Tanner 49). Mili often shot from above, standing on a ladder, creating "a balcony-like effect. The viewer sees all, is in some cases encircled by the musicians, but always maintains a distance through Mili's elevation of the vantage point" (49). While the noted shot of Holiday was not taken from the extreme height of some of the others, which are all but bird's-eye-view images, the angle makes it possible to see Holiday more clearly than one would from the audience Mili has assembled, seated on folding chairs in the foreground.

Unlike Peterson's earlier photograph, Mili's depicts the singer as "just one of the band": "this striking photo of her singing *among the musicians instead of in front of them* would have made her a memorable figure" (Szwed 73, emphasis added). Though her back is to most of the musicians, Holiday seems to be singing as much to drummer Cozy Cole, at the extreme right of the photograph, as to the audience, which is visible only from behind. The angle of the photograph makes it seem as though the photographer was a member of that audience, one who, in his ardor at what he's been hearing, jumps to his feet and captures the group in the middle of their performance. With her hair wrapped in a scarf and her body in a dark-colored dress, Holiday finds herself in the middle of a crowd of musicians and on-lookers. Arms bent and hands jutting forward, she is all action in this shot, as opposed to the peaceful, reserved quality of Peterson's image. Once again, the light catches her face, highlighting her painted lips and bright teeth—with her mouth curved into what is almost a grimace—but it also illuminates the other musicians, most notably the African American guitarist positioned directly behind her, and Cole's drums, close enough to Holiday that she could almost reach out and chime a cymbal.

The image may seem cluttered, but thanks to the lighting and the raised vantage point of the camera, most of the members of the band, and several of the onlookers, remain distinct individuals. Capturing the wide-eyed, side-long look of the trombonist and the rearing back of the slick-haired clarinetist provides additional focal points, thereby emphasizing the fact that Holiday is one of the group, not the stand-out performer one most often thinks of singers as being. Even the audience members are not uniformly focused on her, with some turned towards Cole and others, in the second row, seeming to look over Holiday's shoulder at the musicians in the background. While this photograph may "have made her a memorable figure," as Szwed asserted, it is because of her connection to her fellow musicians, whom Mili presents as far more than the sidemen they appear to be in Peterson's photograph. In short, this photograph highlights Holiday's musicianship, her ability to fit in rather than stand out from the rest of the band, in keeping with her increased stature over time. Mili's photograph announces that Holiday is not "just" a singer; she is an equal participant in the music being created, "on the fly," by the likes of Ellington and Williams. In this way, she transcends the mythos of the lone singer, so prevalent in photographs of her and other vocalists, and is seen as a true musician, one of the qualities that has allowed her music to endure over time.

Gottlieb's close-up of Holiday in mid-song, circa 1948, is undoubtedly the first image that comes to mind for many Holiday enthusiasts. Here, we get Holiday the chanteuse, independent of any history or context. It takes added information from the photographer to fill in such context. According to Szwed,

> [i]f Billie Holiday is thought of as a tragic figure who nevertheless created beauty out of pain, Gottlieb's most reproduced photograph seems to confirm this. "Her voice was filled with anguish," Gottlieb said of the image. "I also tried to catch the beauty of her face. She was at her most beautiful at that particular point in time. [In prison] she couldn't get any drugs or alcohol. Her voice was at its peak. I caught this close-up of her in a way that you really could see the anguish that must have been coming out of her throat" [89].

Interestingly, for as iconic as the image has become, it was not published until 31 years later, in Gottlieb's *The Golden Age of Jazz*. Perhaps Holiday, who had already been to prison and lost her cabaret card, which all but banned her from appearing in New York clubs, was "too hot to handle" for most publications, though she did appear in a remarkable performance at Carnegie Hall that same year. Nevertheless, seeing this photograph outside of this historical context, one is confronted simply by the sheer effort it takes to sing at the level of Billie Holiday.

Once again, we see Holiday with her head back and mouth open, displaying those same painted lips and white teeth that were so prominent in Mili's photograph. Here, the focal point is so close that one can see the texture of her lips, skin, and make-up, and almost feel the weight of the sparkling earring caught in the spotlight. Eyes closed, right eyebrow plucked and slightly arched, Holiday seems to be singing with abandon. Her throat stands out, as is fitting for a singer, and the contours of her neck are so prominent that it makes me want to touch my own for comparison's sake. This is the epitome of Barthes' "punctum," as Gottlieb captures Holiday at the perfect moment, in the type of "happy accident" that cannot be planned for during a live performance. The viewer can see what looks like a curtain behind Holiday, but beyond that, the setting is a mystery. Holiday could be fronting a trio or an orchestra, performing in a smoky club or a concert hall. If we see Holiday the "tragic figure" in this photograph, as Szwed and Gottlieb assert, it is because we imbue the image with all that we know about the Holiday mythos. One could imagine a similar photograph of Ella Fitzgerald or Sarah Vaughan eliciting a very different reaction. Left with what we have, however, most viewers make the shift from singer-in-action to tragic figure as effortlessly as Holiday looked in Peterson's photograph, nine years earlier. The photograph itself does not tip its hand, though; it could just as easily open itself to the "multiple meanings" Sontag refers to in *On Photography*. As such, all we can say for certain is that looking at this image "is to encounter a potential object of fascination" (23). Except that our fascination with Holiday's voice and mythology can lead many viewers to read the "tragic figure" into Gottlieb's image of her.

What Pinson writes about Herman Leonard's style when depicting vocalists could be said about any of the photographs of Holiday I have discussed so far: "[t]he vocalist is exposed and vulnerable to all of the gazing eyes in an audience or viewers of a photograph" (82). Perhaps this is the creeping-in of the Holiday mythos, once again, but the interesting thing about images of her is that she never seems phased by these "gazing eyes." Confined in the recording studio, in Peterson's photograph, Holiday seems relaxed. At Mili's jam session, she fits in with everyone else, using her body to clear space for herself among the men. In Gottlieb's close-up, she sings with seeming abandon, closed eyes shutting out the world around her. Finally, in Herman Leonard's famous 1949 photograph, we see Holiday before the microphone with an almost wry smile on her face. Leonard, one of the deans of jazz photography, was a World War II medic who had studied photography from the age of 12 (Pinson 3–4). He balanced a burgeoning studio-photography career with "paying his way into jazz clubs at night by providing images of the performers to club owners, musicians, and occasionally magazines" (Cawthra 104). Over the course of his career, particularly between 1945 and 1959— when "[h]is photographs of not-yet-famous jazz musicians [...] provide a link to the United States at that time and its cultural and social values"— Leonard created photographs that "are so refined in appearance that many have become 'classics,' representing the standard of jazz photography" (Pinson 8, 7). Pinson, the author of an entire book on Leonard's work, considers the 1949 Billie Holiday photograph to be among "a core group of photographs that are the staple of [Leonard's] collection" (119).

This photograph captures Leonard's style to perfection. Pinson writes that Leonard's "photos best capture the myth of jazz, the image and the face of jazz musicians as nostalgic homage" (62). In order to create this "nostalgic homage," Leonard got to know the musicians as well as he could: "I want to record as closely as I can with as much understanding of that individual's personality as I can, the quality of that person, the essence of that person" (qtd. in Cawthra 119). What a challenge, then, to photograph the jazz chameleon, Billie Holiday. He did so in typical Leonard style, using dramatic backlighting to focus the eye's attention on the subject, and also illuminating the smoky nature of the club, as he did most famously in his shot of Dexter Gordon at the Royal Roost from the previous year. In the photograph of Holiday, the light catches the smoke in the background, bringing even more attention to the subject of our fascination, Barthes' *studium*. Cawthra asserts, "Holiday is delivering a visual performance that, combined with Leonard's lighting technique and sense of timing, makes for an iconography that transcends whatever words she may be singing" (117–118). The same could be said of Gottlieb's photograph, stripped of the type of context that exists for Peterson's image of Holiday recording "Strange Fruit." But what, exactly, is it about this photograph that leads Cawthra and Pinson to celebrate it?

Of course, part of the appeal is the "nostalgic homage" that Pinson refers to. In addition, Leonard's photograph is intimate in a way that the previous ones were not, either due to the context—the recording studio in Peterson's, the presence of an audience and the distance between subject and viewer in Mili's, and, paradoxically, the extreme closeness of Gottlieb's—or to the very attributes that make this photographic unique. Like Mili, Leonard shoots Holiday as though the camera is merely the eye of a member of the audience, like a present-day, smart-phone-toting fan. Significantly, he has also found the "sweet spot" that puts viewers in the moment but is not either too close or too distant. Holiday truly fills our line of sight, with nothing but the edge of the piano and the slightest bit of curtain to frame the photograph and the ubiquitous smoke obscuring the back wall, with its angelic embellishment.

While Holiday seems to be singing to reach the back of the room, the viewer, up front, can feel the "'sculptural' dimensionality" Cawthra attributes to the photograph (117). Her proportions are slightly more round than in Gottlieb's image of the previous year, and her hands have returned to the forefront, as they did in both of the earliest photographs. Here, they are raised before her, similar to Mili's image; but in Leonard's it seems as though she's about to reach out for something, or someone. She seems to be shaping the words as they come out of her mouth, providing a physicality that mirrors the other-worldly quality of the smoke behind her. The V of her blouse—according to Cawthra, the "tailored, contemporary ensemble [that] is the analogue of the male beboppers' natty suits" (117)—allows space for the viewer to admire the workings of that famous throat, once again. It bulges above the ridge of the collarbones, showing the effort behind this effortless-looking singing, like the churning feet of a swan beneath the water's placid surface. Holiday is once again at ease, harkening back to Peterson's image, now a decade in the past. All of these parts, combined with the way the light brightens her white blouse, serve, broadly, as the photograph's transcendent *punctum*. For once, instead of fixating on a specific detail, the viewer wants to absorb *everything*, such is the extent of Leonard's accomplishment. Holiday's entire being has become the "object of fascination," in Sontag's words, her photographic image matching jazz fans' nearly-insatiable appetite for stories about the singer.

What are we left with taking all four of these images into account? The settings are relatively diverse, considering the unified element of capturing Holiday in performance. We see her in the recording studio, a photographer's studio-cum-performance-space, in what Cawthra refers to as a "fugitive image" (90), and in what seems to be a nightclub. We see her at ease, as "one of the gang," and as tragic chanteuse. Finally, we see her however we want to see her: the "race woman" of "Strange Fruit," the musician's musician of Mili's studio, as Gottlieb's tragic singer or Leonard's songstress in search of a connection with her audience. Ultimately, we see her the way we want to see her, reading into the photographs biographical backstory or historical and musical context. The "Mystery" of Farah Jasmine Griffin's book title remains. Can anything alter such a perception?

John Berger's point about "[a]ll photographs hav[ing] been taken out of a continuity" is worth returning to for a moment (*Understanding a Photograph* 58). So far, I've considered photographs that support Berger's point, but thanks to the archival work of Grayson Dantzic, Holiday aficionados have recently been rewarded with another, fuller portrait of the singer. Noted jazz writer and archivist Dan Morgenstern has described the photographs Grayson's father, Jerry Dantzic, took of Billie Holiday as "captur[ing] Holiday in a manner quite unlike any other photographer: intimate but never intrusive" (qtd. in Dantzic 135). This intimacy is what separates them even from

Leonard's excellent 1949 photograph. Grayson, explains in "Jerry Dantzic's Billie Holiday," his father "was hired as a freelance photographer [in April 1957] by Decca Records to shoot Billie Holiday during her Easter Week engagement at Sugar Hill in Newark, New Jersey" (135). The results of these shoots, plus additional photographs taken at William and Maely Dufty's Manhattan apartment and during the second New York Jazz Festival, on Randall's Island, are collected in the recently-released *Billie Holiday at Sugar Hill*. William Dufty is noted, in Holiday lore, as the co-writer of Holiday's autobiography, *Lady Sings the Blues*, and Maely was one of her closest friends. The trio were so close, in fact, that she was godmother to their son, Bevan (Dantzic 135). This bond, in addition to Dantzic's decision to shoot on-the-fly, with only available light, helps to explain the relaxed, casual air of the photographs. We may never know the "true" Billie Holiday, but the photographs taken by Dantzic are the closest we may come to compiling a comprehensive portrait of the singer; for, as John Berger argues in "Uses of Photography," "[t]he aim [of photography] must be to construct a context for a photograph, to construct it with words, *to construct it with other photographs*, to construct it by its place in an ongoing text of photographs and images" (*About Looking* 64, emphasis added). Where the huge quantity of photographs of Holiday taken over decades by numerous noted and obscure photographers provides a composite view of the singer, taken out of the continuum Berger notes, Dantzic's work gives us a clearer image of Holiday during a focused, four-month period, through which viewers are privileged to see her not just in performance but in casual, private moments as well.

In discussing what goes on when one poses for the camera, Barthes states, "I do not stop imitating myself, and because of this, each time I am (or let myself be) photographed, I invariably suffer from a sensation of inauthenticity, sometimes of imposture" (13). This may be true of studio portraits and the type of one-off photographs taken to mark significant occasions, but Dantzic's near-constant presence at the periphery of Holiday's life over the course of these months must surely have resulted in her letting down her guard at times. Like many public figures, Holiday knew how to manipulate the image she presented to the camera, but Dantzic's unobtrusiveness worked in his favor, especially in the shots taken at the Duftys' apartment. In those images, Dantzic catches Holiday in action: looking away from the camera, at Maely, while standing before the kitchen sink or cuddling and entertaining her godson. Even the behind-the-scenes shots at Sugar Hill capture aspects of her that will be unfamiliar to all but the most passionate aficionados. These images find her smoking, doing her hair and make-up, and even being zipped into her evening gown. The onstage shots present the more familiar Holidays: the chanteuse, the musician among her tribe, the applause-seeker. Taken together, these photographs, while not quite as impressive, artistically, as Gottlieb and Leonard's, provide viewers with as much access to the woman behind the myth as we are likely to get.

In arranging his father's photographs—which, as he explains in the afterword were not always shot sequentially, as his father tended to grab half-finished rolls of film at various moments and shoot through the rest of the exposures, regardless of where such pictures fell chronologically—Grayson Dantzic has created a compelling story of the four months his father spent following Holiday. He begins with her walking the streets of Sugar Hill and sitting in the Douglas Hotel, both with her husband and alone, before shifting to the club where she was appearing. In doing this, we see Holiday interacting with others—the owner/manager of Sugar Hill, her band, and even her pet Chihuahua—alone preparing to go on stage and from various angles and distances while in performance. The images from the second New York Jazz Festival follow a similar trajectory, and the two performances are separated by the photographs taken at the Duftys' apartment, where viewers are treated to a Holiday so relaxed that it challenges the tragic intensity that Gottlieb, and others, have associated with her. If anyone truly knew Holiday, it would seem to be William Dufty, her co-writer and close friend. The fact that he knew all of the scandalous stories—including the ones that did not end up in the book due to fear of legal action, as Szwed covers well in his book— and still chose to make her godmother to his son suggests that there is more to the Holiday story than the scandalous behavior often connected with her name. To see her cuddling and playing with her godson creates such cognitive dissonance that I returned to the captions accompanying the photographs, as though they would explain the circumstances surrounding such an unusual depiction of the singer. Nevertheless, the portrait we receive of Holiday from this painstakingly-assembled book is one that should deepen and broaden our appreciation for the woman behind the Lady Day mythos.

Considering the mutually-beneficial relationship between jazz and photography, Cawthra argues that "[w]hile jazz as a musical practice can exist without photography, and while photography certainly has not required a relationship with jazz to develop its own history, the two have interacted in powerful and not necessarily predictable ways" (10). This power is even more significant when considering a figure like Billie Holiday, a woman whose life was as mercurial and mythic as anyone in the history of the music. If it is true that seeing is believing, and that a picture is worth a thousand words, then the images of Lady Day discussed above, and the many that fall outside the parameters of this essay, are worth all of the scrutiny that we can give them. In "America, Seen Through Photographs, Darkly," from *On Photography*, Sontag asserts, "[t]o photograph is to confer importance" (28), which is certainly true in Billie Holiday's case. While Holiday's music will remain a supreme example of the art form forever, the images of her, and the millions of words spent analyzing her work and attempting to demythologize the woman behind the voice, will undoubtedly captivate all who fall under her spell.

NOTE

1. Claxton's book Young Chet covers Baker's rise in the years 1952–57, including photographs in the studio and on the bandstand. These photographs capture Baker dressed casually in a knit shirt and slacks, crooning into the microphone in the studio; shirtless, trumpet in hand, with his wife Halema; and blowing his horn in any number of settings. Decades later, photographers such as Claxton, Bruce Weber, and John Claridge would depict a far grimmer reality—Baker aged beyond his years, with deep lines etched into his face, a lost, faraway look in his eyes, and cheeks sunken-in from a beating that had left him without several teeth.

WORKS CITED

Barthes, Roland. *Camera Lucida*. Translated by Richard Howard. New York: Hill & Wang, 1981.
Berger, John. *About Looking*. New York: Vintage International, 1980.
Berger, John. *Understanding a Photograph*. Edited and introduced by Geoff Dyer. New York: Aperture, 2013.
Cawthra, Benjamin. *Blue Notes in Black and White: Photography and Jazz*. Chicago: University of Chicago Press, 2011.
Dantzic, Jerry. *Billie Holiday at Sugar Hill*. Reflection by Zadie Smith and afterword by Grayson Dantzic. London: Thames & Hudson, 2017.
Dyer, Geoff. Foreword. *Camera Lucida*, by Roland Barth, translated by Richard Howard. New York: Hill & Wang, 2010, pp. xi–xix.
Griffin, Farah Jasmine. *In Search of Billie Holiday: If You Can't Be Free, Be a Mystery*. New York: Ballantine, 2001.
Holiday, Billie, with William Dufty. *Lady Sings the Blues*. Introduction by David Ritz. New York: Harlem Moon, 2006.
Pinson, K. Heather. *The Jazz Image: Seeing Music Through Herman Leonard's Photography*. Jackson: University Press of Mississippi, 2010.
Sontag, Susan. *On Photography*. New York: Anchor Books, 1977.
Szwed, John. *Billie Holiday: The Musician and the Myth*. New York: Penguin, 2015.
Tanner, Lee. *The Jazz Image*. Introduction by Nat Hentoff. New York: Abrams, 2006.

Shouting Back

Cohering Lady Day Through
Kevin Young's Jazz Poem Anthology

Taylor Joy Mitchell

Since her death, Billie Holiday and her voice has continuously crept into American popular culture. On the music streaming services Pandora and Spotify, Holiday maintains 2.2 million listeners with 156 albums and 1,237,978 monthly listeners. Her voice lingers on in backdrop soundtracks to Netflix's *Stranger Things* and video games—mostly apocalyptic games like *Fallout* and the first-person shooter game *Bioshock*. She also often serves as a cultural marker of the hip, those-in-the-know, as in 1995's *Clueless*, when the well-dressed, retroist homosexual Christian asks Cher, the popular blonde, if she likes Holiday as they settle into his vintage 1954 Nash Metropolitan; Cher answers with "I love him." Holiday is even used to honor a vigilante's triumphant return to saving innocent lives in Alan Moore's 1986 graphic novel *Watchmen*: the Nite Owl, whose masculinity is in question, blasts her version of "You're My Thrill" on his crowded Owlship. Each allusion serves a different purpose and offers up a different image of Holiday, images that can act as a foil to the singular tragic image of the downfall that posthumously haunts Holiday.

Besides these popular culture homages to Holiday, many poets have scripted verse in honor of Holiday; most reproduced is Frank O'Hara's "The Day Lady Died," but in the 59 years since Holiday's death, more than enough poems have been written that poet Kevin Young has gathered some of them into a section in his collection *Jazz Poems* by Everyman Press. Each poet celebrates different aspects of Holiday's life and career and, as a unit, they recreate that very sacred space of performance as a fusion of language and musicality, illustrating the impermanence of jazz through a static form.

Depending on the poem, Holiday's image mutates, creating a kaleidoscope of Holidays to fulfill the unique needs of the lamenting poet. Decades after her death, these and other poets are still pinning for Holiday, her voice, her presence. When analyzed as a whole, the 13 poems that make up "Muting (for Billie Holiday)" act as a traditional jazz elegy—an instrumental tribute written for inspirational musicians. In their mourning for Holiday, the poets in Young's 2006 anthology fulfill the basic poetic goal of the elegy, with an added call-and-response strategy that invokes blues history. Young's organization forces readers to consider the way the poems speak to each other, and, in turn, provide a fuller image of Holiday.

Elegies in Jazz Form

Usually written in praise of someone who recently passed, eulogies and elegies are a steadfast part of remembering the dead. Online advice from WikiHow on "How to Write a Eulogy" tells authors to take all the time they need when crafting this formal memorial. The irony of this advice is that time is an insult when speaking of death, as the finite notions of time and the brevity of life appear even more oppressive when the funeral program must be printed. Unlike the eulogy, elegies are tributes to the dead usually composed in song or poem, rather than formal prose. When broken down to basic elements, a traditional elegy includes the three stages of loss: lament, grief and sorrow, and then "praise and admiration of the idealized dead, and finally consolation and solace" ("Elegy"). Modern and contemporary poetic elegies have shifted from the personal to communal in order to express "a broad feeling of loss and metaphysical sadness" ("Elegy"). Like Robinson Jeffers' "Pearl Harbor" or Peter Balakian's "A-Train/Ziggurat/Elegy" for 9/11 victims, these elegies express grief of widespread cruelties or acts of inhumanity.

When the elements of poetic elegies are applied to music, specifically jazz, a whole new genre emerges, one with roots in the music city of New Orleans. Jazz elegies sprang from jazz funerals, which musicologist David Brent Johnson situates in the early 1900s, thanks to the confluence of strong European and African American cultural influences. In the beginning, performers preferred the term *funeral with music*, as jazz was just a part of the funeral (Sakakeeny). Later, jazz funerals began to mimic the elements of poetic elegies, with personal and communal grieving occurring in stages. Regardless of who is being honored or what brass is braying, jazz funerals begin with a lament—the band plays dirges or somber religious hymns—and end with consolation, celebrating the dead with musicians playing up-tempo songs and second liners dancing (Sakakeeny). This cathartic dancing acts as a salve for the sorrow.

Post–1945, the music moved out of funeral parlors and into recording studios (Johnson). Modern jazz elegies now involve jazz artists composing and recording tributes shortly after the death of inspirational musicians (Johnson). Johnson points to Lennie Tristano's "Requiem," a blues written for Charlie Parker in 1955, as a classic example of a modern jazz elegy and claims that dozens have been recorded since. During the 1970s—when the music industry stopped promoting jazz—an explosion of jazz elegies were written in homage to the innovators who had died and the music that ceased (Feinstein 146). Poet and essayist Sasha Feinstein claims that five artists "dominate" the poetic jazz elegy, with Holiday topping the list (144). Feinstein suggests that coupled with artistic talent, her drug addictions and early, tragic death inspired poets to give her back some of the acclaim she should have garnered while alive (144). Quite possibly, the fact that she did not get to live out her career, leaving behind only abstractions about what could have been, inspired poets to create exacting and precise images. As a genre, then, these jazz elegies, according to Chantal McStay, "attempt something next to impossible: to commemorate and preserve music that's defined by its immediacy and transience." This attempt can be performed at funerals, recorded in studios, or, as Young's collection proves, captured in poetic line breaks.

Young's Elegy for Holiday

Young's collection includes all of the basic elegiac elements and, through its specific organization, reflects back many different kinds of Holidays. While each poet personally commensurate Holiday's loss, as a series, the poems showcase the communal grieving for Holiday that our culture cycles through. Unlike the innumerable popular images of her, which presents "contradictory, incomplete, or questionable" stories "based on ... her miserable childhood in and out of institutions, her arrests for prostitution and drug use, her abusive relationships, her rapid physical deterioration, and her early death," this collection tries to fill in the gaps and highlight the contradictions (Szwed). This is emphasized by the poem Young uses as an epigraph to the section: Hayden Carruth's "Billie Holiday." Possibly his first jazz poem and least optimistic of the rest of his jazz poems, Carruth's "Billie Holiday" recreates Holiday's contradictory nature: her downfall is due to her competing emotions of pain, pride, and compassion. Carruth has Holiday call and respond to versions of herself; in her nightly songs she questions whether "you" can "conceive" her song, but rather than wait for a response from the audience, Carruth imagines Holiday proclaiming her own lyric "Don't explain" (219). And the poems following this epigraph do not try to explain; rather, structurally speaking, they trace the arcs and themes of Holiday's life, simultaneously repeating and reflecting on specific aspects of Holiday's life in order to leave readers with a new image. The collection reifies William Spiegelman's description of the poet in *How Poets See the World: The Art of Description in Contemporary Poetry*: "the poet uses his tropes, a simile within a metaphor, to compare a thing to itself as well as to something else[.] ... [T]he poem is an act of repetition as well as of reflection. It makes its own images out of [the] original one, sloughing a skin like a snake, getting farther away from an original (and becoming an image of an image of an image) while simultaneously revealing the new skin underneath" (135). For instance, the collection of 13 poems begins with her voice—what is most often praised and appropriated about her as a performer. The collection then moves onto poems that grapple with race and love, two arenas in which the outspoken Holiday struggled, before concluding with poems about her death and legacy.

As a collection, these poems reveal different Holidays depending on the gender, race, and ethnicity of the poets. Seven are males, four are white, and two are Asian. Some poets are young and others are old enough to have seen Holiday perform live. Some like Tony Hoagland's "Poem in Which I Make the Mistake of Comparing Billie Holiday to a Cosmic Washerwoman" have been criticized for its "mechanisms of diversion" when discussing race relations (Broek 11), and others, like O'Hara's "The Day Lady Died" and Rita Dove's "Canary" have garnered critical acclaim since publication. Once removed from their original context and placed in this order, these poems begin to operate in sequence to each other; they speak to each other in sometimes specific, others times subtle ways. When reading Young's Holiday section, "uncanny links" between the poems emerge, connections that would not occur if poems were organized by poet or chronologically (McHugh xviii). As editor of 2007 *Best American Poetry*, Heather McHugh speaks to these connections as "consequential," resulting in a sequence that "can have its way" with editors and readers alike (xviii). Because of Young's deliberate organization, these elegiac Holiday poems necessarily call and respond to each other.

Jazz and Poetry

Using poetic jazz elegies to commemorate Holiday merges two distinct genres that complement each other well: jazz and poetry. First recited to music strummed on lyre, poetry's natural complement was song. It was not until much later that poems were relegated to print. In the aftermath of WWI's social upheaval, poetry operated more like jazz and experienced new forms, relished in improvisation, and "shared [with jazz] the jagged forms of rhythmic syncopation" (Feinstein 16). Defining jazz poetry, as evidenced by Feinstein's

Jazz Poetry From the 1920s to the Present, is complicated, and "writing about jazz poetry is, as they say, like dancing about architecture" ("A Brief"). The most basic definition states that a jazz poem "must be informed by jazz music" (Feinstein 2). This could include a poem written about the essence of jazz, a lyric narrative about a jazz musician, or a poem that appropriates jazz rhythms. Jazz poems have been written since the 1920s and incorporate a variety of topics and styles from formalists' sonnets to the Beats' spontaneous prose. From the 1950s, poets recited works backed by jazz musicians; these performances showcase the collaboration of jazz and poetry, what Amiri Baraka refers to as "speech musical" because the "music and words extend each other" (246). The recordings of the 1970s and 80s, often rooted in black culture, included "strong imagistic sense" with scatting and jazz rhythms (Wallenstein 612). By the 1990s, enthusiasts collected jazz poems into print anthologies. Sascha Feinstein and Yusef Komunyakaa published 132 poets in their 1991 *The Jazz Poetry Anthology* and diversified their selections in *The Second Set: Jazz Poetry Anthology, Vol. 2.* In 1993, Art Lange and Nathaniel Mackey edited *A Moment's Notice: Jazz in Poetry and Prose.* The most recent collection is Komunyakaa's and Sandy Evans' 2013 *Testimony, A Tribute to Charlie Parker: With New and Selected Jazz Poems.* Beyond proving that the "jazz aesthetic has been a compelling literary force," these anthologies, stated in the preface to the *Second Set,* "inspire engaging discussions on the nature of jazz poetry" (Young; Feinstein and Komunyakaa xii).

One discussion these anthologies provoke is why Young's anthology is structured so differently from the others. For example, both *Jazz Poetry* and the *The Second Set* are organized in alphabetical order by poet. *A Moment's Notice* is also organized by author, but organizes those writers chronologically. In *Jazz Poems,* Young bucks all of the traditional structures. According to his foreword, he organizes his anthology around "a rough history of jazz," with the first section devoted to early jazz poems and the second to how jazz moved north and east from its New Orleans origins (13). Young creates a section for "Horn," "Rhythm," and "Free Jazz," as well as three sections for the commanding figures of jazz: "Bop (Bird and Beyond)," "Sheets of Sounds (Coltrane and Co.), and "Muting (for Billie Holiday)." Unlike "Bop" and "Sheets," which include poems that are not specifically devoted to Parker or Coltrane, every poem in "Muting" is directly related to Holiday. Devoting an entire section to Holiday, and concluding with this section, places emphasis on Holiday in Young's "rough history." One reason to end the anthology with her could be that, since her death, Holiday has "been the subject of more jazz-related poems than any other singer" (Feinstein 49). Another could be, as Feinstein suggests, to offer a posthumous, fitting tribute to Holiday. Regardless of why, ending *Jazz Poetry* with Holiday reinforces her place in jazz history: as readers close the text, the residual image of Holiday looms and lingers.

Young uses five eulogize Holiday's voice: Hughes' "Song for Billie Holiday," Lewis Allan's "Strange Fruit," Holiday's and Arthur Herzog's "God Bless the Child," his own work "Stardust," and C.D. Wright's "The Secret Life of Musical Instruments." Even though these poems speak to multiple of aspects of Holiday's life, her voice serves as the touchstone. Beginning with Hughes' poem, Young consciously gives a song back to Holiday through Hughes. Hughes "blazed the trail for jazz poets," as he was "arguably the first to fully embody a jazz aesthetic, going beyond either the label or trend of jazz to have it affect his poetic language" (Wallenstein 603; Young 12). Thus, in this collection's context, he sets the stage for the following poets—particularly those who will later try to capture Holiday's ability to sing so sweetly about sorrow. Hughes claims that jazz was "the inherent expression of Negro life in America; the eternal tom-tom beating in the Negro soul ... the tom-tom of joy and laughter, and pain swallowed with a smile" (qtd. in Young 17). Ample in allusion, Hughes' jazz poems are often "understated and references to the source of his narrator's pain are oblique, as if the cool detached tone could perhaps influence a change in fortune" (Wallestein 603). "Song for Billie Holiday" is no different. Most likely the only poem written for Holiday while she was still alive, it opens and closes with questions that are not meant to be answered, questions about what could possibly "purge" the speaker's "heart" from sadness. In typical Hughes' fashion, the poem captures loss; this one does so by focusing on the connections between Holiday's voice and instrumentation. Even though Hughes is writing a song for Holiday, the sorrow in Holiday's voice comes through in lines that reference "chance winds" that are "dusted with despair." Hughes follows that despair in the third stanza with a somewhat hopeful concluding couplet, one that neatly balances contradictions. He refers to her voice as that of a "muted trumpet" and her instrumentation as "Cold brass in warm air." These contradictions "suggest the song can indeed cut through this haze of depression" (Feinstein 49). Hughes' poem, a direct response to Holiday's singing, ends on a single-word line: "Where?" Like in Hughes' famous "Dream Deferred," these rhetorical questions are meant to "provoke the auditor," not be answered (Wallenstein 604). However, because of Young's organization, the "Where?" in "Song for Billie Holiday" gets answered in a new, refreshing way: answers can be found in her voice, her songs.

In direct response to Hughes' question about where one could find the salve to sorrow, Young includes two poems that were made famous by Holiday's voice: "Strange Fruit" and "God Bless the Child." These are the only two poems in which Holiday's own voice can be "heard." Situating these two poems early in the anthology places prominence on Holiday's voice as a jazz musician. Being able to "hear" Holiday takes on extra significance in the predominantly masculine realms of jazz and poetry. While not written for her or by her, "Strange Fruit" has come to stand in for Holiday in many ways. Her guttural rendering of the lyrics haunts listeners and poignantly expresses the tragic weight of black history, a weight still burdening the current generation. Cafe Society's white owner Barney Josephson instructed Holiday to sing this song at the conclusion of each of the three nightly sets (Carvalho 112–113). To solidify the spectacle that would become Holiday's signature song, Josephson commanded Holiday to walk off the stage when the notes ceased and the shaft of light on her face dimmed (Carvalho 113). She was not to entertain an encore. Josephson said, "People had to remember 'Strange Fruit,' get their insides burned by it" (qtd. in Carvalho 113). In "Blood at the Root: "Strange Fruit" as Historical Document and Pedagogical Tool," Chris Stone claims that "Regardless of how rapturous the response, she granted no encores, no curtain calls." No call and response from her; just the opportunity to listen.

As if to comment on Holiday's refusal to grant her audience an encore to "Strange Fruit," Young posits "God Bless the Child" a collaboration between Holiday and Arthur Herzog, Jr., right after "Strange Fruit." He could have included any of the jazz poems that take on the politically-charged nature of "Strange Fruit," like Joy Harjo's or Cyrus Cassells' poems of the same title. Instead, Young followed Allan's poem with Holiday's, as if an effort to give back to Holiday. Unlike "Strange Fruit," written and commodified by a "coterie of white men" (Carvalho 114) who appropriated Holiday's black, female body to make the song famous, "God Bless the Child" was written by Holiday in collaboration with Herzog. Besides Herzog's unsubstantiated claims to writing the all of the lyrics, the lyrics to "God the Bless the Child" are mainly attributed to Holiday, and Young credits her as first author on the poem. Hence, Young's choice to include "God Bless the Child" after "Strange Fruit" eases a fraction of the abuse black women have suffered in the racist, sexist music industry. "God Bless the Child," according to Holiday's autobiography, stems from an argument with her mother over money: she credits her mother with the song's qualifying line at the end of the chorus. In printing the lyrics to "God Bless the Child," Young forces readers to remember what Holiday sounded like when she sang the song: a survivor who must bless herself amidst unavoidable inequalities.

After readers can "hear" Holiday's voice in this section, Young responds by continuing to amplify Holiday's voice with his own "Stardust." Originally published in Young's 2001 To Repel Ghosts, "Stardust" is an elegy of epic proportion—dually dedicated to painter Jean-Michel Basquiat and Holiday. "Stardust" was part and parcel of a larger poem, "Discography One," which is dedicated to five of Jean-Michel Basquiat's musical inspirations and subtitled "made from original masters": Louis Armstrong, Charlie Parker, Billie Holiday, Lester Young, and Max Roach. Like the dedications, "Stardust" re-appropriates one Basquiat work, transferring his "Discography One" paint-ing into a poem. To add another layer, Basquiat's "Discography One" was a reproduction of Charlie Parker's record jacket for *Now's the Time*. For jazz enthusiasts, the connection to Parker's *Now's the Time* gets stronger because Young consistently references Miles Davis and Parker's recording of "Billie's Bounce." The song was originally recorded by Davis and Parker on November 26, 1945, a date Young purposefully includes in the second to last stanza. One way to read these "Billie Bounce" references is that Young misremembers one Billie for another. In *Clawing the Limits of Cool: Miles Davis, John Coltrane, and the Greatest Jazz Collaboration Ever*, Farah Jasmine Griffin and Salim Washington suggest that the relaxed manner might be in honor of Billie Hol-iday's relaxed phrasing during her performances (62), but according to Brian Priestly in *Chasing the Bird: The Life and Legacy of Charlie Parker*, the title actually refers to Billie, the secretary of Dizzy Gillespie's agent (58). This wrongful association, this mislabel, echoes much of what happened to Hol-iday's image, and how her image gets repurposed by artists and capitalists alike—something Basquiat and Young both lament. Basquiat even expressed his desire to design a tombstone for Holiday, one that would properly honor her (Hoban). In Young's original lament to Holiday, his multilayered misla-beling of Holiday in "Stardust" mimics the trickster theme running through the five poems in "Discography One." For instance, Young depicts Armstrong as both king and devil, a signifying King Louie monkey; Young applies a sim-ilar trickster strategy in his section on Roach, when he opens the poem with a reference to Kafka's *The Metamorphosis* and accuses white rock 'n' roll artists of capitalizing on their borrowings from blues and jazz musicians without ever properly acknowledging the inspiration. Is Young messing with jazz enthusiasts who know that the song is not really about Holiday, or he is paying homage to the multiple, multifarious depictions of Holiday, ones she didn't have control over when she was alive?

Removed from its original context, "Stardust" in the "Muting" collection loses its dual dedication and becomes solely focused on Holiday. This poem returns Holiday to the spotlight, acting as an example of what the ambitious poet-editor is trying to accomplish with this collection. As editor, Young maintains the rights to insert his poem anywhere, and it's telling that he does so in the section on her voice, right after readers "hear" Holiday. The place-ment suggests an urgency, as if Young wants readers to read his poem while "God Bless the Child" lingers, as if his representation of Holiday equals or rivals the one she created on stage singing that song. This urgency is echoed in the third stanza, which consists wholly of the famous line from "God Bless the Child." Beyond the urgency, "Stardust's" references to "Billie's Bounce" now better refer to Holiday's own ups and down with life and the law. Like Hughes, Young shows Holiday's contradictions. For instance, Young compares the ways Holiday can be "all scat" one minute and later alone, "detoxed, thawed/in time" (225). Young's use of the jazz term for improvised singing here doesn't refer to Holiday's singing. Although she is known for taking many liberties with a song's melody, Holiday mainly avoided scatting. Thus, Young is more likely referring to her lifestyle, one of contradictions when at times she stands proud and others seems dependent on partners who turn out to be abusive. This contradiction is mimicked on Okeh's 1942 release of "God Bless the Child." On side A's "God Bless," Holiday strongly asserts economic theories. Then, on side B's rendition of Duke Ellington's "Solitude," Holiday's voice characteristically lingers behind the notes, and the lyrics have her sitting in despair, waiting and praying. This contrast reminds readers about Holiday's complexity, which seems to be the source of her magical, ethereal nature, and makes Young's "Stardust" title a fitting tribute.

After Young's "Stardust," readers are provided one last poem that focuses on Holiday's voice: C.D. Wright's "The Secret Life of Musical Instruments." Originally published in her 1983 *Translations of the Gospel: Back into Tongues,* Wright dedicated this Holiday elegy to Claudia Burson, a jazz pianist from Fayetteville, Arkansas. Since Wright's poetry often pays homage to the Ozarks in Arkansas, this poem maintains a sense of place while honoring the power of music to corral the "faithless" to a "reckoning" (227, 228). Wright's image of Holiday—the woman on the tour bus with the boys in the band—is akin to Young's: she's complicated but irresistible. While the boys dream, she smokes incessantly and yet "her hair never smells" (227). Other connections between Young's and Wright's poem images of Holiday stand out when they are juxtaposed in this collection, most notably off-hand references to licks and salt. A lick in jazz is a standard pattern of notes or phrasing, and salt, symbolic and scared as a mineral needed to sustain life, can also be seen as a standard. Together, though, the words are reminiscent of Biblical references to salt of the earth. In "Stardust," the words lick and salt appear right after Young's Holiday is "locked up": "licked—the salt/the boot—refused/a chance to belt//tunes in the clubs—" (225). The references to boots and belts, weapons of abuse, contrast with the image of Holiday refusing to sing, refusing to be licked, and instead licking the salt for sustenance. Wright's image of Holiday reinforces this sense of strength, as her Holiday "blows white petals off her lapel" and "tastes salt" (227). In Wright's version, tasting salt seems to lessen the bitterness of life, represented by the fallen petals. Tasting salt also reinforces Holiday's dedication to her craft, as this Holiday tastes salt under a "copacetic moon" and in company of "instruments do not sleep in their dark cribs" (227). Not only can the sentinel instruments be read as Holiday herself or her voice, copacetic points to Holiday's power as a performer to "keep cool" and communicate with "strangers" and the "young and crazy victims of love" (227). As Young ends this section on Holiday's voice and her strength, these five poems speak back to Carruth's epigraph, in which his Holiday posits the unanswered question "Do you conceive my song?" (219).

Moving from her song and her voice, the collection pivots to a focus on race with Terrance Hayes' "Lady Sings the Blues" and Hoagland's "Poem in Which I Make the Mistake of Comparing Billie Holiday to a Cosmic Washerwoman." Readers, however, are prepared for this transition, as both Young's and Wright's poem hint at the racism Holiday endured as an entertainer. For instance, in "Stardust," Young includes "three-/fifths" after detailing how Holiday was jailed for drug possession (244). This "three-/fifths, the law" reminds readers less of a drug amount and more of the 1787 Three-Fifths Compromise denigrating blacks as less human (224). And Wright's description of the moon over Holiday as copacetic should also remind readers of the ways blacks were denigrated. With possible origins dating to black slang from the late 19th century, copacetic was Bill "Bojangles" Robinson's catchphrase (McCabe). Bojangles' catchphrase and nickname reflect the sunny disposition he adorned as a black performer for mainly white audiences in the early 20th century (Jones). As a term, bojangles can have negative connotations since it refers to an on-command street entertainer who is otherwise lazy (Jardim). When both of these terms are situated within the entertainment industry— where racism still flourishes—things can hardly be considered copacetic. Copacetic, then, captures the tightrope task both Robinson and Holiday had to navigate as entertainers of white, black, and mixed audiences. Thus, Young's choice to include these two poems, after poems focused on Holiday's voice, should makes readers aware of how racism collided with the entertainment world. This collision is further exacerbated in Young's jazz poetry collection because while the world of jazz has long been known for its racial divisions— hot and cool jazz charts serve as just one example—the world of poetry has also often been criticized for housing mostly white people (Spahr and Young).

The collection's first foray into poems about race is Hayes' poem "Lady Sings the Blues," which details a family history, an intimate moment when a mother takes her son to see Diana Ross play Holiday on the big screen. Originally published in *Muscular Music* in 1999, "Lady Sings the Blues" opens with a focus on voice, repeating in the first and fourth stanzas how "if flowers could sing" they would sound like Holiday (229). This initial focus on the voice provides yet another transition between the first five poems and these two, especially because Hayes' speaker harkens back to the "legendary scene" of Holiday singing "Strange Fruit" with the single shaft of light on her face, as she "unpetals her song" (229). However, the speaker immediately recalls readers from too deep a reminiscence. The fifth stanza opens with "This should be Harlem, but it's not" (230). Naming Harlem jolts a comparison of Holiday in a nightclub in the 1930s with Ross on a Hollywood screen in the

1970s—an "imitation of the inimitable" (Graham). The stark comparison begs readers to reassess the popular film and Hollywood spin. Although Holiday's tragic encounters with racism were hinted, the film relegates racism to the south and drug addiction, mostly ignoring the repercussions of structural racism Holiday dealt with in the entertainment industry. Hayes' speaker suggests as much by stating Ross' eyes were "not quite sad enough" and commenting on how—because she is the star—her beauty persisted unnaturally through the scenes in which Holiday's hair would not have held. In the tenth stanza, the speaker's mother is the only "blue" one in the theater when the "houselights wake" (230). She grabs her son's hand and says, "Billie didn't sound like that" (230). Hayes ends his poem with a reference to a heart aching for a father in a "distant place" (230). Here readers get a glimpse of a black woman sharing her disappointment with her son, a black family sharing their disappointment in the white Hollywood reproduction and commodification of Holiday.

Young's inclusion of Hoagland's work, right after Terrance Hayes' poem "Lady Sings the Blues," exemplifies the call and response in blues music as well as Young's desire to keep Holiday's memory alive. Unlike Hayes' very personal and specific poem, Hoagland's poem deals with universal symbols of black life. But beyond the comparison of the individual to the universal, Young most likely included this poem here because Hoagland includes a character named Terrance in his poem; this Terrance reprimands Hoagland's speaker for making assumptions about music and culture that he does not understand. This Terrance reprimands Hoagland's speaker for assuming Holiday serves as a "symbol for the black soul" and reiterates that the "night is not African American either, for your information, it is just goddamn dark" (231). Presumably this persona is based on the black poet Hayes, since Hoagland has praised Hayes' work for "its bravery of feeling" and him as a poet who "likes to go to the difficult places of culture and self" (qtd. in Broek 11). The speaker's mention of "teenage genius" bursting on the literary scene with "his dictionary and hip-hop shovel" reinforces that this Terrance should stand in for the poet Hayes: Hayes published poetry collections *Muscular Music* and *Hip Logic,* in which he writes about the hip-hop scene, and he devised a poetic form known as the Golden Shovel. In Hayes' "Golden Shovel" poem, a homage to Gwendolyn Brooks, the last words of each line were borrowed from Brooks' "We Real Cool." This form not only memorializes the original poet, it offers a new reading of history, one that doesn't erase or simply build from, but rather inscribes the past into the present. This form makes a specific argument about the past and the present, how memory is often anchored to something specific that the present triggers.

In Hoagland's poem, the speaker makes his own argument about time, consolidating the past and future with lines like "But here in the past of that future/Billie Holiday is still singing" (232). This tactic of keeping Holiday in the present, pinning her down in print for the present, gets replicated throughout Young's collection. One way Hoagland keeps Holiday alive is by illuminating conversations on language and race. Beginning with a title that some may claim as an escapist clause (an acknowledgment of mistaking Holiday for a washerwoman), Hoagland's work illustrates cultural misunderstandings about race and drips of white privilege. For instance, when Hoagland directly references Hayes and indirectly references his poetic form, he does so with race and racism clearly in mind. After all, in his poem, the future literary genius, who isn't "any color we ever saw before" is "rewriting *Moby-Dick—The Story of the Great Black Whale*" (232). This characterization of Hayes can be classified into the categories Major Jackson refers to in his "A Mystifying Silence: Big and Black": white poets, like Hoagland, are "content to: populate their poems with people of color; exoticize and extol the virtues of ethnic life and so-called 'primitive' cultures; make passing presumptive and ostracizing remarks about nonwhites; or cunningly profit from the loaded meanings and connotative power black and other dark-skinned peoples have come to signify in white readers' imaginations" (22). Hoagland's poem, even with the apologetic title, capitalizes on the connotative power of Hayes' poetic ability, and, by connecting Holiday to darkness, stains, heaviness, and washing, Hoagland fails "to describe the full spectrum of people of color" (Jackson 22). Through the basic descriptions of a big, dark washerwoman, Hoagland lazily relies on the racist "structures of language and received thinking" (22). And when compared with Hayes' more specific descriptions of Holiday, Hoagland's poem reveals complicated feelings toward race and reinforces Young's call and response structure for these Holiday elegies.

A main aspect of call and response associated with blues music, particularly as it moved from field hollers to the church gospels, is the act of listening. Hoagland ends his poem with Terrance and the speaker sitting in the car by the "dashboard glow," and the speaker "imagine[s]" Terrance "pointing at the radio/as if to say, Shut up and listen" (233). Unlike Hayes' poem, Hoagland doesn't use quotations or italics to denote actual speech, so this kind of listening becomes a highwire act for the presumably white speaker and a potentially white audience, of Hoagland's poem and Young's collection. This kind of listening echoes another poet's concluding lines about Holiday: in "Dark Lady of the Sonnets," Amiri Baraka's ends with "Sometimes you are afraid to listen to this lady." This fear, according to Jasmine Griffith's analysis "Baraka's Billie Holiday as a Blues Poet of Black Longing," is for those "naive and unprepared" to hear a voice that "embodies a blues ethos of both tragedy and comedy" (316). As a "representative of the collective history of black people in the United States" Holiday's voice is where listeners can learn—if they actually listen—"what it means to be black in America" (316). Committed to racial equality and calling herself a "race woman," Holiday used her voice as a political platform to get her audience to listen to the ways racism could destroy (Hobson [1] 443). So when Terrance reprimands Hoagland's speaker into listening, it's ironic in light of the poet's title; maybe Hoagland's speaker should be afraid because, if he actually listened to Holiday, he would have to acknowledge the unrelenting racism policies and practices she experienced. Baraka's command "to listen" is issued as a warning to readers, whereas Hoagland's is more likely to implore—quite possibly why Young included Hoagland's poem because it's the kind of ending Young's collection seeks: one that implores the reader to note the contradictory aspects of Holiday's life and speak back.

After these poems' racial commentaries, Young includes poems dedicated to the Holiday's love life with Sonia Sanchez's poem "For Our Lady" and Janet Choi's "What I'm Wild For." This transition from race to love stresses how the tradition of jazz and blues developed within a sexual "ideological framework that was specifically African-American" (Davis). In *Blues Legacies and Black Feminism*, Angela Davis analyzes Holiday's love songs in an effort to illuminate their "simultaneous ability to confirm and subvert racist and sexist representations of women in love" (164). Similar to Hoagland's beseechment to listen to Holiday's ruminations on race, Davis argues that Holiday's otherwise diminished and often-forgotten love songs "demand close listening to and reading of … for the purpose of proposing feminist reinterpretations" (164–5). Therefore, when Young switches from race to love, he aptly begins with Sanchez's poem, whose speaker calls out the country's "wite mind" and wishes for Holiday to have found a "blk/man" for a generous lover (234). Here, Sanchez points out how the racial indignation Holiday faced in her personal and public life was inextricably linked to the sexist mistreatment she received. Originally published in Sanchez's 1970's *We a BaddDDD People*, "For Our Lady" defies a clear gender politics, as the speaker suggests that Holiday might have been rescued from her tragedies if she was involved in a positive heterosexual relationship with a black man. According to this speaker, Holiday's fraught love life kept her from being "permantentlee warm" and possibly stunted "the jazz of [her]/songs" (234). Because the speaker ties Holiday's hopes to a black lover, Holiday seems less able to act as a strong, revolutionary or "race woman." The stripped down "u" in Sanchez's poem, as Elizabeth Frost argues in *The Feminist Avant-Garde in American Poetry*, does not have the ability to have "swung/gainst this country's wit mind," leaving readers with a possibly diminished view of Holiday (234.) While this "u" is thus weakened without a particular lover, Holiday's potential in Sanchez's poem is unfathomable—there "ain't no tellen" what ways Holiday could have "pushed us from/our blue nites" or what unimaginable places she could have "led us" (234).

As if to better explain Holiday's unfulfilled love life, Young includes Choi's "What I'm Wild For," a poem that boldly adopts Holiday's voice as the speaker. In terms of call and response, the "I" in Choi's poem seems to balance out Sanchez's exposed "u," and rather than only alluding to her bad lovers, Choi details the sexual violence Holiday experienced, opening with how her childhood rape "broke" her (235). In the first stanza, the "I"—seemingly too mature for her age—comes to revile her mother's prostitution, wanting to "fling that in her face" (235). In this stanza alone, the "I" must deal with incomprehensible violence and sexism, like when a musician removed her underwear, tossing them into her face. Choi follows that up in the second and third stanzas with the ways sexism infiltrates different institutions such as prisons and the military. "Behind/the warden's back, behind Jim Crow's back," Holiday witnesses a variation of "love" in prison, as "dykes … touch hands" that stands in stark contrast to the physical relationships in the first and third stanzas. The third stanza introduces some of the ways soldiers loved Holiday. Unlike the female prisoners' caring relationships (touching, feeding), the soldiers' violence (begging, tearing) better reflects Holiday's multiple abusive relationships and simultaneously showcases how cultural institutions dictate who and how people can express their emotions. As Choi's poem concludes, the speaker states what Holiday is really "wild for." After all of the abuse, Choi's Holiday only wants a home-cooked meal and a "few grains of dope and the shakes" she gets when singing "Strange Fruit" (236). No longer chained to her body, Holiday's "notes break clean," and her voice "fl[ies] over the band" (236). The audience exclaims that "no one sings/hunger like you do, or love" (236). This conflation of her voice, hunger, and love echoes the collection's opening focus on her voice and reinforces the importance of her love songs.

As the audience in Choi's poem praises Holiday's voice and relinquishes the earthly pressures on her body, the poem leads into final section of collection, where Young capitalizes on keeping Holiday's legacy alive. The final poems include O'Hara's "The Day Lady Died," Dove's "Canary," and Inada's "The Journey." Already well-documented, O'Hara's and Dove's works don't try to pin down Holiday, catalog her as a memory in their family photo album, or as a symbol for all of black culture. Rather, these two poems act as a fitting tribute for Young's Holiday tribute. O'Hara's breathless, personal poem redistributes the weight of the personal pronoun of the "I" used in Choi's poem. O'Hara's mundane *Lunch Poems* from the 1964 paint concrete images that move from the trivial to the significant, and his "The Day Lady Died" forces readers to consider cultural questions like where they were on days of specific tragedies. Without naming Holiday throughout the entire elegy, O'Hara demonstrates the weight of her death on the community through the bank teller Miss Stillwagon, who, according to the speaker, grants him the courtesy of not checking his balance for the first time. When O'Hara concludes with the austere image of Holiday "whisper[ing] a song along the keyboard," he does what many of the poets in Young's collection strive to do: reinscribe Holiday into the breathless listener of today. In this way, O'Hara's elegy, which begins with a specific time (12:20 p.m.) and interchanges tenses ("go get a shoeshine"; "will get off the 4:19"; "go back where I came from"; "thinking of leaning on") ends up effectively conflating the past audience at the Five Spot with a present one, making Holiday live on all of these decades later.

This poetic tendency gets extended in Dove's "Canary." Published in Dove's *Grace Notes* from 1991, "Canary" begins using a third-person, past tense to describe Holiday's "burned voice" and "ruined face," and then quickly moves into a second stanza seemingly directed at Holiday with the second-person, present tense. The speaker encourages Holiday to take all the time "you" might need to pamper herself with "your mirror and your bracelet of song" (239). The final stanzas also shift between universal proclamations about why besieged women must cultivate myths and Holiday's specific defense strategy to move beyond the "posthumous narrative that pins her as a tragedy" (McStay). Similar to O'Hara's, Young's, Hayes,' Hoagland's poems, Dove's shifts create alternate timelines that juxtapose Holiday's tumultuous past with a present lacking her presence. And yet, Dove's poem is far from tragic, as Holiday gets to live out her myth as a mystery.

While firmly rooted in the past tense, Inada's "The Journey" continues the redemptive thread of these legacy poems. Published in 1970, "The Journey" uses the first-person and contains three characters, Miles Davis, Holiday, and the speaker, huddled in a boat. Davis had "his trumpet in a paper bag" and Holiday's gardenias were "wind lashed" (240). They row away from the "moan[ing] and smolder[ing]" city into the open sea (240). Once in the boat, Davis' horn, Holiday's voice, and the speaker's rowing all converge, getting "caught" by the "current" (241). Although they weep after floating, signing, and playing all night, the poem concludes with the characters "soar[ing] in a spiritual" (241). Like Choi's Holiday floating above the audience, these characters also soar above. Following this final image, the speaker exclaims, "Never have I been so happy" (241). This delight reflects how Young wants Holiday's image to live on. Young claimed in his foreword that Inada's poem evokes an "afterlife" for jazz music, one that traces its roots in spirituals, connections to blues, and inspiration to rock 'n' roll.

In parallel fashion, these elegies evoke an afterlife for Holiday, one that moves her beyond tragic labels. For instance, even though five of these poems mention Holiday's drug use, as a collection, the poems showcase how Holiday "had as many shadows as lights" (239). Because these poems expose the complexities of Holiday's life, they are not depressing. They accomplish what William Ford notes in *The Second Set, Vol. 2: The Jazz Poetry Anthology* about being able to contemplate alienation without being alienated. For Ford and the poets of this collection, Holiday's contemplation was "why [she] could sing 'Fine and Mellow' while smiling so sweetly to Count Basie" (211). This seeming contraction speaks back to Carruth's poem, the epigraph to the collection, in which Holiday challenges listeners to "conceive her song" without trying to explain it (219).

Recognizing the futility of trying to explain Holiday, Young's collection gathers jazz elegies that allows readers to peek beyond the loud labels of tragedy that often pin Holiday down. This might be one reason why Young titles his section "Muting." The gerund muting implies a deadening, muffling or a softening, a reduction in intensity. In music, a mute refers to physical addition to an instrument, a device fitted to purposely alter the sound: by affecting the timbre, a mute reduces the volume or the timbre. Mutes range in style, and jazz and blues musicians as early as the 1920s were using solo tones, buzz wahs, wah wahs, and derbies. These particular devices provide a characteristic sound, and greatly influenced the jazz community. For example, the buzz wah sounds like a bunch of unruly kazoos attached to a horn. As an unusual, albeit recognizable sound, the buzz wah is reminiscent of descriptions of Holiday's voice: instantly recognizable and impossible to replicate in performance. Hence, Young's title intimates an image of Holiday that is less amplified and rare. Contemporary jazz singer Cassandra Wilson, who released a tribute album to Holiday on what would be her 100th birthday, reiterates the importance of this more subtle, scarce image of Holiday: "For all the praise that Billie Holiday gets as a vocal stylist, she's seldom acknowledged as a musical genius. She was the first to prove that you could make soft sounds and still have a powerful emotional impact. She was understating jazz long before Miles ever stuck a mute in his horn; she was the true 'Birth of Cool'" (qtd. in Himes). Taken as a whole, then, the jazz elegies in Young's collection acknowledge Holiday for more than the tragedies of her life, and by doing so, they try accomplish the inconceivable. As McStay alludes, these jazz elegies emulate the essence of the moment, "the grain of the voice. The physicality of the performer. The improvisations and flourishes and intangibles that exist for one night only." Thus, while Young's collection "Muting: for Billie Holiday" always already acknowledges the impermanence of Holiday's existence, through its call and response structure, she mutates and moves on, making Young's collection ultimately uplifting.

Works Cited

Baraka, Amiri, ed. *The Music: Reflections on Jazz and Blues.* New York: William Morrow, 1987.

Blair, Elizabeth. "The Strange Story of the Man Behind 'Strange Fruit.'" *NPR Music,* 5 Sept. 2012. www.npr.org/2012/09/05/158933012/the-strange-story-of-the-man-behind-strange-fruit.

"Brief Guide to Jazz Poetry." *Poets.org,* 17 May 2004. www.poets.org/poetsorg/text/brief-guide-jazz-poetry.

Broek, Michael. "Weird and Bathetic: Tony Hoagland, 'The Office,' and the Confessional Mode." *The American Poetry Review*, vol. 41, no. 6, Nov./Dec. 2012, pp. 11–15.

"Elegy: Poetic Form." *Poets.org*, 14 Feb. 2014. www.poets.org/poetsorg/text/elegy-poetic-form.

Feinstein, Sascha. *Jazz Poetry from the 1920s to the Present*. Westport, CT: Prager, 1997.

Feinstein, Sascha, and Yusef Komunyakaa, eds. *The Jazz Poetry Anthology*. Bloomington: Indiana University Press, 1991.

Feinstein, Sascha, and Yusef Komunyakaa, eds. *The Second Set, Vol. 2: The Jazz Poetry Anthology*. Bloomington: Indiana University Press, 1996.

Fleming, Colin. "The Legacy of Billie Holiday's 'God Bless the Child,' 75 Years Later." *Salon*, 26 Sept. 2017. www.salon.com/2017/09/26/billie-holiday-god-bless-the-child/.

Friedwald, Will. *Jazz Singing: America's Great Voices from Bessie Smith to Bebop and Beyond*. New York: Da Capo Press, 1996.

Griffin, Farah Jasmine, and Salim Washington. *Clawing the Limits of Cool: Miles Davis, John Coltrane, and the Greatest Jazz Collaboration Ever*. New York: Thomas Dunne, 2008.

Himes, Geoffrey. "What Makes Billie Holiday's Music So Powerful Today." *Smithsonian*, 7 April 2015. www.smithsonianmag.com/arts-culture/what-makes-billie-holiday-so-powerful-today-180954893/.

Hoban, Phoebe. "Basquait: A Quick Killing in Art." *New York Times Books*, 1998. archive.nytimes.com/www.nytimes.com/books/first/h/hoban-basquiat.html.

Hobson, Janelle. "Everybody's Protest Song: Music as Social Protest in the Performances of Marian Anderson and Billie Holiday." *Signs*, vol. 33, no. 2, Winter 2008, pp. 443–448.

"How to Write a Eulogy." *WikiHow*, n.d. www.wikihow.com/Write-a-Eulogy.

Jackson, Major. "A Mystifying Silence: Big and Black." *American Poetry Review*, vol. 36, no. 5, Sept./Oct. 2007, pp. 19–25.

Jardim, Suzane. "Recognizing Racist Stereotypes in U.S. Media." *Medium*, 26 July 2016. medium.com/@suzanejardim/reconhecendo-esteri%C3%B3tipos-racistas-internacionais-b00f80861fc9.

Johnson, David Brent. "In Memoriam: Jazz Elegies." *WRTI*, 25 May 2014. wrti.org/post/memoriam-jazz-elegies.

Jones, Jae. "In the Words of Bill 'Bojangles' Robinson 'Everything's Copacetic.'" *Black Then*, 23 June 2018. blackthen.com/in-the-words-of-bill-bojangles-robinson-everythings-copacetic/.

McCabe, Charles. "Copacetic." *SFGate*, 12 Oct. 2007. www.sfgate.com/entertainment/article/COPACETIC-2518694.php.

McHugh, Heather, ed. *The Best American Poetry, 2007*. New York: Scribner, 2007.

McStay, Chantal. "Rita Dove's 'Canary.'" *Paris Review*, 17 July 2014. www.theparisreview.org/blog/2014/07/17/rita-doves-canary/.

Priestly, Brian. *Chasin' the Bird: The Life and Legacy of Charlie Parker*. Oxford: Oxford University Press, 2007.

Sakakeeny, Matt. "Jazz Funerals and Second Line Parades." *Encyclopedia of Louisiana*, 2 Oct 2017. www.knowlouisiana.org/entry/jazz-funerals-and-second-line-parades.

Spahr, Juliana, and Stephanie Young. "The Program Era and the Mainly White Room." *Los Angeles Review of Books*, 20 Sept. 2015. lareviewofbooks.org/article/the-program-era-and-the-mainly-white-room/#!.

Spiegelman, Willard. *How Poets See the World: The Art of Description in Contemporary Poetry*. Oxford: Oxford University Press, 2005.

Stone, Chris. "Blood at the Root: 'Strange Fruit.'" *OAH Magazine of History*, vol. 18, no. 2, Jan. 2004, pp. 54–56.

Szwed, John. "Billie Holiday." *Oxford Bibliography*, 28 June 2018. www.oxfordbibliographies.com/view/document/obo-9780190280024/obo-9780190280024-0006.xml.

Wallenstein, Barry. "Poetry and Jazz: A Twentieth-Century Wedding." *Black American Literature Forum*, vol. 25, no. 3, pp. 595–620.

Werbanowska, Marta. "Kevin Young's 'Discography One'—An Exercise in Post-Soul Poetics." Spring Academy on American History, Culture & Politics, Conference, March 2014, Heidelberg, Germany.

Young, Kevin, ed. *Jazz Poems*. Everyman's Library, 2006. https://www.jstor.org/stable/10.1086/521057?seq=1#page_scan_tab_contents.

Reevaluating *Lady Sings the Blues* and *What's Love Got to Do with It*

Ambivalent Representations of Black Female Artistry

Jesse Schlotterbeck

The majority of critics who have tackled the musical biopic observe that this is a genre defined by compromises given the difficult task of representing a life story in a feature length film. Since the musical biopic is unequivocally a popular genre, this transformation often comes with all the trappings of Hollywood filmmaking—romance, success, happy endings, and pat psychological motivations. In short, critics are usually left with much to critique with the biopic. The films studied here are no exception; *Lady Sings the Blues* (1972) and *What's Love Got to Do with It* (1993) qualify and contextualize their lead subjects in ways that are disappointing. They are also, still, remarkable films in terms of Hollywood history and the evolution of the musical biopic genre.

Both films are clearly celebrations of black female artistry. At the same time, however, the achievements of Holiday and Turner are contextualized and qualified. For example, both biopics emphasize the relational self (whether a male partner or mainstream rock producers) above the autonomous self. As represented in *Lady Sings the Blues* and *What's Love Got to Do with It,* these black female stars are not fully celebrated as independent individual artists. This is largely due to the prominence of other contextual aspects of their lives: the workings of the entertainment industry, producers, lovers, collaborators, and social evils. This essay works as a corrective to extant scholarship, which tends to criticize *Lady Sings the Blues* as too conservative and more positively evaluate *What's Love Got to Do with It* (with notable exceptions, such as the bell hooks piece). I note the trade-offs that both films take in the representation of black female artists. Instead of a narrative-of-progress from 1972 to 1993, I find more to celebrate than is often granted with *Lady Sings the Blues* and aspects of *What's Love Got to Do with It* that should trouble critics more than they currently have.

In what is largely a white- and male-dominated genre, the prominence of black female artists is also notable in *Lady Sings the Blues* and *What's Love Got to Do with It*. *Lady Sings the Blues* is, in fact, at the late date of 1972, the first film to narrate the life of an African American woman working in any artistic medium.[1] Yet, the extent of the film's success must be tempered with more careful analysis.

These films cannot be out and out celebrated as groundbreaking since their landmark status was achieved alongside numerous compromises. With *Lady Sings the Blues,* the celebratory narrative of the film is mitigated by the fact that Diana Ross' performance as Holiday is stereotypically feminine. She is overly emotional, easily influenced by others, and dependent on a life-partner to stabilize her. The feminist narrative of *What's Love Got to Do with It*, starring Angela Bassett as Tina Turner, is achieved by way of elevating rock and pop music over Motown music. Many critics evaluate *Lady Sings the Blues* as more regressive and *What's Love Got to Do with It* as more progressive than I do; I aim to correct this contrast by demonstrating the way that both films display significant compromises and achievements.

My reading of *Lady Sings the Blues* and *What's Love Got to Do with It* as ideologically ambivalent in their portrayals of African American female artistry is at odds with the current literature on these films The critical approach that most defines my reading of these films is outlined by Robert Ray in *A Certain Tendency of Hollywood Cinema*. Here, Ray offers a corrective to the tendency of academics to read Hollywood film as politically transparent. As I summarize in a previous publication, "Ray argues that the most successful Hollywood films are not those that are the most conservative or liberal, but those that are maximally ambivalent or ambiguous" (189).[2] Both *Lady Sings the Blues* and *What's Love Got to Do with It* can be read in this manner: as films that, however consciously, try to maximize their popularity by striking an ideological balance between progressive and conservative aspects of representation.

Lady Sings the Blues

Though the idea for a Billie Holiday biopic was explored as early as the mid–1950s by print biographer William Dufty, this provisional project was

he Silent Majority's anxieties" (107–108). Comments from the film's own pro-
uction staff validate Storhoff's thesis that the film is best read as "a crossover
ext, created to win the sympathies of both a white and an African American
udience. In its effort to provide for all possible viewer positions, *Lady Sings
he Blues* negotiates racial, gender, generational, and political issues" (Storhoff
05). In the featurette included with the release of *Lady Sings the Blues* on
VD (2005), co-screenwriter Suzanne de Passe qualifies that "we [the pro-
uction staff] always made the distinction that this was a film that happened
o have black people in it, but it wasn't a black film in that only black people
ould watch it." Notably, this characterization accurately describes Gordy's
elong approach to record recording as well; in the example of Motown, and
en the Holiday biopic, he sought black artists with the aim of widespread
ommercial appeal.

   While Storhoff is accurate to note conciliatory aspects of the film's rep-
sentation of racism, it is difficult to imagine how the film could both try
 accurately represent the 1930s, while clearly pointing towards events of
e 1970s as well. By necessity, most of this movement across time must be
plicit—as part of the reception context, or indicated in the role of casting
970s musical star in the lead role. Given the films that preceded it, such
St. Louis Blues, Lady Sings the Blues* still deserves a measure of credit for
ng the first musical biopic to tell the story of a black musician while still
phasizing the importance of race and racial discrimination in the subject's

   Initially, in fact, Storhoff promises a more even-handed reading of the
n, which emphasizes the film's availability to all audience segments: "In its
ort to provide for all possible viewer positions—from the Silent Majority
servative of the early 1970s, to the African American proud of the real-
Holiday's achievements, to the viewer primarily interested in Diana Ross'
eer—*Lady Sings the Blues* negotiates racial, gender, generational, and polit-
 problems with complexity and subtlety" (105). By the conclusion of the
cle, however, Storhoff shifts to a more familiar academic account of Hol-
ood filmmaking—that social and cultural portrayals are almost always
e conservative than progressive. Storhoff points to a long list of Holiday's
aracter traits in describing the film's sexist and conservative tendencies:
iday has multiple emotional breakdowns; she has drug problems and is
eed of a stable spouse to give her life stability (107–110). While Storhoff's
ment is coherent, it is also made without identifying any of these char-
r traits as broadly typical of musical biopic protagonists.
   Male leads, especially in post-classical era biopics, also possess signifi-
 flaws and are almost always in need of a significant other to stabilize
. Carolyn Anderson and Jonathan Lupo's essay "Off-Hollywood Lives:
y and Its Discontents in the Contemporary Biopic" and Glenn D. Smith

never financed (Sutton 305). The successful production of *Lady Sings the
Blues* (1972), more than ten years later, was the brainchild of Motown Records
owner Berry Gordy, who also wanted to use the film to promote his contract-
artist Diana Ross in the lead role, establishing her ability as a solo artist after
the breakup of The Supremes. Gordy's decision was a success, as *Lady Sings
the Blues* earned $19.7 million at the box office, nearly ten times its budget
of $2 million, and was nominated for five Oscars. ("The Numbers") This
financial success indicates that the film's producers struck an effective balance
in making a film that appealed to a broad range of the American public.

   In *Critical Readings: Media and Gender*, Cynthia Carter and Linda
Steiner discuss the threat of "symbolic annihilation" for marginal groups in
society if they are not fully or adequately represented in mainstream culture:

> A key concept generated by an early generation of media content researchers was that
> of "symbolic annihilation." This term initially used by US mass communication
> scholars George Gerbner (1978) and Gaye Tuchman (1978) to describe the claim that
> powerful groups in society suppress the less powerful by marginalizing them to such
> an extent that they are rendered virtually invisible as a representable group [13].

Lady Sings the Blues remains a vital and important breakthrough film in that
it was the first full-length feature film to tell the life story of a black woman
artist. As such, the film is a step against the "symbolic annihilation" of black
women as visible, vital parts of the American public. Landmark works in
popular culture are rarely achieved without numerous compromises. Consider, for example, current debates about the comparative merits of *Love,
Simon* (2018), the first gay teen drama financed by a major studio. In 1972, in
terms of mainstream Hollywood filmmaking, *Lady Sings the Blues* was an
analogously important first step in the evolution of the musical biopic—an
enduringly popular film genre.

   Lady Sings the Blues deserves a measure of credit for making racism a
much more visible subject than any of its precursors about black male artists.
For example, compared to the Holiday film that would be released 14 years
later, Paramount's *St. Louis Blues* (1958), starring Nat King Cole as the composer and cornetist W.C. Handy, is notably more tepid in its engagement
with social issues. Both John C. Tibbetts and Krin Gabbard, authors of the
most extensive studies of the musical biopic to date, point out that *St. Louis
Blues* strategically avoids any critical engagement with race. In addition to
the erasure of racial prejudice, Gabbard discusses the necessity of casting the
mild-mannered crooner, Nat King Cole, in the lead role: "Cole functioned
as a healthy alternative to the unsavory image of the drug-crazed, psyched-
up black jazz artist that had been thoroughly inscribed on the American
mind by the late 1950s" (Gabbard 99). The casting of Cole stands out as a
compromise envisioned to attract a wide range of viewers, including those
potentially threatened by the default image of the jazz artist.

The years between *Lady Sings the Blues* and the first musical biopic about a black male artist (*St. Louis Blues*) had seen African Americans become more prominent cinematic performances. The two most significant developments regarding African Americans and film in these intervening years help explain the double-sidedness of *Lady Sings the Blues*. To better understand the place of *Lady Sings the Blues* in film history, we ought to take note of recent trends in film performance (the ascendance of Sidney Poitier as a star actor and the emergence of *blaxploitation* film) that informed the reception context. These changes in black film culture and production are reflected in *Lady Sings the Blues*, a work best understood as trying to reach both blaxploitation audiences and audiences who would be more inclined to favor Poitier.

By the early 70s, popular cinema was at a tipping-point, torn between two ways of representing black life on screen; one built around the idealized star image of Sidney Poitier, whose erudition and restraint made him equally appealing and off-putting for audience identification and the other, featuring more rebellious, forceful characters such as Richard Roundtree as *Shaft* (1971) and Melvin Van Peebles as the lead in *Sweet Sweetback's Baadasssss Song* (1971). These independent and defiant characters were sometimes seen also, borderline caricatures of African Americans as over-sexed, angry, and violent.

In *Lady Sings the Blues*, as compared to Poitier or *blaxploitation* films, African American characters fall in between such starkly divided performances of assimilation or resistance. Black men are sometimes portrayed as predatory hustlers, and other times as well-intentioned companions. Holiday's extraordinary musical talents are, of course, made clear, but she is also portrayed as self-destructive and indecisive. The film's most questionable fictionalization expresses these contrasts. Where, in actuality, Holiday had had a series of variously unreliable companions, the film invents a long-time idealized love interest with Billy Dee Williams as Louis McKay. In his article about adaptation of Holiday's life-story, including print and aural versions, Matthew Sutton importantly points out that McKay, himself, worked "as a paid 'technical advisor' on the film, contributing another voice (and agenda) to the telling of Holiday's posthumous story." He continues, "McKay's self-interested cooperation in the film underscores a questionable assumption it shares with Dufty's book: for all her talent, Holiday's seemingly innate tendency to self-destruct can only be curbed with luck and the heroic intervention of a good man" (307). Following Sutton's argument, it hardly seems excusable to create a "dream prince charming" to compliment Holiday's equally consistent helplessness and dysfunction, but, as Donald Bogle argues, the depiction of such a lavish, glamorous courtship, however sexist, remained a landmark in its own right: "It was a new sensation to watch a black man actually court and cajole a black woman. Rarely before had the movies given

audiences the idea that black characters could be romantic" (24 to this romantic focus, *Lady Sings the Blues* also attempts to realities of racism, and its terrible effect on Holiday's life.

Selected scenes from the film clearly illustrate the attem to engage critically with race and racism. For example, early in currently performing at an African American night club, is members of a traveling jazz band interested in hiring her t them. The film, here and in the following examples, does blindness. Holiday is shocked, not that these white men believ enough to play with them, but that their collaboration c acceptable. She asks, "a colored singer with a white band though, turns out to be successful, and Billie is soon accep important member of the group. In many shots of Ross' H band, she is normally blocked in the center of the frame, in is the most talented and important member of the group. In of course, Diana Ross, herself, is a bigger star than any of the in the film. Dramatically, *Lady Sings the Blues* effectively painful incongruity of the fact that Holiday is both the most of this band, and, through everyday experiences of racism, everyday existence that her bandmates do not.

After Holiday has established herself as a successful a Reg, lines up a sponsorship opportunity. Holiday is snubbed from landing a spot with Sun Ray soap in favor of a lesser She dismisses the snub later, saying, "they're trying to sell s one knows we don't use it. Heh. Give a bright complexion, p This scene illustrates the way that *Lady* persistently foreg as a pervasive force in Holiday's everyday life and the soc

When the group travels to the Deep South, Ross' F necessity, the inconvenience of segregation, waiting by the gets to comfortably dine inside a restaurant. When Holid; virulent, direct expressions of Southern hatred, this is stand. Two incidents lead the fictive Billie to a nervous after she unexpectedly encounters a lynched black man band travels past a Ku Klux Klan rally. Holiday can nc emotions, and tries to scream at the Klansmen while her her. Gary Storhoff argues that *Lady's* portrayal of racism is—has been insidiously transformed so as to comforta nicious social attitudes only in the past and the South. Hi; this encounter with the Klan rally: "Her hysterical res; immediate, localized to southern racism, and intensely emphasizing racism as a peculiarly southern problem ago (the 1930s) and the far away, is clearly intended to abs

Jr.'s "Love as Redemption: The American Dream Myth and the Celebrity Biopic" both cover the tendency of contemporary biopics to portray deeply flawed male leads. In this respect, it could be argued, Ross' Holiday is somewhat typical of most Hollywood biopic protagonists, whatever their gender or race. Like the stars that Anderson, Lupo, and Smith Jr., analyze in their articles, such as Ray Charles and Ed Wood, Holiday is also a flawed person. The tendency to portray flawed-leads is so common in this genre (of both male and female protagonists) that Dennis Bingham has coined a specific subgenre to the biopic, "the warts-and-all film" (380). The opening scenes of *Lady Sings the Blues*, in which Ross' Holiday appears in a padded jail cell after taking a series of mugshots clearly qualifies it as a film which intends to include some "warts" in addition to the singer's achievements.

Additionally, in his eagerness to outline a typical conservative viewer, Storhoff creates a straw spectator: "The film thus frames its retrogressive argument: If only Billie had known her place—as loyal wife and obedient daughter, if only Billie had restrained her hubristic desire for fame and wealth in favor of home and family, if only Billie had understood the tacit boundaries for African American women that the Silent Majority takes for granted, then Billie would have been safe, innocent, and happy" (112). While aspects of Billie's characterization, such as her emotional volatility and codependence, do contribute to a sexist framework for understanding this life-story, Storhoff's implied spectator who wishes Holiday never had a performance career at all is unfairly pessimistic if not impossible to imagine.

Given that Storhoff focuses, in part, on the role that drug use played in Holiday's life as a point of excessive emphasis in the film, it is worth considering that the film (had it left this part of her life entirely out) could have been criticized for sanitizing her story too much. In a 2017 article in *The Ringer* about the rarity with which women are designated musical "geniuses," there is discussion of the fact that female performers are often regarded more critically for living a life of excess. Linday Zoladz writes,

> Very often, women who live as freely and hedonistically as the average man are criticized by outside forces for not behaving correctly, for not taking proper care of their bodies. [Joni] Mitchell, a lifelong chain-smoker who sometimes burned through four packs a day, has often been accused of, as [David] Yaffe puts it, "not being a devoted custodian to her own instrument."

Zoladz's analysis of Joni Mitchell biographies finds problem in the fact that the singer's smoking habit is frequently criticized; this is in contrast to male stars. Do Leonard Cohen or Tom Waits receive similar criticism for their smoking habit? Definitively not. Taking this view into account, if the producers of *Lady Sings the Blues* wished to produce a film that pleased a broad audience, it is easy to envision a version of the film that minimized, if not eliminated entirely, Holiday's drug-use.[3] This imagined alternate film could, then, have been criticized precisely for avoiding this aspect of her life and presenting a more sanitized version of the star. A too functional, too hagiographic version of Holiday could have invited criticism for being too stereotypically feminine as well.

In the recent academic text on feminism and psychology, *Woman's Embodied Self: Feminist Perspectives on Identity and Image*, Joan C. Christler and Ingrid Johns summarize the double-binds that still define the ideology of womanhood:

> Every day women receive instructions about how their bodies should look, should function (or not function), and should behave. Instructions come from advertising and other media, from religious texts and leaders, from medicine, from government, and from other women [11].

As cultural critics, we would do well to remember that works which tell women's stories effectively find themselves in this thicket of potential double-binds. While Christler and Johns are thinking, principally, of the lives of ordinary women, I argue that these weighted expectations are also placed on cultural works about women's lives as well. The authors continue, summarizing the range of expectations that apply to female subjects:

> Women learn that their bodies should be feminine, beautiful (but not look like they tried too hard to achieve their beauty), sexy (but not slutty), pure (but not prudish), slender (but curvy in the right places), youthful (if they are adults), mature (if they are adolescents), healthy, fit, and able-bodied. Women should be warm, approachable, giving, yielding, and cater to others' needs before their own. Women should look, do, and be what is impossible [11].

Without giving *Lady Sings the Blues* a free pass for any of its representational choices, it is worth remembering that the demanding and often contradictory expectations of womanhood will also apply, by extension, to any author or filmmaker who chooses to represent a woman's life. For its audience, *Lady Sings the Blues* was destined to attract criticism for failing to negotiate all aspects of Holiday's life and personality in a way that both made her an admirable, impressive artist as well as an actual human being that was not presented unrealistically.

The promotional poster for the film evidences some awareness of the competing representational demands for this film. A drawn-hand both holds a microphone upward, while handcuffs also dangle from the lower arm. The poster condenses the difficult work of the film itself in addition to the struggles of Holiday's life. The microphone's indication of transcendence and stardom and the cuff's representation of the potential for failure and downfall concisely represent the double-sidedness of cultural work that tries to appropriately summarize an important figure in a way that will also appeal to a diverse mass audience. *Lady Sings the Blues* is an imperfect film; yet, it remains a landmark work and critics (especially decades after its release) should not let the presence of notable compromises draw all our attention to the extent that we lose sight of the important cultural work it also did—as the first feature length biopic to tell the life-story of a black female artist.

What's Love Got to Do with It

As opposed to the negative academic reception to *Lady Sings the Blues*, typified by Storhoff's article, the critical reception of *What's Love Got to Do with It* (1993) has been far more complimentary. Yet, in celebrating this Tina Turner biopic as a feminist film, scholars have overlooked the fact that the singer's movement toward independence is paired with the elevation of rock and pop music over Motown.

In *The Musical: Race, Gender, and Performance*, Susan Smith argues that Tina Turner biopic ought to be commended for its feminist approach to the musical. Comparing *What's Love Got to Do with It* to 1950s era classical musicals such as *The Pirate, A Star Is Born,* and *Love Me or Leave Me* that also evince anxiety about the power of female voices, Smith argues that *What's Love Got to Do with It* is, unequivocally, the most progressive of these films: "In offering such an emphatic celebration of the woman's emancipation, *What's Love Got to Do with It*'s ending also marks a significant development in the musical's ongoing fascination with the great female singer," with a lead who fully "breaks ties with the male protagonist … the female singer finally asserts her autonomy as a performing self in her own right" (116). While Smith accurately notes *What's Love*'s open engagement with gender politics— most notably the celebration of an independent woman at the conclusion— she misses the way that the most significant binary through which Ike and Tina are opposed is their stance on rock 'n' roll. Whereas Ike Turner is staunchly protective of black music and angered by the emergence of the "English invasion," Tina Turner openly embraces it. This antagonism is expressed twice, once in a brief sequence and again in an extended sequence, the final act of the film.

In the first sequence, Ike Turner and Tina Turner are briefly interviewed about rock'n'roll. Following a montage of "home movie" footage, accompanied by a radio DJ enthusing over and "Do Wah Diddy Diddy," the "hot sound of the British invasion." This song, about a love at first sight, also signifies the suddenness of rock's emergence. The melodramatic language of this pop song, the *so much, so soon* of falling in love, also describes the narrative of rock's dominance, of the popular audience falling for this white sound (or, white *performers*) and forgetting the black ones.

What's Love makes use of a faux-documentary or television aesthetic here, as the image switches to a grainy, handheld aesthetic that functions as a reality effect. A subtitle identifies this as a station interview and an off-screen voice asks them both, "So what's your take on the new English music invading the States?" By this point in the film, Ike Turner's abusiveness has been established, and this unresolved conflict between them is palpable even before they speak. In a long-take two-shot, Ike is visibly perturbed by the question. The interview clearly provokes some anxiety in Tina as well, but she, nevertheless discloses, "Well, Ike said there ain't nothin' new about it. It ain't nothin' but black music. I mean, Negro music with an accent. But, uh, I like a lot of it." Tina smiles while answering the question, hoping to defuse the tension introduced by Ike's sullen silence. When Ike doesn't add anything further, the interviewer prompts him, "Ike, I sense you don't feel fully appreciated here?" With this, Ike stands and leaves the room.

In the film, Tina and Ike's musical preferences are, at multiple key plot points in the film, distinguished as open versus restrictive. Where Tina is open to being recorded by Phil Spector, Ike is opposed to it. In an even more crucial scene, Tina is savagely beaten by Ike after she tells him that many of the songs he has written sound similar. The possibility of a broader range of musical experimentation, as well as the possibility of white involvement in their production is persistently repellant to Ike Turner, and consistently attractive to Tina Turner. While this difference in range of musical interests is historically accurate it also works, potentially, to appease audience members who might assume, however consciously, that pop and rock music is better than Motown music.

The film's final, triumphant act is enabled by Tina's collaboration with a white producer, modeled after the singer's business partnership with Roger Davies in the early 1990s. The Davies character is equivalent to Louis McKay in *Lady Sings the Blues*. As Dennis Bingham notes, a common character in biopics featuring female leads is "the male authority figure or driving force, the man who approves of her work and impresses upon her how great she is" (329). In *What's Love Got to Do with It*, this function is first performed by Ike, then Davies. When Tina meets with her would-be-producer, she assures him that she is not "about" being sad regarding her fallout with Ike. Davies asks, "So what are you about?" "Rock and roll!" Tina replies, continuing, "I'm talkin' about the energy of it, fun stuff, you hear it in the music of Bowie and Jagger. That's the stuff I want to do, not that old sad sack stuff I used to do with Ike…. It took me a long time to get Ike out of my system, and now that I've done that, I'm ready." Her producer offers her a cheers "to you," and she corrects him, "to us." This scene is followed by an emphatic performance of the film's title track, "What's Love Got to Do with It," a song best classified as pop or pop rock, in front of a large and appreciative audience. Halfway through the performance, Bassett is replaced by Turner herself—suggesting that the film has moved close enough to an authentic version of this star performer that this transition is authorized. At this point, according to Smith, Turner has triumphantly emerged from under the thumb of a controlling and abusive man, but we should not lose sight of the fact that this end is also achieved by her abandoning "sad sack" songs of her rhythm and blues days. The implication of this narrative is familiar: rock represents greater freedom and artistry than blues (or rhythm and blues).

In the dominant history of late 20th-century pop music,

[W]hite rockers are routinely celebrated as enigmatic artists while their black counterparts are made out to be simpleminded conduits of energy and fun. "The Rolling Stone Illuminated History of Rock and Roll" once described Motown as a "wholly mechanical style and sound." The Beatles, by contrast, were hailed as mop-top Beethovens [Ross].

Granting the dominance of this covertly racist history of popular music, it is still surprising that *What's Love Got to Do with It*'s parallel narrative, which naturalizes the replacement of blues with rock, escapes the notice of critics whose primary interest in the film is its social and political content. bell hooks discusses the way that *What's Love Got to Do with It* portrays Ike in a deservedly negative light next to the positive portrayal of Tina. hooks aptly draws our attention to the film's presentation of a mostly-still-glamorous woman as opposed to the abjection of spousal abuse:

[N]o fucking woman—including Tina Turner—is beautiful in her body when she's being battered. The real Tina Turner was sick a lot. She had all kinds of health problems during her life with Ike. Yet the film shows us this person who is so incredibly beautiful and incredibly sexual. We don't see the kind of contrast Tina Turner actually sets up in her autobiography between "I looked like a wreck one minute, and then, I went on that stage and projected all this energy." The film should have given us the pathos of that [112–113].

This fits a tendency of mainstream films featuring African American women (such as Stephen Spielberg's 1985 adaptation of Alice Walker's *The Color Purple*) to balance these positive portrayals against violence abuse at the hands of African American men. I surely agree with hooks that domestic abuse ought to be known and visible in the cultural representations remembering Ray's observation that "the film historian … has an array of factors to consider, each of them 'right' as an object of study, each becoming 'wrong' only if the historian's attention fixes on one as the sole explanation of cinema"— and that we attend to any singular element of the film at our own risk. (7) *What's Love Got to Do with It*, while breaking ground in its focus on a triumphant black woman, does so by way of larger stereotypes about the violent black man and/or presumptions about the relative unimportance of the disgruntled "race records" artist in the broader history of popular music.

Conclusion

In this respect, *What's Love Got to Do with It* shares a tendency with *Lady Sings the Blues*—both films depict the extraordinary achievements of these female African American singers but are also compelled to balance the particularity and progressive potential of their subject alongside more compromising and conservative representational choices. Extant literature on these films is unduly dismissive of *Lady Sings the Blues* as a univocally conservative film, and unduly celebratory of *What's Love Got to Do with It* as a progressive film. Examined again, both films are defined by compromise and a measured balance between representational strategies that are, selectively, conservative, progressive, and mainstream. In the case of the Tina Turner film, her success comes at the cost of the integrity of black artists to stand apart from the (white) mainstream since these spheres (contrasted with Tina's openness to rock and pop) are associated with Ike's abusiveness. *Lady Sings the Blues*, by contrast, portrays Holiday as out of control next to the fictionally perfect man who stabilizes her. My corrective reading works to destabilize a narrative of progress in which the 1993 film is, naturally, more progressive than the 1972 film.

The promotional poster for the film evidences some awareness of the competing representational demands for this film. A drawn hand both holds a microphone upward, while handcuffs also dangle from the lower arm. The poster condenses the difficult work of the film itself in addition to the struggles of Holiday's life. The microphone's indication of transcendence and stardom and the cuff's representation of the potential for failure and downfall concisely represent the double-sidedness of cultural work that tries to appropriately summarize an important figure in a way that will also appeal to a diverse mass audience. *Lady Sings the Blues* is an imperfect film; yet, it remains a landmark work and critics (especially decades after its release) should not let the presence of notable compromises draw all our attention to the extent that we lose sight of the important cultural work it also did—as the first feature length biopic to tell the life-story of a black female artist.

Notes

1. In their study of biographical films, Carolyn Anderson and Jonathan Lupo note a significant increase in the genre's depiction of African American subjects in recent years. In the classical era (from the 1930s to the 1960s), less than five per cent of biographical films featured black subjects. In the 1990s, this number increased to more than 20 percent (Anderson and Lupo, "Hollywood Lives," 93).

2. Taking *The Godfather* as an example, I summarize Ray's explanation of the film's success "by way of its appeal to diverse, seemingly oppositional segments, of the audience." For Ray, it is little coincidence that *The Godfather* was both extraordinarily profitable—setting a new box office record of $86 million in 1972—and successfully combined "right" and "left" qualities of early 70s film cycles—defined on the right side by Charles Bronson (Death Wish), Clint Eastwood (*Dirty Harry*), and Steve McQueen (Bullitt) features and on the left by films

like *Bonnie and Clyde, Easy Rider,* and *The Graduate*—to maximize profitability by satisfying both sectors of the audience" (189).

3. The aforementioned opening scene of LSTB implies Holiday's arrest on drug charges—but not explicitly.

WORKS CITED

Anderson, Carolyn, and Jon Lupo. "Hollywood Lives: The State of the Bio-Pic at the Turn of the Century." In *Genre and Contemporary Hollywood,* edited by Steve Neale. London: British Film Institute, 2002, pp. 89–102.

Anderson, Carolyn, and Jon Lupo. "Off-Hollywood Lives: Irony and Its Discontents in the Contemporary Biopic." *Journal of Popular Film and Television* 36.2 (Summer 2008): 102–111.

Bingham, Dennis. *Whose Lives Are They Anyway? The Biopic as Contemporary Film Genre.* New Brunswick: Rutgers University Press, 2010.

Bogle, Donald. *Toms, Coons, Mulattoes, Mammies, and Bucks: An Interpretive History of Blacks in American Films.* New York: Viking Press, 1973.

Carter, Cynthia, and Linda Steiner. "Mapping the Contested Terrain of Media and Gender Research." In *Critical Readings: Media and Gender,* edited by Carter and Steiner. Maidenhead, England: McGraw Hill Education, 2004, pp. 11–36.

Christler, Joan C., and Ingrid Johnson-Robledo, eds. *Woman's Embodied Self: Feminist Perspectives on Identity and Image.* Washington, D.C.: American Psychological Association, 2018.

Gabbard, Krin. *Jammin' at the Margins: Jazz and the American Cinema.* Chicago: University of Chicago Press, 1996.

hooks, bell. *Reel to Real: Race, Sex, and Class at the Movies.* New York: Routledge, 1996.

"Lady Sings the Blues." *The Numbers.* http://www.the-numbers.com/movies/1972/0LASB.php. Accessed 30 June 2018

Ray, Robert B. *A Certain Tendency of the Hollywood Cinema, 1930–1980.* Princeton: Princeton University Press, 1985.

Ross, Alex. "Rock 101: Academia Tunes In." *The New Yorker,* 14 and 21 July 2003. http://www.newyorker.com/archive/2003/07/14/030714crmu_music. Accessed 30 June 2018.

Schlotterbeck, Jesse. "Masculinity, Race, and the Blues in the Bizpic *Cadillac Records.*" In *Anxiety Muted: American Film Music in a Suburban Age,* edited by Tony Bushard and Stanley Pelkey, 188–204. New York: Oxford University Press, 2014.

Smith, Glenn D., Jr. "Love as Redemption: The American Dream Myth and the Celebrity Biopic." *Journal of Communication Inquiry,* vol. 33, no. 3, July 2009, 222–238.

Smith, Susan. *The Musical: Race, Gender, and Performance.* London: British Film Institute, 2005.

Storhoff, Gary. "'Strange Fruit': *Lady Sings the Blues* as a Crossover Film." *Journal of Popular Film & Television,* vol. 30, no. 2, Summer 2002, 105–114.

Sutton, Matthew. "Bitter Crop: The Aftermath of *Lady Sings the Blues.*" *a/b: Auto/Biography Studies,* vol. 27, no. 2, Winter 2012, 294–315.

Tibbetts, John C. *Composers in the Movies: Studies in Musical Biography.* New Haven: Yale University Press, 2005.

Zoladz, Lindsay. "Joni Mitchell: Fear of a Female Genius." *The Ringer,* October 16, 2017. https://www.theringer.com/music/2017/10/16/16476254/joni-mitchell-pop-music-canon Accessed 30 June 30.

Easy to Love

Representations of Billie Holiday in Contemporary American Poetry

Tara Betts

Since Billie Holiday's notoriety as a singer began, poetic renderings seemed to rapidly follow. Aside from references to her, and her songs, in countless poems, Holiday has been a subject for literary-minded and various cultural groups, including poets from the New York School, Beat poets, Black Arts Movement poets, women, as well as poets who fall outside of that purview. Aside from this wide range of poets looking at Holiday as a muse, she recorded "Strange Fruit"—one of the most haunting, enduring, and often covered, songs which adapted its lyrics from a poem by Lewis Allan (also known as Abel Meeropol). This broad range of poets looking toward Holiday as a central figure in their poems, or a touchstone, indicates Holiday's enduring relevance as a vocal presence and cultural legend.

Although tracking every reference to Billie Holiday in poems verges on impossible, Holiday's presence is clear when examining readily available anthologies that celebrate jazz. By elaborating on Billie Holiday's appearances in anthologies such as *Jazz Poems*, *The Second Set*, a handful of individual poems, Alexis De Veaux's book-length verse biography *Don't Explain: A Song for Billie*, and Carole Boston Weatherford's 2008 young adult poetry collection *Becoming Billie Holiday*, this brief discussion could serve as a beginning to document Holiday's appearances as a literary character that poets return to again and again, even as the decades extend far past her birth. Although many poets reference Holiday, there are not many poems that focus solely on Holiday herself. Many of the poems feature Holiday as a symbolic moment of tragedy or vocal virtuosity. She is the woman done wrong, the woman who falls victim to addiction, the woman who wrestles with the aftermath of sexual assault, and the ever-present bitter fruit of racism that pervaded her life. Herein, poems that feature Holiday as their central figure and content, the connections between those poems, and how the poets celebrate and complicate the representations of Holiday, are the main concerns to be approached.

Carole Weatherford's Becoming Billie Holiday

Becoming Billie Holiday by Carole Boston Weatherford and illustrated by Floyd Cooper functions like a young adult verse novel comprised of short, accessible, first-person poems written from the perspective of Holiday herself. Although almost every other book focuses on the heroin addiction that decimated Holiday too soon, *Becoming Billie Holiday* celebrates how this young girl was persistent, resourceful, honing her skills with talented musicians, and supporting her peers and her mother. The opening poem "Intro: What Shall I Say?" starts with Holiday speaking as an adult looking at a picture of herself in *Time* magazine, being written up as "Woman of the Year," and how proud her mother was of all she had accomplished. After that introductory poem, the rest of the book chronicles her odd jobs to make ends meet, many times when her mother Sadie would leave her with others like "Aunt Eva" and her great grandmother who was a former slave who had 16 children with her master Charles Fagan.

The great grandmother's son, Charlie Fagan, was the only child who survived. However, these women were not enough to keep her from being shuttled into a home for wayward girls or being sexually assaulted by a neighbor. The poem "I'll Never Be the Same" tells how a neighbor Mr. Rich visits while Sadie was out with her boyfriend, Wee Wee. Young Holiday tries to fight off Mr. Rich; when young Holiday is later examined by a doctor, her rape is confirmed. Billie is returned to the home for girls and her attacker is jailed, but she ends her account with being the same as she was before she was attacked, but her "childhood was spent" (35). In a collection for young people, a few poems subtly address how prostitution helped fund her life as a young adult in New York City, and there is even a poem discussing how young Holiday could not bring home men to the apartment that she shared with Sadie, who did not say one word about young women who came home with her daughter and called her "Bill," which subtly alludes to Holiday's bisexuality. The book closes with "Coda: Strange Fruit" where Holiday herself squares up to sing the politically-charged song that challenged racism. This song fueled civil rights activists, and has become a widely-covered composition among artists across musical genres and generations.

Holiday's Vocal Guile in Poems by Angela Jackson and Rita Dove

As readers become familiar with poems about Holiday as a collective body of work focusing on her from different cultural points of view and varying degrees of sexual politics. One poem that directly discusses Billie's sensuality is Angela Jackson's poem "Billie in Silk" which appears in *The Second Set: The Jazz Poetry Anthology* edited by Sascha Feinstein and Yusef Komunyakaa as a follow-up to the first *Jazz Poetry Anthology*. This poem originally appeared in Jackson's 1993 collection *Dark Legs and Silk Kisses*. "Billie in Silk" talks directly to Holiday in the first person. At the end of the first stanza, spider imagery starts with an orchid in Holiday's hair that then becomes a spider whose shadow hangs in Holiday's eye (91). This spider-likeness builds until the poem reaches an italicized fourth stanza, which ends with describing a dragline—the initial strand cast by a spider to begin establishing a web. This dragline shows the power of Holiday's voice resides not in volume or size, but in the intangible factors of its unrest and how it can fool us into swinging and following its reverie. By the time the poem ends, the speaker finally says something to Holiday. The speaker comments on the loneliness of being "black and bruised" then hands Holiday an orchid described as "spideresque-petaled, glorious/full of grace" (92). So, it is no surprise that Billie Holiday becomes a vehicle for the gradual craft and technique that spiders exhibit as they build their webs.

Rita Dove's often-anthologized poem "Canary" from her 1989 book *Grace Notes* also appears in Feinstein and Komunyakaa's *The Second Set*. "Canary" relays that same sense of vocal guile. The three short stanzas total up to 11 lines, but it reveals the power of a woman even as she is in decline. Dove describes Holiday's voice as burned with "as many shadows as lights" like "a mournful candelabra" in the first stanza which underscores the multiple lights and shadows appearing in her vocals. The specific turn toward her signature gardenia under that "ruined face" (46) hints at the physical results of the sorrow in Holiday's voice and her countenance.

The second stanza is a parenthetical note, as if Dove is sharing a personal aside with Holiday herself. Although "Now you're cooking" can refer to a drummer or a bass player finally making a song pick up in intensity, but it also alludes to the tools of cooking, or preparing, the heroin that weakened Holiday. This double entendre is followed with "magic spoon, magic needle" in the following line that further describes the paraphernalia used in heroin ingestion. The words "light," "burned," and "cooking" in the three stanzas work together as if the immolation of Holiday is slow, but devastating nonetheless. The immolation of Holiday in this poem is therefore not self-induced but projected onto her indirectly by Dove.

Furthermore, the most compelling turn of this poem resides in its last three lines, where Dove describes besieged women as an invention for audiences that desire a tragic mythology, women like Holiday who serve "to sharpen love in the service of myth." (46) When Dove concludes the poem in this fashion, she is not just focusing on Holiday's ruin, she is also considering the artifice and the social conditions that make women victims and survivors of love, rather than those who are rewarded by love's possibilities. The act of embodying an intangible mystery makes women like Holiday impossible to contain, even though such women are never quite free. Those lines are offered as another aside preceded by "Fact is," as if the speaker is leaning over and looking intently toward the reader; they then are punctuated by a final imperative line commanding women to "be a mystery" if they "can't be free" (46). This poetic facet makes it clear what Holiday achieved with her artistry.

Farah Jasmine Griffin's Consideration of Holiday's Legacy

Moments like these in Jackson and Dove's poems make it clear why Farah Jasmine Griffin chose to discuss Holiday in her 2002 book *If You Can't Be Free, Be a Mystery: In Search of Billie Holiday.* Griffin's consideration of Holiday's art, life, representations of the singer's life, and how contemporary vocalists and writers take cues from Holiday, construct the prominent overarching idea of the book—that these various representations have obscured knowing the actual truth about Holiday, while still celebrating and complicating our understanding of her work and presence. Griffin discusses the resistance to white men being so prominent in detailing this black woman's narrative, and how many white men who knew her have corralled her image and how it is documented. By challenging those perspectives and including other artists and texts, Griffin offers a more nuanced understanding of Holiday and grants the singer, who has more poems written about or referencing her "than just about any other jazz artist, save John Coltrane," a more accurate depiction (Griffin 152). Griffin focuses her brief discussion primarily around Rita Dove's "Canary," Frank O'Hara's "The Day Lady Died," Amiri Baraka's "The Lady," and Betsy Scholl's "Don't Explain" from the award-winning poetry collection of the same title.

Betsy Scholl's poem briefly relates a daughter's conversation with her mother as the daughter throws her father's old cassettes out of a car window while crossing the bridge over the Raritan River in New Jersey. Aside from the title, Holiday does not appear until the poem's midpoint. While talking with her mother, the mother insists that she will tell the daughter more over the phone. At first, the daughter's questions seem innocuous, then take a turn toward "darker things—" (69). Scholl follows the long dash with a question addressed to the mother. She asks her mother if she knew that Billie Holiday washed floors and played Louis Armstrong in a whorehouse while the mother was in school (69). This is delivered as a single question broken into four lines then punctuated by the mother's potential wincing at the very image of what Holiday did to survive while the mother was a schoolgirl. By introducing this image, Holiday invokes a moment of unjust treatment of an immensely talented young black girl, then references a Nine Inch Nails cover of a Jimi Hendrix as a comparable raging "love *and* hate" that rings through the emotional landscape where the daughter reads her dead father's letters and listens to old cassettes.

Aside from the image of a white rock band profiting from a pioneering black musician, there is another questioning of privilege that Holiday never experienced, and Scholl is abundantly clear about it. Holiday never went to private school or had the opportunity to live like carefree schoolgirl. This listening concludes the poem by mentioning Holiday and a poor cassette recording of old records. The daughter's listening breaks down the grounding that Holiday's distinct voice provides. Hearing her father's voice in his letters and his old cassettes brings the daughter down to the place where the emotional core is evoked and even rising above technical virtuosity in music where a voice like Holiday's deteriorated after a hard life.

Holiday's genius becomes even more evident in poems like those by O'Hara, Scholl, and in other later works, because they catalog their own experiences with Holiday as an enduring presence weaved into the cultural fabric of their lives, and she cannot be extricated from how each poet looks at the world surrounding them. O'Hara published "The Day Lady Died" in his 1964 collection *Lunch Poems*. As a poet of the New York School, it's evident how he basically walked the streets of New York on his lunch break from his office job, yet was still stunned by the loss of Holiday. Strategies employed in post–O'Hara poems mirror his approach of detailing the motions and tasks that amount to background noise as Holiday's presence rises around deliberately controlled and emotional moments. Holiday may not be a muse, but she can be centered as the main influential subject. This balance of emotion and control appears in Janet Choi's "What I'm Wild For" and Lawson Fuson Inada's "The Journey" which both appear in *Jazz Poems*.

Kevin Young's Jazz Poems *and His Poem* "Stardust"

Kevin Young's thematic anthology *Jazz Poems* dedicates a section entitled "MUTING (for Billie Holiday)" consisting of 12 works related to Billie

Holiday. This section includes Abel Meeropol/Lewis Allan's "Strange Fruit" and "God Bless the Child" by Holiday and Arthur Herzog, Jr. In addition to Young's poem "Stardust," Young features poems by C.D. Wright, Terrance Hayes, Tony Hoagland, Sonia Sanchez, Choi, and Inada. Notably, the diversity of the poets and their own experiences with Holiday's work shape the poems and how they approach Holiday. Dove and O'Hara's poems are included here, and the section is introduced by Langston Hughes' "Song for Billie Holiday." Hughes' 1948 poem is comprised of three stanzas—the first rephrases the rhetorical question asking what might cleanse the "sadness of the song" three times, then moves into a second stanza that personifies sorrow as if it is Billie herself with "dust in hair" that is "dusted with despair." In the final stanza, sorrow seems to join that trumpet's "cold brass" and her sound is so intense that it blurs this "Bitter television" that only projects images and sounds (221). It doesn't create sounds like a trumpeter or even Holiday herself as she sings.

Kevin Young's poem "Stardust" is one of the more recent poems in the "MUTING" section of the anthology. Like Rita Dove, Young uses short lines to play with the double *entendres* of slang that Holiday would have been familiar with as well. In three-line stanzas with three- to five-syllable lines, Young creates a shorthand that reveals details about Holiday and her vocal abilities. His short lines attest to Lady's ability to sing the blues, and other colors and possibilities to create a palette of sound, even though she was short-changed by some of the disadvantages that she experienced. The break in the word "shortchanged" allows Young to say she changed a chord like a musician or the tenor of how her chosen genre operates. She was not limited by the hue of the blues. Instead, she created with a range of colors that might be considered unexpected for a black women singing blues and jazz at that time. The next two stanzas refer to the songs "God Bless the Child" and "Billie's Bounce." When Young mentions "Billie's Bounce" a second time, he states that "Miss Holiday's up/on four counts" which can refer to counts in a musical measure, but connects to the next line so it reads "four counts/of possession"—a drug charge that Holiday received. After "possession," a comma and enjambment breaks the phrase "three-/fifths, the law" (224). In addition to loosely referencing the common adage, "possession is nine-tenths of the law," the fraction of three fifths is historically charged for black people in America, who at one point were counted as ⅗ of a human being by slave masters and senators who wanted to manipulate legislative districts. Since Billie Holiday was not contrite and unwilling to bow, she was "locked up" and didn't lick "the salt/the boot" and clubs then refused her as being an "ex-con," Holiday's income began to dry up (225). The Depression era-query "Brother/can you spare/a dime" sounds like a lived reality for the singer, but going into the next line means, the line reads "Brother/can you spare/a dime/bag?" where a dime bag can be an obvious reference to marijuana.

The next few stanzas runs through scats and riffs until she is "detoxed, thawed/in time//for Thanksgiving" (Young 226) so Holiday was clean and warmed up around the time of the November holiday, and recording "Billie's Bounce," "Warming Up a Riff," "Thriving on a Riff" and other songs in a session with Miles Davis, Bud Powell, Max Roach, Curley Russell, and Charlie Parker as the leader (Ramsey 65). The last line "Day cold as turkey"— describes November 26, but also hints at quitting a substance "cold turkey" as well. The enjambment of these short lines described above and the Emily Dickinson–like em-dashes throughout establish these multiple meanings throughout the poem.

"Lady Sings the Blues" by Terrance Hayes presents different views of looking at Holiday in three short sections separated by dinkuses. There is smoke, Holiday "unpetals her song" and a cigarette flares. "Amber amaryllis, blue chanteuse" fills in color in a fashion that hints at flora when Hayes states "If flowers could sing they'd sound like this." In the second section, Hayes is describing himself as a boy in a movie theater with his mother watching Diana Ross play Billie Holiday in the 1972 film *Lady Sings the Blues*, and the pair watch movie where Holiday is portrayed like "a burnt-out cliché" (230). When Hayes arrives at the third and final section, his mother's dissatisfaction is open enough for her to say "Billie didn't sound like that." The poem demonstrates how Holiday can permeate yet another intergenerational relationship, much like Betsy Scholl's "Don't Explain."

"Permanentlee" Warm: Women Recognizing and Remembering

In the same vein as her fellow Black Arts Movement writer Angela Jackson, Sonia Sanchez directly addresses Holiday in "Our Lady Day" which originally appeared in her 1970 chapbook *We a BadddDDD People*. Instead of addressing Holiday's power and dexterity as an artist, Sanchez places the impetus for care and love on black men who did not make Holiday "feel/permanentlee warm." Scholar Elisabeth Frost describes how Holiday and the men around her could have saved Holiday to make other music altogether and live a longer life:

> But to be "permanentlee warm," to be nurtured by a man who is capable not just of killing but of loving, also means revolutionizing conceptions of gender within the black community. Black self-love still awaits black women and men; "ain't no tellen" where such a road "wud have led us" [Frost 88].

That black self-love is easier to practice now, decades later, even as some of the conditions for African Americans, particularly African American women, have become more complicated, and in some ways, improved.

Women are considering that the dependency on men is far less significant than self-determination. In short, women are considering how they can save themselves and document their own legacies. In addition to scholars like Farah Jasmine Griffin, Emily Lordi, Shana Redmond, and Angela Y. Davis exploring the multi-faceted role of Billie Holiday as an artist with craft and dignity, there are so many women of color who have creative control over their careers in rich, varied ways in popular music—Janelle Monae, Erykah Badu, Mary J. Blige, Me'shell Ndegeocello explore ways to empower themselves through narratives that they steer and perform. There are also vocalists like Madeline Peyroux, Dianne Reeves, Cassandra Wilson, Nnenna Freelon, and Alice Smith who comprise a short list of women who've gathered influence from women like Holiday as well. These women have drawn on the same themes and expanded on them based on the frameworks of artists like Holiday. Their phrasing and political agency is shaped by decisions that Holiday made, and was forced to make. And if we consider Griffin's input on Holiday's life, many of these women have actively sought to sidestep or heal from encounters with trauma much like those experienced by Holiday.

Upon revisiting songs throughout Holiday's catalog where many songs were written by men and notably in Joel Katz's 2002 documentary *Strange Fruit*, Farah Jasmine Griffin discusses how some of the early biographies debated Holiday's ability to write her own story. Griffin quickly follows that comment with an astute observation that even the people prominently speaking about Holiday long after her death as authorities were often men. So, the range of women who are scholars and musicians enacting their own agency and self-love serve as welcome developments, despite intense ongoing policing that attempts to circumscribe black women, black people, and women's bodies in ways that echo the segregation that suffocated Holiday's career.

Another poem outside of Young's anthology also approached Holiday as subject matter. E. Ethelbert Miller published his seven-line poem "Billie Holiday" in his 1994 collection *First Light: New and Selected Poems*. As concise as this poem is, Miller centers Holiday as the main subject from the beginning. The opening couplet, where deaf people hear better than blind people, conveys that a person can notice more than what is heard or seen. The second stanza notes that "some men ... first heard her sing" which implies that someone had missed some qualities about Holiday on the first listen. When the poem concludes with the same men were "attracted to the flower in her hair" which could mean they saw one element of Holiday's appearance and missed the rest; possibly they gleaned more from her work later. Although some could read that last couplet as a sexual objectification of Holiday and the flower, Miller's sparse language is most likely talking about "some men" who are deafened by what they cannot see in women, even Billie Holiday.

Most recently, the online anthology *Love You Madly* edited by Lisa

Alvarado features and focuses solely on poems about jazz artists. Each musician is celebrated by one poet. Daisy Franco's three poems on Holiday are influenced by compositions performed by Holiday—"Harmony," "Dance to a New Beat," and "Different" are prefaced with the song titles "Solitude," "God Bless the Child," and "Our Love Is Different," respectively. Although these poems riff of the lyrics delivered by Holiday, they do not rely on her biographical details, the typically expected imagery of the gardenia, or the drug-related tropes that recur in many poems about the vocalist. Overall, the poems center Holiday as a practitioner of her craft and as a woman with agency despite her challenges. She is centered as a presence and an influential powerhouse in the American cultural landscape.

As more work is generated, published, and anthologized, there will certainly be more poems that center Holiday as a subject, and hopefully, those poems will allow Holiday to reveal her complexities as an artist and a human being. She is not just a voice, a gardenia in her hair, or a persecuted drug addict. Her emotional terrain and her social and political impact is relayed in the poems discussed here. As a growing body of black feminist scholarship and musicology re-envisions and revisits the life and work of Billie Holiday, her work can finally receive the nuanced and wider recognition that it deserves. As poets continue to reference and center Holiday as a subject in their writing, the poetic directions that cultivated her mystery will become a valuable story and lesson for other artists who appreciate Holiday's contribution to music, whether we categorize it as black, American, woman-centered, or jazz.

WORKS CITED

Alvarado, Lisa. *Love You Madly*, 2014. https://www.loveyoumadlypoetry.com. Accessed 27 Apr. 2018.

De Veaux, Alexis. *Don't Explain: A Song of Billie Holiday*. New York: Harper & Row, 1980.

Feinstein, Sascha, and Yusef Komunyakaa. *The Jazz Poetry Anthology*. Bloomington: Indiana University Press, 1991.

Feinstein, Sascha, and Yusef Komunyakaa. *The Second Set: The Jazz Poetry Anthology, Volume 2*. Bloomington: Indiana University Press, 1996.

Frost, Elisabeth A. *The Feminist Avant-Garde in American Poetry*. Iowa City: University of Iowa Press, 2005.

Griffin, Farah Jasmine. *If You Can't Be Free, Be a Mystery: In Search of Billie Holiday*. New York: One World, 2002.

Lange, Art, and Nathaniel Mackey. *Moment's Notice: Jazz in Poetry and Prose*. Minneapolis: Coffee House Press, 1993.

Miller, E. Ethelbert. *First Light: New and Selected Poems*. Baltimore: Black Classic Press, 1994.

Ramsey, Guthrie. *The Amazing Bud Powell: Black Genius, Jazz History, and the Challenge of BeBop*. Oakland: University of California Press, 2013.

Sanchez, Sonia. *We a BadddDDD People*. Detroit: Broadside Press, 1970.

Scholl, Betsy. *Don't Explain*. Madison: University of Wisconsin Press, 1997.

Strange Fruit. Directed by Joel Katz. California Newsreel, 2002.

Weatherford, Carole Boston. *Becoming Billie Holiday*. Honesdale: Word Song Press, 2008.

Young, Kevin. *Jazz Poems*. New York: Alfred A. Knopf, 2006.

The Fruit Is on the Ground

The Impact of "Strange Fruit" on Black Lives Matter

DEVONA MALLORY

Although she died in 1959, Billie Holiday (otherwise known as Lady Day) continues to be one of the most popular and influential artists of all time. One of the main things that seals her legacy is a protest song she recorded in 1939: "Strange Fruit," which depicts the horrific, yet common, act of lynching. The "strange fruit" refers to African Americans hanging from trees, like fruit, to describe or to even warn other blacks not to continue accepting their supposed powerlessness under institutionalized racism. Lyrics such as "Black bodies swinging in the southern breeze," combined with Holiday's haunting and disturbing rendition, has never left the world's consciousness. Prime examples include Kanye West's 2013 controversial sampling of Nina Simone's version of the song called "Blood on the Leaves," a title that is taken directly from the song's lyrics. The song itself, however, has been covered 59 times, including Rebecca Ferguson's 2016 version, which she famously vowed to sing at Donald Trump's inauguration. Trump declined.

This essay analyzes the continuous impact of this song and situates it within the rise of the Black Lives Matter movement, and its attempts to stop the still-relevant horror of lynching. Here, I expand the definition of lynching to discuss the myriad of ways that blacks continue to be abused and murdered and the role Black Lives Matter plays in overcoming these continued racist obstacles of oppression. Furthermore, the Black Lives Matter Movement and the contemporary references to the song, demonstrate that the message of "Strange Fruit" remains as relevant today as the day it was first recorded.

I first encountered this song back in the late 70s when I was about seven years old while watching *Lady Sings the Blues* with my stepmother and step-siblings over a weekend visit. I will never forget Billie (played wonderfully by the Oscar-nominated Diana Ross), leaving her tour bus and running across a black man hanging from a tree. I understood that what I saw dramatized was wrong and unfair. With help from everyone present, my young brain was able to process how the song fit into that scene. According to the movie, this tragic and visceral event inspired Holiday to write "Strange Fruit." Of course as a child, I accepted the simplistic movie version eventually learning that the movie was very inaccurate with certain events in Holiday's life. A few years ago, I learned that the movie fabricated the origin of the song. When I discovered the truth, I was shocked and disappointed. It is akin to discovering as a kid that Santa Claus and the Easter Bunny do not exist. Despite the song's origins, all I know is that this song, like for many people, is a permanent part of my psyche. As Angela Y. Davis describes:

> Billie Holiday never witnessed a lynching firsthand. The fictionalized scene in the film *Lady Sings the Blues*, in which she sees a black man's body swinging from a tree, is a gross oversimplification of the artistic process. This scene suggests that Holiday could only do justice to the song if she had experienced a lynching firsthand. The film dismisses the connections between lynching—one extreme of racism—and the daily routine of discrimination which in some way affect every African American [193].

Hence, one does not need to see a lynching firsthand in order to be affected negatively by the event. The fact that lynchings occur at all is hard enough to handle for most black people. Yet, as Davis discusses, lynching is an extreme form of discrimination, but black people can be discriminated against everyday in a myriad of commonplace and/or extreme ways. Conversely, since film is a visual medium, viewers need to see a simplistic visual connection even if the incident is fictionalized. In other words, the film suggests that the people needed to see Holiday witnessing a lynching in order to write a song in response. The film suggests that the truth does not matter—only the dramatic and immediate impact.

Still, no one can totally blame the film for the fictionalization since the movie is based on Holiday's also factually-challenged autobiography *Lady Sings the Blues*. In her autobiography, Holiday provides her version of the song's origins:

> It was during my stint at Café Society that a song was born which became my personal protest—"Strange Fruit." The germ of the song was in a poem written by Lewis Allen [sic]. I first met him at Café Society. When he showed me that poem, I dug it right off. It seemed to spell out all things that had killed pop.... Allan ... suggested that Sonny White, who had been my accompanist, and I turn it into music. So the three of us got together and did the job in about three weeks [Holiday with Dufty 82–83].

Obviously, Holiday identifies with the song to the point where she claims that she is one of the songwriters.

In any case, it makes a good story of tragedy and possible redemption. Holiday wanted the title of her autobiography to be *Bitter Crop*, the last two lines of the song, but the publishers disapproved because of its controversial nature and possible future lack of sales (Margolick 33; Davis 187). Although she did not write the song or witnesses a lynching, Holiday still related to the lyrics because Holiday's father eventually died of a possibly curable illness when a white hospital refused him admittance (Davis 187). Therefore, her father experienced another type of lynching since he became a victim of a racist health care system that did not bother to help a sick man when needed. In a way, she and every African American that have ever existed have contributed to "Strange Fruit." Literally and figuratively, the blood of African American victims still nourishes and alternately poisons the roots.

Originally, lynchings occurred when a community would get together and hang someone utilizing vigilante justice in areas where there was minimum law enforcement. The concept eventually segues into an act of terrorism designed to murder slaves and free black people who "stepped out of line" or as a warning to other blacks to stay subjugated—the very thing that "Strange Fruit" discusses. Traditionally, as part of the ritual the men are castrated and mutilated and the women raped (Davis 188–189). Sometimes the bodies of these unfortunate victims are also burned. The last humiliation is the photographs and postcards of black people hanging in front of a crowd of happy whites who seemingly just stepped away from the picnic baskets to enjoy the view (Davis 188–189). The fruit is strange, indeed. As David Margolick chronicles: "According to figures kept by the Tuskegee Institute—conservative figures—between 1889 and 1940, 3,833 people were lynched; ninety percent of them murdered in the south, and four-fifths of them were black. Lynchings tended to occur in poor, small towns" (37). Back in 1939 when "Strange Fruit" was released, lynchings of black people were on the decline. In fact, only three people were "officially" lynched that year (37). Lynchings may have been on the decline at the time; however, African Americans were still living under the discriminatory Jim Crow laws, especially in the south.

Interesting enough, "Strange Fruit" is not written by a black person. The song first appeared as a poem written by Abel Meeropol, a Jewish English teacher from New York City. Meeropol's songwriting pseudonym is Lewis Allan, a named that is derived from his stillborn sons (Margolick 35). A communist for many years before leaving the party, he has certainly been against the racism against blacks. He wrote the poem in 1937 after seeing a photograph of the lynching of Thomas Shipp and Abram Smith on August 7, 1930, in Marion, Indiana (38). Meeropol states in 1971: "I wrote 'Strange Fruit' because I hate lynching and I hate injustice and I hate people who perpetuate it" (qtd. In Margolick 31). First, the poem was published as "Bitter Fruit" in a teachers' union newsletter in January 1937. Eventually, Meeropol changes the name and adds music. Holiday does not have the honor of being the first singer of the song in public. That privilege goes to Meeropol's wife, Anne. She sings the song at various leftist get-togethers (39). When communists Ethel and Julius Rosenberg where executed in the early 1950s for espionage by the U.S. government, Meeropol and his wife adopted their sons (27).

In late 1938 or early 1939, Meeropol goes to the Café Society, the first racially integrated club in New York City to convince Holiday to sing the song, which she eventually did in early 1939 (Margolick 42–44). Barry Josephson, the white owner, gave permission, but with three provisos: Holiday has to close all three nightly sets with the song, service must stop, and the room must be completely dark, "save for a pin spot on Holiday's face" (qtd. in Margolick 51–52). As Holiday also comments after the song is over, "My instruction was to walk off, period" (52). These actions give the song the extra emotional and visceral impact needed to increase the reaction of the audience. Meeropol comments about Holiday's interpretive performances later:

> She gave a startling, most dramatic and effective interpretation, which could jolt an audience out of its complacency anywheres [sic]. This was exactly what I wanted the song to do and why I wrote it. Billie Holiday's styling of the song was incomparable and fulfilled the bitterness and shocking quality I had hoped the song would have. The audience gave her a tremendous ovation [qtd. in Margolick 48].

The above passage shows Meeropol's utmost respect and admiration for Holiday. He loves the raw passion and innovation that she brings to the song, which is exactly what he wants to emphasize. This may be the reason why despite so many other wonderful diverse and talented artists such Nina Simone and Tori Amos have recorded different versions, still when most people think of "Strange Fruit," they think of Billie Holiday. According to Margolick, besides Anne Meeropol, the song was song by "progressive friends at gatherings in hotels and bungalow colonies around New York, by members of the local teachers' union, by a black vocalist named Laura Duncan (including once at Madison Square Garden), and by a quartet of black singers at a fund-raiser [sic] for the anti–Fascists during the Spanish Civil War" (39). Interestingly, the co-producer of the fundraiser, Robert Gordon, was also directing Billie Holiday at the Café Society at the time (Margolick 39). It remains unknown whether or not Gordon encouraged Allan to approach Holiday to sing the song. In any case, because the song became so popular, Holiday decides to record the song. However, her label, Columbia, rejected it because of the subject matter (Margolick 65). Fortunately, she was allowed to record the song for Commodore, a smaller label at the time (Margolick 65). On Thursday, April 20, 1939, "Strange Fruit" is recorded with another

Holiday standard, "Fine and Mellow" on the flip side of the record (Vail 31). That day two other songs were recorded. The main reason why the poignant bluesy yet turbulent love song "Fine and Mellow" may have been put on the flip side was to possibly balance out the tremendous impact of "Strange Fruit," but that is conjecture. Despite the name of the song, the only thing fine and mellow was the melody. The lyrics goes from a lovey-dovey romanticism to love's problematic realism. Regardless of the subject matter, even the name of the song suggests something easy and light in comparison—something the record company probably decided to market as such for record sales.

One of the most controversial rumors and statements is that Billie Holiday initially does not or never understands the meaning of the song. Interestingly enough, this accusation comes from Barry Josephson and other white men (a group that does not include Meeropol who always holds Holiday in high regard) who happen to be around at the time and later biographers. Once Josephson quips: "At first I felt Billie didn't know what the hell the song meant" (qtd. in Davis 186). Josephson even states that he tells her to sing the song despite her reluctance. He quotes Holiday as saying, "You wants me to sing it. I sings it" (qtd. in Davis 185). According to one biographer, Holiday, who was not formally educated (which was not uncommon at the time), preferred cheap romances and comic books (qtd. in Davis 186). Still, as she is an African American woman living in racists conditions, she does not need to be educated to understand the discrimination, abuse, and murders of black people under slavery and afterwards. In fact, many critics do not dispute that Holiday sings not only her life but humanity's as well. For example, the crooner Tony Bennett once said, "She didn't sing anything unless she lived it" (qtd. in Margolick 29). Sylvia Sims, a singer who is a contemporary of Holiday's, marvels at the songtress' prowess: "wherever you saw her, and I went to see her everywhere possible—you saw the world in that face. You saw everything that was alive, all the beauty and misery of life. There was an aura about this face that was celestial and otherworldly" (qtd. in Margolick 111). It seems Holiday knew that by emoting the agony and ecstasy of life that she was taking her listeners to an emotional space that made her listeners uncomfortable because of the lynching story line. However, with ending the song, Holiday symbolically is asking the listeners to stop the atrocity of lynching and racism. One critic continues this idea, "[s]he was really happy only when she sang. The rest of the time she was a sort of living lyric to the song 'Strange Fruit,' hanging, not on a poplar tree, but on the limbs of life itself" (qtd. in Margolick 24). Holiday knows the messages that she conveyed in her song could and would change the world for the better. During Holiday's lifetime, she does not have to see a firsthand account of a lynching to understand the full effect of its racially charged message. Being a black woman, Holiday has been discriminated against on a regular basis with the Jim Crow laws in full effect. Hearing about black people being lynched through word of mouth and newspaper articles had to impact her as a marginalized human being. She did not need to see a lynching to feel the horror and pain of that event and to use those emotions for singing her truth. The same goes for Meeropol. He did not see a lynching firsthand, but his outrage became his artistic outlet.

As Davis posits, "I have considered these conflicting accounts of the genesis of Billie Holiday's 'Strange Fruit' because they reveal … the extent to which her stature as an artist and her ability to comprehend social issues were both disparaged and defined as a result of plans conceived by savvy white men" (187). Even as Holiday's biographers have debased Holiday intellectually, racially, sexually, socially and gender-wise with their comments, her rendition of "Strange Fruit" demonstrates a social awareness that challenges these characterizations. Still, as Davis continues, "Josephson's depiction of Holiday is problematic at best: he paints her as illiterate, ignorant, and passive woman, willing to sing 'Strange Fruit' simply because he asked her to do it. His attempt to recapture her speech—'You wants me to sing it. I sings it'—is reminiscent of the worst king of minstrel caricatures of black 'dialect'" (186). Josephson's and the other white males alleged statements gives one a knee-jerk reaction of "Yessa Massa!" Obviously this is another attempt of paternalism, where good meaning and all-knowing, godlike white man came in to save the unintelligent and ignorant black people from themselves.

This characterization suggests that black people have to be lead, like mindless sheep with white shepherds, to the Civil Rights Movement. In opening the Café Society, Josephson opened the door for racial integration, but would not open the door of black autonomy. Even somewhat "enlightened" whites may have barriers of hypocrisy that they do not even realize they possess. This concept is the equivalent of white people advocating for civil rights but not wanting any blacks moving next to them in the suburbs. Furthermore, because of the song's fame and social impact, white men like Josephson and others desire to grab most of the glory for themselves.

At first, Holiday may not have known the meaning of the word "pastoral," but how many do? It does not seem to be a word that the average person may know. In fact, I did not learn of the complete background of the word *pastoral* until graduate school. Stemming from Vergil's *Eclogues*, which was written between 44 and 38 BC in ancient Rome, the original meaning of pastoral, shepherds (sometimes the shepherds are city men in disguise) come together in an idyllic country setting to talk about the harsh, brutal reality of that time, which is in direct contrast to the setting. The more modern meaning of the word just has to do with a romanticized view of the country in its natural splendor ("Pastoral" 862). Holiday may not have known initially what "pastoral" meant, but she sure knew that a lynching would damage a perfect country setting forever, as suggested in the song's lyrics which certainly ties into Vergil's initial definition. About singing the song, Holiday stated once, "it affects me so much that I get sick. It takes all the strength out of me" (qtd. in Margolick 85). Does her statement demonstrate ignorance of what she is singing? The answer is no. I doubt the song "Sunny Side of the Street" affected Holiday nearly as much. However, despite her continuous reaction, "Strange Fruit" was part of Holiday's repertoire until she died in 1959. Obviously, she felt the song should be heard as often as possible especially with regards to its social impact.

Therefore, the social impact of this protest song is something that cannot be denied. One of Holiday's biographer's observed "the liberal atmosphere of the club, with its clientele of 'New Dealers,' and the humanitarian principles of the owner, made it a receptive setting for the presentation of the song's dramatic anti-lynching lyrics" (qtd. in Davis 190). In other words, having "Strange Fruit" being performed in an integrated nightclub by an up and coming black female singer creates the perfect atmosphere to launch the song into legendary status.

The song's reception back in 1939 was mixed and continues to be until the present day. At the time of its release on vinyl, the sales were inflated by the record company probably for public relations reasons, but in reality, the sales were small. Yet, many people heard the song without buying it. The subject matter and lyrics may have been just too overwhelming and graphic for some to hear on a regular basis. However, despite the lack of initial sales, Meeropol, who eventually became a very prolific songwriter, and his sons have earned over $300,000 on the song over the years (Margolick 71–72). Regardless, the music mogul Ahmet Ertegun states the song is "a declaration of war … the beginning of the civil rights movement" (qtd. in Margolick 19). As David Margolick mentions:

> Proponents of federal anti-lynching legislation urged that copies of the song be sent to congress, where Southern senators were about to filibuster another bill to death. "Let them constantly feel the terror of lynching, the threat of democracy which is inherent in the flouting of democratic processes," a magazine called *The Fraternal Outlook* urged its readers in March 1939 [79].

Hence, the song may not have been a "bestseller" initially, but over time, "Strange Fruit" becomes a legendary, influential, and thought-provoking cry for racial and social justice. Most of the people that have heard the song over time cannot help being viscerally and emotional impacted—even if they have no personal experience with this horrific crime. On the other hand, some people never get the message of the song. According to Holiday, one woman in Los Angeles asked her, "[W]hy don't you sing that sexy song you're so famous for? You know, the one about the naked bodies swinging in the trees" (Holiday with Dufty 85). This woman's statement demonstrates the oversexualization and eroticizing of blacks. Even Josephine Baker, who wore a banana skirt and no top and would dance on a jungle-themed stage, rose above these negative notions because she subversively undercut them. However, in this woman's mind, African Americans swung from the trees, like Tarzan, because they were noble savages, not murder victims. Also, swinging brings up connotations of wild and uninhibited alternative sexual lifestyle stereotypes, which many blacks and other people of color continue to endure. This idea is the modern equivalent of swinging from the chandelier.

Along these lines, another type of lynching exists. A type that unfortunately has become commonplace—modern lynching. In today's world, just casually searching for the term modern lynching online, is not used just against African Americans being hung, it's used for anyone that may or may not be disenfranchised from society. For example, some people claim that the still living black celebrities Bill Cosby and O. J. Simpson are victims of lynching. There are instances where white journalists refer to the term with regards to white people. One prime reaction to this recent phenomenon is the *Newsweek* article published on December 9, 2017, entitled "Roy Moore and Trump Are Not Facing a 'Lynch Mob' Despite What White Politicians Say." In other words, the word lynching has become a catch-all idea for anyone who is deemed to be publicly and/or legally shamed and/or accused of a crime that may or may not have merit. Still, no matter how the meaning has changed throughout history, every time I hear about another allegedly suicidal African American person (mostly men) found hanging from a tree or another shot by a white policeman on video despite being cooperative, I always continue to refer to "Strange Fruit" in my mind. We are living in an age where people are being lynched not just with a rope, but with a gun and other weapons as well (Eric Garner was choked by a cop using an illegal chokehold).

Since Trayvon Martin's murder in 2012, there seems to be an open-season on black men especially: "[I]t is not an exaggeration to concur with those who believe that black men in America are an endangered species, hunted like wild animals in a blood sport" (Goffe 81). Furthermore, "the Malcolm X Movement found there was a 'war against black people' and that a black person had been 'executed' every 28 hours in 2012 by police, and by security guards and by vigilantes associated with the police" (Goffe 82). The names of murdered black people read like a litany: Trayvon Martin, Michael Brown, Eric Garner, Sandra Bland, John Crawford, and the more recently Philando Castile. The names go on and on and they are too numerous to mention them all. Of course, there were notable cases previously such as Amadou Diallo in 1999 and Sean Bell in 2006. However, they "seemed" to be isolated incidents. Still, the main difference between these killings and the most recent ones is that most of these were filmed usually with someone's cell phone and posted online. With the exception of the Rodney King case over 20 years ago, documenting most of these past incidents rarely occurred due of the lack of technology. Nowadays, despite the myriad of beatings and murders caught on camera, many of the police officers involved have been exonerated in criminal court, including in King's case.

Holiday and Meeropol's legacy of advocacy still occurs today. In 2013, to turn the tide on any version of "lynching," the initially national Black Lives Matter (BLM) organization starts when three black lesbian activists named Opal Tometi, Patrisse Cullors, and Alicia Garza create a Twitter hashtag to protest of the murder of the 17-year-old Trayvon Martin at the hands of George Zimmerman and has fought for black rights all over the world ever since. In 2014, BLM became an official organization when it protested the murder of Michael Brown in Ferguson, Missouri (Joseph 19). BLM's motto is "This is not a moment, but a movement" (*BlackLivesMatter.com*). The organization's website proclaims: "When we say Black Lives Matter, we are broadening the conversation around state violence to include all of the ways in which Black people are intentionally left powerless at the hands of the state. We are talking about the ways in which Black lives are deprived of our basic human rights and dignity" (*BlackLivesMatter.com*). In fact, another Peniel Joseph describes the movement in this manner:

BLM has moved beyond many of the blind spots and shortcomings of its predecessors, embracing the full complexity of black identity and forging a movement that is far more inclusive and democratic than either the Panthers or civil rights activists ever envisioned. Many of its most active leaders are [lesbian] women and feminists. Its decentralized structure fosters participation and power sharing. It makes direct links between the struggles of black Americans and the marginalization and oppression of women, those in [LGBTQ] communities, and other people of color. It has made full use of the power and potential of social media, but it has also organized local chapters and articulated a broader political agenda [19].

It is commendable that three black lesbians have started this movement. Homosexuals in the black and mainstream communities have been disenfranchised and discriminated against for many years. BLM is attempting to not only connect these fragmented areas of racism and discrimination with each other so everyone can fight for the rights of everyone; just not African Americans. These female activists have picked up the torch from Holiday and have started a new revolution against lynching in all its forms, figuratively and literally, to help people around the world. Holiday may not have intended to be an activist, but she sure became one by singing one of the top protest and political songs in the world. BLM fights for the rights of all the different types of discrimination that black people may go through. Also, BLM demonstrates that we, regardless of ethnicity or differences, are in the struggle for equal rights together which echoes the message of Meeropol and Holiday.

Unfortunately, because of the continuous murders of blacks by police especially, we have a long way to go in the struggle for equality and autonomy.

Despite the song's message and notoriety, the United States as of July 2017 still does not have an anti-lynching law. In the late 19th century, Ida Wells, the famous African American journalist and activist, made the anti-lynching campaign her life's work. The last attempts to pass a law occurred in 1921 and 1935 (Davis 191). Still, "'Strange Fruit' was a frontal challenge not only to lynching and racism but to the policies of a government that implicitly condoned such activities, especially through its refusal to pass laws against lynching as well. The song was thus an undisguised rallying cry against the state" (196).

A more explicit way that "Strange Fruit" still resonates happened when President Trump asked the African-British singer Rebecca Ferguson to sing at his inauguration. The singer who recorded an album of mostly Holiday songs entitled *Lady Sings the Blues*, declined saying she would do it only if she got to sing "Strange Fruit" with her comments:

> I've been asked and this is my answer. If you allow me to sing Strange Fruit, a song that has huge historical importance, a song that was blacklisted in the United States for being too controversial. A song that speaks to all the disregarded and downtrodden black people in the United States. A song that is a reminder of how love is the only thing that will conquer all the hatred in this world, then I will graciously accept your invitation and see you in Washington. Best Rebecca X [Jamieson].

Since she did not perform at the inauguration, the offer must have been declined. Furthermore, the assumption could be made that the "X" may be another version of Malcolm X or just part of the endearment of Xs and Os.

Besides the constant versions continuing to be recorded, the song has traversed into other mediums. In 1944, Lillian Smith, a progressive southern white woman, wrote a best-selling yet controversial novel about an interracial relationship called *Strange Fruit*. Allegedly, the title is inspired by Holiday's song (Goodreads.org). A movie of the same name came out in 2004 (*IMDB*). The movie, which is set in the South, deals with a young gay black man's homecoming to discover why his also gay friend was lynched when they were children. However, two of the most recent manifestations are geared toward children and adolescents. In 2016, in conjunction with the Christian Theological Seminary, The Salt Project, and WFYI created a 15-minute video on *YouTube*, named "Strange Fruit—The Story Behind 'The Song of the Century.'" This video combines biblical passages with a rap or spoken word version of the song infused with the song's history and followed by a great song performance by Marietta Simpson and Tyron Cooper.

Next, in 2017, Gary Golio published a wonderful book for ten- to 12-year-olds called *Strange Fruit: Billie Holiday and the Power of a Protest Song*. The book features beautiful illustrations by Charlotte Riley-Webb. This book takes the history of the song and discusses lynching with a lot of sympathy and depth in a way that helps kids to understand the meaning of the song without scarring them for life.

Reaching across time, "Strange Fruit" has not only been a part of the Civil Rights Movement, it has become part of many a top songs list and has won numerous awards.

Ironically, almost 80 years since "Strange Fruit" was recorded, things have not changed very much. Although we have had an African American president for two terms, we still have a long way to go with regards to race relations. With the advent of cell phones, social media, and the internet, police brutality against blacks has been filmed and disseminated to the world within seconds. Now, Black Lives Matter and other like-minded organizations have continued over time to pick up the torch and continue to fight against the oppression of African peoples all over the world utilizing "Strange Fruit" as a rallying cry. "Strange Fruit" continues to have social and political clout even though the situations have been updated and modified with the changing times. Now, the "fruit" has not only been hanging on the trees, but has dropped to the ground for everyone to see. The scent of magnolias has been replaced with the smell of gunpowder and Starbucks while the initial Southern pastoral scene can be any neighborhood in America. The blood has spilled out from the roots onto the streets. No one is immune from its effects.

WORKS CITED

"About Us: What Does #BlackLivesMatter Mean." Blacklivesmatterwww. Accessed 1 June 2017.

Blau, Max. "What Really Happened to the Man Found Hanging in Piedmont Park? How Social Media Fueled a Rumor that the KKK 'Lynched' a Black Man in Piedmont Park." Atlantamagazinewww. Posted 12 July 2016. Accessed 3 June 2017. http://www.atlantamagazine.com/news-culture-articles/what-really-happened-to-the-man-found-hanging-in-piedmont-park/

Davis, Angela Y. "Strange Fruit." *Blues Legacies and Black Feminism: Gertrude "Ma" Rainey, Bessie Smith, and Billie Holiday*. New York: Pantheon, 1998, pp. 181–197.

Dogan, K. H., S. Demirci, and I. Deniz. "Why Do People Hang Themselves on Trees? An Evaluation of Suicidal Hangings on Trees in Konya, Turkey, Between 2001 and 2008." Abstract. *Journal of Forensic Sciences*, Jan. 2015. Reprinted on PubMed.gov. Accessed 1 June 2017. https://www.ncbi.nlm.nih.gov/pubmed/25088533.

Goffe, Leslie Gordon. "Modern Day Lynching? Black America v. White Police." *New African*, Oct. 1, 2014, pp. 80–83.

Golio, Gary. *Strange Fruit: Billie Holiday and the Power of a Protest Song*. Illustrated by Charlotte Riley-Webb. Minneapolis: Millbrook Press, 2017.

Holiday, Billie, with William Dufty. *Lady Sings the Blues*, 4th ed. New York: Lancer, 1972.

Jamieson, Amber. "Rebecca Ferguson Says She Will Play Trump Inauguration If She Can Sing Strange Fruit." TheGuardianwww. Posted 2 Jan. 2017. Accessed 5 June 2017. https://www.theguardian.com/us-news/2017/jan/02/rebecca-ferguson-says-she-will-play-trump-inauguration-if-she-can-sing-strange-fruit.

Jarvie, Jenny. "Black Man Found Hanging in Atlanta Park Stirs Fear and Ugly Memories." latimeswww. Posted 10 July 2016. Accessed 2 June 2017. http://www.latimes.com/nation/la-na-atlanta-hanging-20160708-snap-story.html.

Joseph, Peniel E. "Why Black Lives Matter Still Matter." *The New Republic*, May 1, 2017, pp. 16–19.

Kuhn, David Paul. "Exit Polls: How Obama Won." Politicowww. Posted 5 Nov. 2008. Accessed 5 June 2017. http://www.politico.com/story/2008/11/exit-polls-how-obama-won-015297.

Lady Sings the Blues. Directed by Sidney J. Furie, performances by Diana Ross, Billie D. Williams, and Richard Pryor. Paramount, 1972.

Margolick, David. *Strange Fruit: Billie Holiday, Café Society, and an Early Cry for Civil Rights.* Edinburge: Canongate, 2000.

Meeropol, Abel (Lewis Allan). "Strange Fruit." Commodore Records, 1937.

"Pastoral." *Merriam Webster's Encyclopedia of Literature,* 1995, pp. 862.

"Strange Fruit—The Story Behind 'The Song of the Century.'" *WFYI Online/YouTube.* Accessed 1 June 2017. Posted 7 Feb. 2015.

Vail, Ken. *Lady Day's Diary: The Life of Billie Holiday 1937–1959.* Castle Communication, 1996, p. 31.

About the Contributors

Anna Maria **Barry** is a researcher at the Royal College of Music Museum in London. Her research focuses on singers and explores their relationships with literature, visual culture and celebrity culture. She has published on a range of these topics and writes regularly for a number of popular magazines.

Tara **Betts**, author of the poetry collections *Break the Habit* and *Arc & Hue*, is also a coeditor of *The Beiging of America: Personal Essays About Being Mixed Race in the 21st Century* and *Adventures in Black and White*. Her prose appears in *Sounding Out!* and *The Lauryn Hill Reader*.

Matthew **Duffus** is an instructor of English and director of the writing center at Gardner-Webb University. His areas of interest include composition, creative writing and American literature from 1865 to the present. His first novel, *Swapping Purples for Yellows*, was published in August 2019.

Tammie **Jenkins** holds a doctorate from Louisiana State University in Baton Rouge. Her publications include "Moving Beyond the Veil of Double Consciousness: Making the Past, Present in Toni Morrison's *Song of Solomon*" and "Visualizing Cultural Spaces: (Re) Imagining Southern Gothicism in the Film *Midnight in the Garden of Good and Evil*."

William **Levine** has served on the English faculty at Middle Tennessee State University since 1998, where he teaches a course on the literature of jazz and the blues nearly every semester. He has published numerous articles on later 18th-century British poetry and historical aesthetics but has also been engaged in music journalism for nearly 20 years.

Devona **Mallory** is an associate professor of English at Albany State University in Albany, Georgia, where she is chair of the Gender Studies Committee and teaches classes in women's literature, world literature, and composition. She has published extensively on #BlackLivesMatter.

Jessica **McKee** is an assistant professor of humanities and director of the writing center for the Academic Advancement Center at Embry-Riddle Aeronautical University. Her research interests include popular culture, gender studies and American literature. She teaches Holiday in her "Rhythm and Prose" course, which introduces students to the intersections of music and literature.

Taylor Joy **Mitchell** is an assistant professor of humanities at Embry-Riddle Aeronautical University. Her research explores the inextricable relationships between sexuality, gender and race in popular media. Often focusing on polarizing figures, like Hugh Hefner or Colin Kaepernick, she analyzes how and why these figures become American icons.

Fernando Gabriel **Pagnoni Berns** is a professor at the Universidad de Buenos Aires (UBA)—Facultad de Filosofía y Letras (Argentina) where he teaches seminars on international horror film. He is the director of Grite, a research group on horror cinema, and has published in a number of edited collections on a variety of topics.

Michael V. **Perez** is an assistant professor of humanities and communication at Embry-Riddle Aeronautical University. His poems have appeared in *Crab Orchard Review, Route Seven Review, BLOOM, The Journal of Florida Studies*, and *Glass Poetry Journal*. His contributions to edited collections include "Pretty Is Not Enough" in *Sontag and the Camp Aesthetic* and "Dazzle, Gradually," about Truman Capote, in *Queer/Adaptation*.

Jesse **Schlotterbeck** is an associate professor of cinema at Denison University, where he teaches courses on film analysis, film history, and film theory. His scholarship focuses on American film genre, in particular musicals, biopics and film noir. His work appears in the *Quarterly Review of Film and Video* and the collections *Howard Hawks, Film Noir Prototypes* and *Film Noir*.

Claudius **Stemmler** is a doctoral candidate at the University of Siegen, from which he obtained a master's degree in media studies. Having previously worked as an intern on the exhibition *Film and Games: Interactions* at the Deutsches Filmmuseum, Frankfurt, he is researching Japanese video game designer Hideo Kojima.

Index